THE POLITICS OF RITUAL IN AN ABORIGINAL SETTLEMENT

SMITHSONIAN SERIES IN ETHNOGRAPHIC INQUIRY

William L. Merrill and Ivan Karp, Series Editors

Ethnography as fieldwork, analysis, and literary form is the distinguishing feature of modern anthropology. Guided by the assumption that anthropological theory and ethnography are inextricably linked, this series is devoted to exploring the ethnographic enterprise.

THE POLITICS OF RITUAL IN AN ABORIGINAL SETTLEMENT

Kinship, Gender, and the Currency of Knowledge

Françoise Dussart

SMITHSONIAN INSTITUTION PRESS
Washington and London

Production Editor: Ruth G. Thomson
Designer: Janice Wheeler

Library of Congress Cataloging-in-Publication Data
Dussart, Françoise.
The politics of ritual in an aboriginal settlement : kinship, gender, and the currency of knowledge / Françoise Dussart.
p. cm.—(Smithsonian series in ethnographic inquiry)
Includes bibliographical references and index.
ISBN 1-56098-393-0 (alk. paper)
1. Women, Walbiri—Rites and ceremonies. 2. Women, Walbiri—Kinship. 3. Women, Walbiri—Religion. 4. Mythology, Walbiri—Australia—Yuendumu (N.T.) 5. Sex role—Australia—Yuendumu (N.T.) 6. Kinship—Australia—Yuendumu (N.T.) 7. Dreamtime (Australian aboriginal mythology)—Australia—Yuendumu (N.T.) 8. Yuendumu (N.T.)—Social life and customs. I. Title. II. Series

DU125.W3 D87 2000
305.48′89915—dc21 00–036548

British Library Cataloguing-in-Publication Data available

Manufactured in the United States of America
07 06 05 04 03 02 01 00 5 4 3 2 1

♾ The paper used in this publication meets the minimum requirements of the American National Standard for Information Sciences—Permanence of Paper for Printed Library Materials ANSI Z39.48-1984.

For all the *juju-ngarliya* of Yuendumu

CONTENTS

ILLUSTRATIONS

MAPS

FIGURES

ACKNOWLEDGMENTS

Few writers start book projects anticipating that their research and writing will take ten years to complete. Certainly I didn't. I can only hope that the immediacy this book has lost has been replaced by a measure of insight emerging from repeated consideration of and reflection on my ethnographic data and theoretical suppositions. The use of ritual as a currency of knowledge that gives coherence to Warlpiri social identity is not a subject of analysis that presented itself to me in the early months of study. Countless field trips, notebooks, private deliberations, public meetings, friendly e-mails, and thoughtful suggestions were needed to give material substance to my theories and theoretical weight to my ideas. The most crucial element of the process, I only now realize, was *time:* time to write, time to *not* write, time to reconsider and revise.

Almost two decades separate my first visit to Yuendumu from the publication of this book. In the intervening years, I have benefited from the guidance and support of innumerable friends, scholars, and institutions. A full list might threaten to double the size of this work. However, this is the one place in which I can gather up and distribute formally the many thanks and acknowledgments handed out piecemeal from the back of trucks and the front of conference halls.

I received long-term support from a number of institutions. The Australian National University and the Australian Institute of Aboriginal and Torres Strait Islander Studies bankrolled my first two field trips to Yuendumu (1983–1985, 1987). The National Australian Research Unit and the Australian Institute of Aboriginal and Torres Strait Islander Studies partly funded return visits in 1989 and 1991. The Wenner-Gren Foundation, in issuing grant number 5280, also sustained my 1991 trip. The following year, my employer, the University of Connecticut, stepped in as a regular underwriter of research through its Research Foundation, which provided crucial funding in 1992, 1995, 1996, and 1999.

Perhaps the most intellectually stimulating institutional boost came in the form of a residential fellowship sponsored by the School of American Research (SAR) and funded by the National Endowment for the Humanities. The year I spent at SAR, in Santa Fe, New Mexico (1995–1996), allowed me to transform a notional argument about the interconnectedness of gender and kinship into four rough chapters. More than three years later, as a visiting research scholar at New York University, I made the final editorial changes on the page proofs.

I have enjoyed my collaboration with a team of editors at the Smithsonian Institution Press. I want to thank first Daniel Goodwin and Robert Lockhart, who enthusiastically read the first chapters of the manuscript. Peter Cannell, Joanne Reams, Scott Mahler, and Ruth Thomson, gifted and knowledgeable in the performance of book publication, nurtured my writing immensely. On the graphic level, Jane Goodrum and Mike McChesney, who prepared and designed the illustrations that Janice Wheeler then integrated, greatly aided the process. I also want to thank the publisher's anonymous readers, who provided me with insightful comments and helped me sharpen my arguments.

So much for the academic and editorial organizations that assisted in the research and publication of this book. On a noninstitutional level, the list of benefactors is much longer and more intimate. First, my thanks go to the people of Yuendumu. It is to them that I owe my greatest and most heartfelt debt. They have been my teachers and friends and (at the risk of stumbling into a Western debate on matters of cross-cultural appropriation) my family. Their insights helped me as a professor, a mother, a writer, and a friend.

A common liability of acknowledgment, when focused on the Warlpiri, is the speech taboo that attaches itself to the names of the deceased. In early drafts of my work, I tried employing pseudonyms to circumvent this problem. I have since abandoned that practice and now refer to friends no longer living by the referential term that the Warlpiri themselves use in such contexts: *kumanjayi*. Doing so, I believe, allows for recognizing assistance while avoiding offense. The many friends who have helped me include: Judy Nampijinpa, Dolly Nampijinpa, Molly Nampijinpa, Uni Nampijinpa, Lucky Nampijinpa, Peggy Nampijinpa, Kumanjayi Nampijinpa, Rosy Nangala, Tilo Nangala, Kumanjayi Napangardi, Maggy Napangardi, Lucy Napaljarri, Tess Napaljarri, Lydie Napanangka, Topsy Napanangka, Jeannie Nungarrayi, June Napanangka, Cecily Napanangka, Jorna Napurrurla, Lorna Napurrurla, Peggy Napurrurla, Long Maggy Nakamarra, Bessy Nakamarra, Kumanjayi Nungarrayi, Kumanjayi Nungarrayi, Kumanjayi Jungarrayi, Kumanjayi Japangardi, Kumanjayi Japangardi, Kumanjayi Jampijinpa, Darby Jampijinpa, Rex Japanangka, Robin Japanangka, Kurt Japanangka, Kumanjayi Japaljarri, Paddy Japaljarri, Kumanjayi Jakamarra, Harry Jakamarra, Kumanjayi Jakamarra, Francis Jupurrurla, Kumanjayi Jupurrurla, Kumanjayi Jangala, Kumanjayi Jangala, and Tom Jangala. These men and women, in various ways and times, provided profound insight into the nuances of Warlpiri culture—its language, its kinship practices, its notions of the Dreaming, its hunting and gathering strategies, and a thousand other matters. I will always try to treat the knowledge they gave me the way they themselves handle ritual material: as both gift and obligation.

The help I received in Yuendumu did not come solely from its Aboriginal residents. Without months of linguistic assistance from many nonindigenous friends there, I would never have gained the verbal competence needed to decode the language of ceremonial action. My non-Warlpiri teachers, all brilliant linguists, included David Nash, Mary Laughren, and Nick Piper; all three of them helped me (and continue to help me) parse out the specificities of Warlpiri syntax and vocabulary. There were others who gave fluency to my fieldwork. These dear friends include Frank and Wendy Baarda, Pam Harris, Christine Lennard, Ann Mosey, and Geraldine Tyson.

Though I have never cared much for Alice Springs, the urban center closest to Yuendumu, my resistance has been regularly tempered by the intellectual, culinary, and emotional generosity of Penelope Evans and Robert Hoogenraad; they offered up books, breakfasts, bedrolls, and means of transportation at any hour of the day or night. Their camaraderie and knowledge about Aboriginal matters remain invaluable. Likewise, I feel fortunate to have received guidance from two local Warlpiri women during my field trips to the fringe camps of Alice Springs. Without the help of Kumanjayi Napangardi and Kumanjayi Nampijinpa I could never have come to understand how Warlpiri ritual expresses itself in semiurban contexts.

The terrain of the Central Desert offers one set of challenges, the landscape of the blank pages quite another. And because I come to both English and Warlpiri as a non-native speaker, the challenges feel especially great. My first guides through the territory of the written word were my dissertation advisors, Nicolas Peterson and Howard Morphy, professors and friends who have beyond devotion been reading and rereading my work since before the days of e-mail. Despite my lapses and circumlocutions (a stubborn legacy of the French) they have been supportive and insightful. So too Fred Myers, whose help, while never formally sanctioned, has always been prompt, rigorous, generous, and wise. To that troika of fine minds and devoted scholars I must add Nancy Munn, Peter Sutton, and Robert Tonkinson, as well as the late Sally White and Annette Weiner.

The list goes on. Without the long and involved mealtime conversations I had with Annette Hamilton and Marcia Langton (usually in Alice Springs); without the collegial departmental exchanges I had with Tom Beidelman (at New York University) and James Faris (at the University of Connecticut); without the curatorial debates I had with Christopher Anderson (all over the world); without the field trips taken with Faye Ginsburg in 1992 and the land claims with Nicolas Peterson, Joh Bornman, and Paul Burke (in the Central Australian Desert); without years of intellectual sorority with Janet Siskind, Anne Marie Cantwell, and Marika Moisseeff; without the support of Robert Alvarez, Meg McLagan, Nick Spitzer, Alan Swedlund, Duane Anderson, and Doug Schwartz at the School of American Research; without the conference invitations of Richard Lee, James Weiner, and Alan Rumsey; without the help of Candace Hetzner and especially Sydney Plum, who proofread my manuscript before I nervously mailed it to the Smithsonian, I would have written a book containing many more mistakes and far fewer insights. (However, they are not to be held responsible for any of the book's shortcomings.) The collective impact of the abovementioned scholars and friends defies the vocabulary of gratitude.

I reserve the final paragraph of what lexicographers call "declarations of retrospective empathic affection" to five individuals who lived through (and in) the writing of this book: my mother, Constance Dussart; Judy Nampijinpa; Dolly Nampijinpa; my husband, Allen Kurzweil; and our son, Maximilian. Kinship can be forged and strengthened in many ways, as those five individuals have taught me.

THE POLITICS OF RITUAL IN AN ABORIGINAL SETTLEMENT

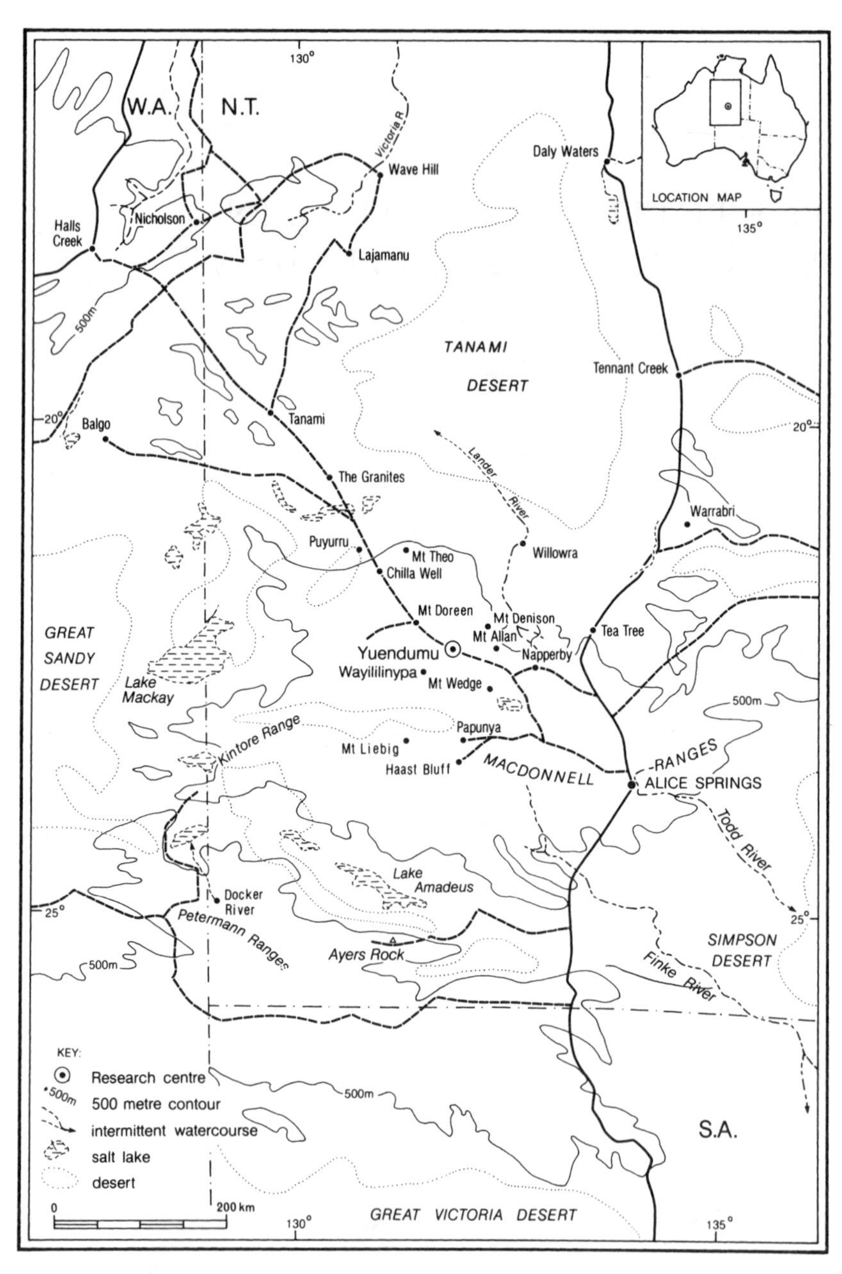

Map 1. Research area (*Source*: research, F. Dussart; del. J. R. Goodrum, Australian National University, 1988)

INTRODUCTION

I arrived at the Aboriginal settlement of Yuendumu in the autumn of 1983, a twenty-three-year-old hybrid of a French and Australian education. Training in the structuralist ideologies of the Sorbonne and empirical methods of my (principally) British-educated professors at the Australian National University precipitated in me a confused, theoretically schizophrenic approach to the discipline of anthropology. Like so many graduate students, I combined overreaching ambition with underdeveloped hypothesis. Among other things, the dissertation I hoped to write was supposed to challenge fundamental Durkheimian dichotomies that placed men in the realm of the sacred and shunted women into the realm of the profane, to obliterate normative models, and to embrace various feminist theories that had held sway in the late 1970s and early '80s. With those modest goals in mind, I chose to study patterns of iconographic representation in the ritual life of the Warlpiri Aborigines living in the Central Australian Desert.

My ethnographic work was intended to be restricted to a detailed analysis of the symbolic vocabulary of women's body painting, so as to allow theory to flourish. But as I dutifully gathered data, filling notebook after notebook with the circles, semicircles, and meanders for which the settlement subsequently gained international recognition in the art world, it started to become clear that my hypotheses were overly deterministic and woefully incompatible with the complex negotiations surrounding the production and use of the visual representations of Warlpiri cosmology. My confusion and dissatisfaction intensified slowly until, two months into a two-year stay (which itself grew into a decade-long study), I found myself jettisoning the theoretical models I had so cavalierly brought to the field. This abandonment coincided with more mundane physical displacement: eviction from the house where I had been living. Being deprived of both a rhetoric and a residence caused me no small measure of distress. I confronted the more urgent of the two liabilities—lack of lodging—by trying to relocate into one of the settlement's peripheral camps, where many of Yuendumu's most active ritual performers (and hence many of my informants) lived. My request, made to Judy Nampijinpa and Lucy Napaljarri, two self-described "big businesswomen"—that is, ritual leaders of the settlement—precipitated lengthy and complex negotiations that revealed with surprising clarity a long-standing rivalry between the two I had previously undervalued.

It became clear very quickly that I was seen by the women to be both a resource and a responsibility. I provided various forms of economic assistance, chauffeured women (and related kin) on hunting expeditions, and contributed in less definable ways to the status and prestige of those with whom I worked. These assets, however, carried concomitant burdens. Any dividend I might generate also necessitated intricate and highly stressful demands of redistribution, which is at the core of Warlpiri social exchange. The women wanted to maximize the benefits my residency might bring while avoiding distributive obligations, a mirroring of many of the kin-based strategies of exchange I would only later come to recognize in the settlement's ceremonial life. Judy and Lucy, close cross-cousins belonging to two competing kin groups, employed tactics of triangulated negotiation and of delegated responsibility that implicated ritually beholden relatives, both male and female, who found themselves obligated to serve as emissaries for the businesswomen. Both women tried to use my request to reify and strengthen their personal status and the standing of their residential group. Judy supplemented her kin-based discussions by intensifying her commitment to my education. She showed me the proper methods of hunting and cooking game (goanna, emu, kangaroo), the techniques for gathering bush yams, and the subtleties of the kinship dynamics needed to nurture the Dreaming during ritual enactment.

Naturally this effort did not go unnoticed by Lucy, who immediately expressed concern to her relatives that the time I spent with a rival might cause me to undervalue their kin group's ceremonial repertoire. More triangulated intervention followed, further increasing the number of individuals involved in the lodging negotiations. Eventually the issue of residency was resolved when Judy exploited her kin ties to a younger (and thus beholden) brother, then the president of the Yuendumu Council. She urged him to provide me with a council house. Though reluctant, he acceded to the request—which, because of her kin status, had the force of a demand—and spoke with the authorities responsible for such housing allocations. He managed to locate a wood-frame structure recently vacated by the Yuendumu Council plumber. The house was situated in neutral territory between South Camp, where Lucy lived, and West Camp, where Judy and her kin group resided. (See map 2.)

While this accommodation positioned me in a geographically nonpartisan section of the settlement, it in no way reduced the competition sparked by the housing request. Quite the contrary. For the next twenty-four months I shared the wood-frame structure with a large number of Warlpiri women and children, initially with one leader's kin group and later with others. As my circle of friends from the different groups widened, so did my awareness of the entanglements of residentially constituted patterns of kinship, gender, and persona found at the core of Warlpiri social identity—a social identity sustained both in the performance of ritual and in the realm of the so-called profane. I saw, too, over time, that to understand fully the motive forces underneath the anthropological labels of kinship, gender, and persona, it would be necessary to explore the highly competitive dynamics of Warlpiri social engagement, and that the engagement might best be observed through the ritual life that brought these elements so demonstrably to the fore. Indeed, within months of relocation, I had shifted the focus of my research from the iconography to the iconographers who created it. In doing so I was able to expand my appreciation of the function of ritual, to see the shapes of a body design as a kind of currency of knowledge, the circulation of which sustained many of the most fundamental aspects of Warlpiri social identity.

The simple lodging request in effect raised an awareness in me of the plurality of issues I had unknowingly avoided in my early days of research: the interplay of kinship and gender; the nuances of authority, persona, and prestige; the extraceremonial obligations associated with ritual and land tenure; the function of competition in the distribution of ritual knowledge attached to that tenure. And by competition, I mean not only the struggle between businesswomen such as Lucy and Judy, but also the struggles between women and men, between individual and kin group, between Warlpiri kin groups, between the Warlpiri and other Aboriginal people, and, to be sure, between the Aboriginal world and the world that has come to dominate it. In facing these tensions, I was forced to abandon the exclusive kin group models that segregated Judy and Lucy, as women, from the male members of their kin groups. For the first time, I began to recognize that these businesswomen could be social actors *and* women *and* members of a kin group, and that the nature of the kin group itself required redefinition. To deny any one of these constituent components was to misconstrue the forces at work in settlement life. That insight prompted further revision of my theoretical premises and an enlargement of the questions that I posed. As so commonly happens in the ethnographic process, a minor episode had a major, almost epiphanic, impact. The dispute between Judy and Lucy provided a key (to be sure, at that point crudely formed) to larger issues of exchange—issues that ultimately gave focus to my work on the resonances of ritual, and the currency of knowledge that circulates to sustain it.

There is, of course, a danger in privileging a personal anthropological anecdote in a work about Aboriginal ceremonial life, since it draws attention away from the subject studied and points it toward the person doing the study. But that danger is present (in fact endemic) in the process of ethnography, whether or not it is acknowledged. Fieldwork implicates the researcher—especially when it is undertaken in a settlement of forcibly sedentarized erstwhile hunter-gatherers. For better or worse, the presence of researchers at Yuendumu, arriving as they do with tape recorders and field notebooks in hand (and more recently computers, video cameras, and VCRs), has had a direct impact on the settlement scrutinized. For that reason, and others, anthropologists have a particular obligation to embrace the reciprocity and exchange methods of those with whom they work. In my case, that meant that while I gathered information on ritual and social structure and began to develop insights into ritual as a currency of knowledge, I also served as a part-time taxi driver, fundraiser for a fledgling art movement, and land claims consultant. In all those roles, as well as in the formal academically sanctioned one that brought me to Yuendumu, I often found myself embracing the spirit of combative compromise surrounding the housing dispute in matters of ethnographic theory. Where I once felt compelled to choose sides in the debates that pitted gender against kinship (at the root of much Aboriginalist literature), I now sought reconciliation, attempting to employ methods and methodologies that would acknowledge the same kind of interdependence and "relatedness" that governed the lives of the businesswomen (and men) with whom I lived.

This effort toward inclusiveness has had repercussions that extended beyond the theoretical. It also has had an impact on the style and tone of this book. What started out as a monograph unwaveringly beholden to much-quoted and little-read ethnographic literature of the Central Desert turned into something different: a work conceptualized and composed for a slightly broader, less specialized readership. This does not mean that I will provide a blow-by-blow description of ritual or even linger at length on descriptive representations of the so-called ritual life. In point of fact, Warlpiri life *is* ritual insofar as the expression of a spiritual connection to the ancestors extends beyond the formal ceremonial sphere. The links can be made manifest in momentary asides during hunting trips or songs sung during sudden pangs of grief over missing loved ones (which can include pieces of land as much as kin). This book is not a spiritual guide to the Dreaming; it is, instead, an analysis of how and why ritual knowledge circulates.

The Warlpiri, as I detail in a later chapter, have a wonderfully rich vocabulary with regard to the accessibility of ritual. Within their ceremonial discourse, they are quick to distinguish the *warraja,* or public, event from a ceremonial representation that they label *tarruku,* or closed. The public event is no less essential to the nurturance of the Dreaming, but it inhabits a more accessible space than the restricted materials to which the uninitiated are denied access.

Anthropology, too, has its restricted vocabularies and closed rituals. Some of the best writing on the Aborigines is also some of the least read by the general public because of a cumbersome reliance on the language of the initiand. With this liability in mind, I have, whenever possible, attempted to sidestep the jargon-spiked chasm of the arcane, though not, I hope, at the expense of complexity or nuance. That is the reason formulations peppering an early version of this work—for example, "If the FZ/FB links to the FBB . . ."—have been replaced by descriptions of the actions of a father's sister, father's brother, and father's brother's brother.

The reason I have at times ventured so far from classic formal terminologies is worth a moment's reflection. Because this work constitutes an act of serial translation—a rendering of a particular aspect and moment of the Warlpiri world in the English of a French woman—I am only too aware of how easily non-Warlpiri (that is, Western) sensibilities can co-opt indigenous vision and voice. Indeed, the matter is further complicated by the Warlpiri themselves, who at times embrace the ethnographer's lexicon and translate it into an indigenous form that can then be retranslated (often unknowingly) to produce ethnography that neatly, if erroneously, legitimates the perspectives of the fieldworker. In short, the ghost of Werner Heisenberg hovers over the anthropologist's enterprise as much as it does over physics. I have found that by writing simply and directly, I reduce the risk of inadvertent projection and mitigate (though by no means eradicate) the liabilities of tethering an indigenous world to theories born from twentieth-century Western discourse. That is not to say I have abandoned the ethnographic literature or all the useful terms it contains, only that I have tried to prevent non-Warlpiri writings from drowning out the voices that gave those writings life.

GENDER, KINSHIP, PERSONA: A BRIEF OVERVIEW

The relationship of kinship to gender has occupied a rich and contentious position in the ethnographic study of Australian Aboriginal ritual. As I stated earlier, the tension between these two concepts can be found at the root of much Aboriginalist debate. And yet the irony in that tension is this: The roots of these seemingly incompatible words are intricately linked. The origins of both *gender* and *kin* have been traced to the Latin *genus,* and to terms of birth, race, kind, and class.[1] One of the paths traveled by the Latin word *genus* moved through the Gothic form *kuni,* then through Old Norse and into the Old High German word *kind,* "child." From there it advanced to the Old English word *cyn* and on to the Middle English word *kin,* so valued by anthropologists. As for the much deployed and falsely conceptualized competitor to *kin, gender,* that word comes to us via the Middle English and Middle French words *gender* and *genre,* from the same Latin root that gave birth to *kinship. Kin* and *gender,* to repeat, share a common lexical ancestry. And to judge from the relationship that these forces retain at Yuendumu, that is as it should be. Far from being oppositional or disconnected, the qualities are inexorably linked. While a detailed exploration of the history of the gender-versus-kinship debate would fill a separate volume, the key moments of the history of these putatively competing concepts in the literature of the Central Australian Desert are worth identifying, since they underline the divergent theoretical presumptions found in the field of anthropology at large.

Many of the earliest ethnographers to work extensively among the Warlpiri—Olive Pink, Nancy Munn, Mervyn Meggitt—adopted a substantially Durkheimian view that subordinated women to men. Their fieldwork, collectively, portrayed Warlpiri women as having little or no access to so-called secret sacred knowledge. The argument was perhaps advanced most forcefully by Meggitt in *The Gadjari among the Walbiri Aborigines,* a monograph that explored "the superior status of men vis à vis women in the sacred situation." He noted:

> A belief in the existence of creative Dreamtime women, superordinate to other totemic Beings, would at the conscious level not only tend to conflict with prevailing ethos but also, I should think, be actually repugnant to most men. Thus, the few myths that treat in detail the activities of Dreamtime women tend to be taken to justify or to account for the relatively inferior position of contemporary women. (Meggitt 1966:23)

Meggitt went on to note that beyond the domain of the so-called sacred, women also held a diminished status in the secular domain as well. But even before Meggitt conducted his fieldwork, alternative perspectives (albeit not among the Warlpiri) could be found in Aboriginalist literature. Two anthropologists in particular disputed the assumptions driving Meggitt's view of women. As early as 1939, Phyllis M. Kaberry portrayed a ritual life in which women shared with men "the same supernatural sanction of the totemic ancestors and the Time Long Past" (Kaberry 1939:273). Displaying more eloquence than Meggitt, if less data, she argued against the view that Aboriginal women were "utterly degraded" (the term is Briffault's), adding that such generalizations "savour of the moralist rather than the scientist; as an unqualified summing up of sexual relations" (Kaberry 1939:270). Kaberry went on to write that though women did not share in the secret ritual life of men, this in no way diminished their "spiritual heritage," one that emphasized "kinship to environment." Women's ceremonies, Kaberry concluded, had an ameliorative effect on the community and its individuals (1939:269).

There would be a danger (in fact, more than one) in attempting a "who's right?" resolution of the differences in Meggitt's and Kaberry's views on the role of women in Aboriginal ritual life. For instance, geographic and cultural distinctions must be acknowledged. Kaberry conducted her fieldwork in the southern Kimberley region of Western Australia, several hundred kilometers to the north and west of Lajamanu, the settlement where Meggitt worked. Furthermore, the Kimberleys circa 1939 and Lajamanu circa 1955 represent profoundly different moments in the history of sedentarization. Nevertheless, these divergent determinations go a long way in defining the parameters of many subsequent feminist and postfeminist analyses of Aboriginal ritual life. Still, it is essential to distinguish sedentary from nomadic circumstance; it is neither beneficial nor even possible to attribute the changing status of women solely to issues of forced sedentarization. To be sure, pre- and postcontact clarifications must be made, but not to the exclusion of an analysis that also acknowledges the dynamic transformations that have occurred in the last fifty years.

Whereas Meggitt and like-minded anthropologists built a male-dominated kin-based model of ritual leadership—one that marginalized women—many of the heirs to Kaberry's suppositions of complementarity and coexistence tended to subsume kinship under issues of gender. The first major analysis of the significance of women in Central Desert ritual life appeared in the work of Catherine Berndt. Berndt, acknowledging Kaberry for removing "a welter of distortion" (Berndt 1965:238), studied the universe of women's Dreamings and ritual activity that emerged after "alien contact" (Berndt 1950:9), documenting the transformation of Aboriginal social relations that accompanied forced settlement. She argued that newly evolved ritual activities had a direct and lasting impact on maintaining social relations. Berndt's long-term commitment to fieldwork infused her work with a subtle understanding of how kinship and gender relations had changed over time, and with an awareness of the necessity to distinguish between pre- and postcontact circumstance when assessing the role of Aboriginal women, a distinction Meggitt had systematically downplayed in his work. Berndt, it must be noted, tempered some of her early work, first conducted in the 1940s, a quarter century later by raising a cautionary note against overly dichotomized views of the ritual life of men and women (Berndt 1965, 1974). This concern coincided with the rise of overtly feminist methodologies that radicalized the study of women's status and injected an economic dimension into the study of Aboriginal ritual. Perhaps the most sophisticated expression of this approach emerged in the work of Annette Hamilton. Starting in the early 1970s, Hamilton conducted research among Pitjantjatjara women living in Central Australia. What made her work especially noteworthy was its comparative nature; she had previously lived with the Gidjingali in northeast Arnhem Land. The two settings enabled her to draw rigorous inter-Aboriginal distinctions based on her own participant observation. In matters of ritual, Hamilton concluded that Pitjantjatjara women, unlike those living in Arnhem Land, had a flourishing secret life, one that was separate from men. This autonomy, while it did not preclude economic interdependence and domination in moments of irreconcilable conflict, allowed for a "fundamental form of sociality which renders each sex powerful to itself" (Hamilton 1981: 69). As such, the Pitjantjatjara could evince a pattern of "homosocial associations" that acknowledged both inequality and autonomy (1981:84).

Hamilton's feminist and Marxian insights were subsequently refashioned by Diane Bell, who added a Leacockian sensibility to the study of Central Desert women (Bell 1983). Bell, like Hamilton, was quick to point out that contact with the dominant society had caused a debilitation of women's ritual and the subordination of its performers. "Where once there was independence," she wrote about the pre- and postcontact change to the status of women, "there now is relative dependence" (Bell 1983:46). However, during her work at Warrabri, a Central Desert settlement composed principally of Kaytej and Warlpiri Aborigines, Bell discovered a domain in which this subordination was mitigated. That domain was the *jilimi,* camps of single women that provided a context of ritual and social separation. The camps, to which men were prohibited access, enabled senior women to emerge as "autonomous, independent ritual actors who actively participate in the creation, transmission and maintenance of the values of their society" (Bell 1983: 226).

This activity was not restricted to rituals performed by women only. On the contrary, Bell showed how women even played a crucial role in certain men's ceremonies. She further argued that the independence women manifested in the *jilimi* counteracted a general weakening of the ritual role of women prompted by sedentarization, and that the *jilimi* contained a secret ritual life inaccessible to men. In this way, she inverted the gender dichotomy but preserved the supposition that secret sacred knowledge was the central criterion by which ritual status could be judged; it was just that the locus of that authority was to be discovered in a domain where previously it had not been seen. Bell suggested that the reason such knowledge, and the power it implied, was overlooked was that male anthropologists were ill equipped to gain access to the secret life of women. By questioning the feasibility of cross-gender research within communities that enacted a segregated ritual life, Bell privileged male/female dichotomies over other variables of culture, including kinship and less commonly applied distinctions of persona and personal prestige.

The gender-versus-kinship debate was considerably complicated by Fred Myers, who began working in the 1970s with Pintupi Aborigines at the settlement of Papunya, some 150 kilometers (about 93 miles) southeast of Yuendumu. Myers chose to sidestep either/or constructions of the debate about kinship and gender, proposing instead to address the "inner logic of Pintupi sociality." This logic, he argued, expressed itself in complex patterns of "relatedness" and "autonomy" mediated by a third pattern Myers tagged "the cultural representation of hierarchy as nurturance" (Myers 1986a:22). These patterns, necessitating ongoing negotiation and exchange, were predicated on the individual's ties to Dreaming sites and to issues of residential organization.[2] While Myers limited his fieldwork mostly to Pintupi men, his analytic premises found applicability to women as well. What made Myers's work so important was its nondichotomous model for exploring the social forces at work in Aboriginal culture. To the entangled variables of kinship and gender he added a sophisticated notion of the individual and the self.

My admittedly selective overview is by no means intended to provide an exhaustive exploration of the issues of gender and kinship in the ritual life of Australian Aborigines. The half dozen or so anthropologists cited are invoked because their contributions, collectively, raise fundamental questions central to an understanding of the roles Yuendumu's businesswomen play in the larger universe of the settlement. Beyond that, the works refer to central debates at the heart of the larger anthropological discourse. The varying methodologies and conclusions of these scholars suggest a certain utility in attempting to draw connections rather than separations among the issues of gender, kinship, and the personal motivation so often found in social action. As the ethnography of the last fifty years implies, any analysis of Aboriginal ritual life and the effect that ritual life has beyond the ceremonial domain must be both geospecific and temporally attentive. And by "temporal" I refer not only to complex issues of pre- and postcontact change in the nature of ritual and the makeup of its constituency, but to the individual timelines that link ritual performers to the ceremonies they reenact.

To that end, this book attempts to address a set of questions that can be stated, reductively, as follows: What sustains ritual and what, in turn, does ritual sustain? How has ritual changed the status of women, and how have women changed the nature (if not the status) of ritual? What relationships do kinship, gender, and persona have to the expression of Warlpiri ritual life and vice versa? How does ritual enactment—the circulation of the aforementioned currency of knowledge—inform the nonceremonial life of the settlement? These questions touch on issues of secrecy, pan-Aboriginality, and other matters that have come to dominate Aboriginalist literature. If these questions seem excessively general, it is because more specific formulations presuppose an understanding of the particular nature of Warlpiri ritual life at Yuendumu, and that understanding can emerge only after the basic structures of the belief system have been described and the specific historical circumstances of Yuendumu as a settlement have been established.

Most of my time at Yuendumu was spent with women and, in particular, the self-described "bosses," or businesswomen, who sustain so much of Yuendumu's ritual life. This bias was an inevitable outgrowth of the physically (if not psychically) segregated nature of settlement life. Where and when possible, I have tried to integrate the voices of men, who often amplified, corroborated, or contradicted the observations made by my principal women informants.

A PLAN OF PRESENTATION

The book begins, as it must, with an exploration of Warlpiri cosmology, the Dreaming known as *Jukurrpa* (chapter 1). Five overlapping meanings of the term are isolated so that a thorough grounding in the lexical and social complexities of ritual then may be explored. These plural meanings require such thorough explication in order to understand how ritual—the ceremonial celebration of the Dreaming—is conceptualized and deployed as a form of social currency. This quintet of definitions is followed by an analysis of the "ideal" template of kinship, a pattern of social connection central to the ritual reproduction of the Dreaming. While the template characterizes the formal rights and responsibilities by which the Warlpiri constitute their cosmology, historical circumstances modifying that template must also be shown. To that end, a brief overview of ritual life at Yuendumu after sedentarization is presented, with special emphasis placed on the kin-based residential component of contemporary social organization.

Chapter 2 advances the study of ritual, kinship, and gender by moving from a general exploration of Warlpiri cosmology to a specific lexical analysis of certain vocabularies—indigenous and adopted—that orbit ceremonial life. Four sets of categorical constructs are isolated, defined, and conflated. In the process, the chapter attempts to show how some of the standard language of ethnography ("circumcision ceremony," "secret knowledge," and so on), as well as certain terms used by the Warlpiri themselves, hide the complex entanglements of gender and ritual maturity in the discussion of ceremonial life. Scrutiny of these vocabularies and their variant applications forces a reevaluation of the notion of gender-specific "secret" knowledge, as well as the presumptive power such "secrecy" establishes. For while Yuendumu's businesswomen have managed to sustain and even enhance their roles in the ritual domains of the settlement—the focus of a later chapter—they have done so without the ceremonial expression of so-called secret ritual knowledge. To provide a sense of the full repertoire of ritual events in which the politics of Warlpiri ceremonial life is played out, chapter 2 concludes with a chronologically ordered evaluation of the rituals marking the ceremonial life cycle of the Warlpiri, followed by an assessment of those performances enacted beyond the formal parameters of certain so-called rites of passage.

With the cosmology reviewed (chapter 1) and its ritual language defined and temporally situated in the trajectory of Warlpiri ceremony (chapter 2), it becomes possible to address the social significance of the expression of that ritual knowledge by scrutinizing the businesswomen who oversee its nurturance. To that end, chapter 3 explores how ritual knowledge is acquired, maintained, and ultimately passed on by the *yamparru* (that is, business leaders) of Yuendumu.[3] The chapter attempts to characterize the highly competitive process of ritual nurturance, one imbued with a value-laden sensibility of "winning." The distribution of ritual knowledge is equipped with a series of checks and balances that reconciles the acquisition of authority with diffusionary egalitarian components permeating Warlpiri society. Though this chapter acknowledges the rigid physical divisions separating women and men, it focuses on the shared qualities of obligation and competition, qualities that serve as a bridge. By devoting the second half of the chapter to a single case study of leadership among women, it is possible to understand the forces by which religious and secular leadership are acquired and expressed, maintained, limited, and ultimately abrogated.

After describing the process by which women become ritual leaders, it becomes possible to characterize how this authority and concomitant prestige can directly inform the actual substance of ritual. That characterization is the subject of chapter 4: an exploration of how one businesswoman was able to integrate personal dreams into a ritual repertoire jointly performed by men and women. This study of how dreams are made (and remade) provides insight into the links among personal prestige, gender, and kinship, and clarifies how supposedly static expressions of Warlpiri cosmology are in fact open to transformation. The insertion of new Dreaming segments into ceremony hints at the way in which ritual knowledge and authority implicate men and women even in gender-restricted ritual events. Other aspects of this conduit must also be explored.

Chapter 5 focuses on the cross-gender negotiations implicating ceremonial (and metaceremonial) knowledge, those exchanges that bring women and men together in various postsedentary contexts of ritual collaboration. The transmission of such currency in the wake of nocturnal dreams, during ceremony, and in the production of acrylic paintings—three domains wherein the gender dynamics implicating ritual knowledge undergo reconfiguration—exemplifies the nonexclusionary nature of "male" and "female" ritual. Indeed, such cross-gender negotiations force us to rethink certain dichotomous representations common to the discourse surrounding Warlpiri social relations. To appreciate how this currency of knowledge is distributed and withheld by (and among) men and women vis-à-vis each other points to the manner in which the most recent generation of ritual performers has undertaken the (re)formation of social identity, a process I characterize as one of "engendering." The term *engendering,* as it is deployed here, captures the oft-neglected movements of ritual material between women and men, a cross-gender negotiation of knowledge that points to how the Dreaming (and its Dreamers) is reproduced through the exchange of ritual material. The term has further utility, for it suggests how the roles of women have expanded in the public expression of the reproduction of the Dreaming, a realignment of rights and responsibilities that shall be addressed in the final chapter of the book. Once the movement of ritual material among women and men has been characterized, it becomes possible to address broader structural expressions of this engendering, seen specifically in the wholesale transfer of performative control, a phenomenon evinced in the evolution of Yuendumu's public—that is, unrestricted—ritual history. Although once the sole province of men, these "open" performances are now conducted primarily by women. Despite this apparently radical realignment of duties, it would be ill advised to limn a picture of contemporary ritual life that overprivileges a gender-based dichotomy of ceremonial power. Closer inspection of the sea change in the public presentation of ritual underscores, in point of fact, a plurality of constants that the Warlpiri—men and women alike—continue to bring both to the ceremonial sphere and to the less formal social relations that this forum of ritual engagement promulgates. Indeed, public events offer up a chance to revisit a number of the overlapping vocabularies infusing previous discussions of "business." The historical shift from *purlapa* (men's public events) to *yawulyu warrajanyani* (women's public events) confirms, among other things, the pervasive influence of residentially constituted kinship: the ongoing significance of seniority, the forces of connectedness, facts of competition in ritual enactment, and the stresses that these forces generate.

Beyond that, a chronological overview of public ritual since sedentarization highlights the function of business in the extraceremonial life of the settlement—specifically in the manner by which the Warlpiri have come to mediate their cross-cultural engagements. And because such rituals figure prominently in, among other things, issues of land reclamation, mining disputes, and less contested forms of cultural representation such as "dot" painting, tracing how the business of "business" has evolved in "open" settings registers Warlpiri efforts to respond both to external pressure and indigenous imperatives. The gender shift in public ritual belies ritual motives shared by Warlpiri women and men, and further obscures a dynamic of performative separation, a bipartite cohesion at the core of Yuendumu's ceremonial life.

During my fieldwork, two of the most active ritual leaders in the display of Warlpiri ritual, both inside Yuendumu and out, were the same two women who found me lodging and who helped me refine my understanding of settlement politics. Judy's and Lucy's early engagement with my concerns naturally prompted a correlative interest in theirs. And what mattered to them was not postfeminist theory or competing models of kin organization, but "business," the planning and performance of ritual. By refocusing my research on their concerns, I found one of the keys to the fieldwork that follows. Understanding ritual fully forced a reconciliation of the supposedly incompatible constructs I had brought with me into the field. The women's insights into "business" provided the means by which I could appreciate gender and kinship as constituent and indivisible components of Warlpiri social identity. And yet the language of convergence or cohesion is, in itself, not entirely satisfactory. The acknowledgment of interdependence is inadequate if the specific nature(s) of the synthesis is (are) overlooked—if the possibility and contexts of primacy between two mutually constituted components of social construction are ignored. In the case of the Warlpiri committed to the nurturance of ritual, where and when issues of gender and kinship collided, it was kin-based residentiality that tended to overwhelm other social pressures. That having been said, it is important also to note that indigenous representations of that residentially conceptualized commitment obviate these theoretical divisions. For Judy and Lucy, the overriding function of "business" was not a declaration of the potency of their gender or of their kin group, but rather the maintenance of the *Jukurrpa* in all its various guises.

I.

THE DREAMING AND ITS KIN

"Past" and "Present" Circumstance

To understand how the Warlpiri organize and maintain their social universe, one must first comprehend the complex, plurally employed concept they invoke when discussing their cosmology: *Jukurrpa.* Variously translated as the "Dreamtime," "Dreaming," and "Ancestral Times," these English-language terms often obfuscate more than they clarify.[1] *Jukurrpa* provides the Warlpiri with links to their past, their land, their ancestors, and each other, reifying contemporary social relations and articulating—in both oral and structural senses—omnipresent connections at the core of the Warlpiri sense of identity. As such, any assessment of kinship and gender relations in ritual, or of the role of the individual in the group, necessitates at the start a thorough grounding in the notion of *Jukurrpa* in all its facets and contexts.

THE *JUKURRPA:* MEANINGS AND MANIFESTATIONS

Contrary to the simplified definitions employed in certain early anthropological literature and the grotesquely reductive appropriations by contemporary New Age "spiritualists" in the West, *Jukurrpa* appears to have at least five distinct, albeit interrelated, meanings—meanings that the Warlpiri use in different contexts to evoke distinguishable components of their cosmology. The term is most commonly applied to a temporally ambiguous moment I shall call (with purposely oxymoronic intent) the

Ancestral Present. It is during this Ancestral Present that the world was physically and spiritually shaped by Ancestral Beings who gave the Warlpiri their moral and ritual order. In this temporal application, *Jukurrpa* alludes to an epoch that is paradoxically—at least by Western notions of time—situated simultaneously in the distant past (*nyuruwiyi*) and in the present (*jalangu*).[2] It was (and is) during the Ancestral Present that the Warlpiri (both human and mythological) were (and are) first linked to the sites and countries they inhabit(ed) and maintain(ed). These Beings emerged (*wilypi-pardimi*) from the ground to make waterholes, rock holes (natural depressions in rocks that catch water), creeks, watercourses, mountains, and hills before returning to the ground and the sky.

The second sense of *Jukurrpa* employs the word as a collective noun for the Ancestral Beings themselves, Beings who formed, and continue to form, the multiple dimensions—geophysical, spiritual, and social—of the Warlpiri world. It is commonly argued that these Ancestral Beings and ancestors (that is, deceased humans) are considered synonymous by the Warlpiri (see Munn 1964, 1973; Glowczewski 1988). The actual relationship between ancestors (*nyurnupatu*) and Ancestral Beings (*Jukurrpa*) is more complicated.

It is true that an individual may refer to a deceased actual father as, say, "the Red Kangaroo" (*Marlu*), implying the *Jukurrpa* Ancestral Being of that name. Such reference is particularly common when the cosmologically constituted connection to that Being can strengthen ceremonial or territorial rights associated with that Being's Dreaming. This does not mean, however, that the deceased parent's persona is instantly folded into, or immediately becomes one with, some larger cosmological force situated in the Dreaming. In point of fact, further interrogation reveals that at least two generational levels must exist between the deceased and a speaker for the deceased to merge fully with the *Jukurrpa*, a process of genealogical amnesia that coalesces humans and Ancestral Beings.[3]

The mobility of these Beings in the distant past (*nyuruwiyi*) varied greatly. Some—for example, the Worm Being, one of whose many characteristics is that it is said to cause toothaches—emerged from the ground, stayed in their home area for an indefinite period, and then returned whence they came. Others traveled widely over the different homes and countries before ending their travels where they started. All of these Beings left "essences" or "spirits" of various kinds in the landscape. These essences—collectively glossed into "ancestral powers" by Munn and "life forces" by Peterson (1969:27)—are principally distinguished by the Warlpiri as *pirlirrpa, kuruwarri,* and *kurruwalpa.*

Munn defined *kuruwarri* in the following way: "The term *guruwari* [*kuruwarri*] can be used in a general sense to refer to any visible mark left by an ancestor in the country, and in addition, *guruwari* in the abstract aspect of 'ancestral powers' are lodged in the country" (1973:119). The Warlpiri continue to use *kuruwarri* in the concrete sense of marks left by ancestors. The more abstract aspects of Ancestral Powers, however, tend to be invoked by the use of the word *pirlirrpa.* In other words, *kuruwarri* is used to identify the visible component of the *pirlirrpa,* including rock paintings, ritual body designs, and specific marks of ritual activity such as footsteps—in short, the traces of the Dreaming. The Warlpiri dictionary (Hale et al. 1982–1988) establishes a synonymity between *kuruwarri* and *Jukurrpa,* and while it is true that the word *Jukurrpa* can be used as an umbrella term for the trace elements of the Ancestral Beings, the gloss misconstrues the synecdochic relationship between the Dreaming and its outward manifestation.

Pirlirrpa, the essence of *Jukurrpa,* is no less prone to definitional problems, since it also has both general and specific meanings. In the larger sense, *pirlirrpa* can refer to the Ancestral Powers "lodged in the country," to repeat Munn's words. It is the potency of this spiritual essence that establishes the effectiveness of the ritual or ritual performer. But *pirlirrpa* also refers to the "spirit" or "essence" of the individual, which enters via the semen of the father and the egg of the mother, and which localizes itself in the two kidneys (Dussart 1989a:103). The *pirlirrpa* spirit from the semen and that from the egg, though lodged in separate kidneys, are linked through the navel. It is this tie that establishes the spiritual essence of the individual. Both the separation and the link are highlighted by the Warlpiri. Male and female elements are found in every individual, distinct and connected, not unlike certain ritual domains in which *pirlirrpa* is maintained.[4]

Kurruwalpa, the other "essence" or "spirit" of *Jukurrpa,* is associated exclusively with the act of conception. Whereas the *pirlirrpa* is linked physically to the individual, wherever that individual may be, the "conception spirits" (identified by Spencer and Gillen [1899] as the "spirit children") are site-specific. After penetrating the mother—through the womb, foot, or navel—in a fashion that animates the fetus, the *kurruwalpa* localize themselves at the site of conception. *Kurruwalpa* are thus geospecific, whereas the *pirlirrpa* are said to imbue an individual, Dreamings, and the ceremonies that invoke the Dreamings. It is the potency of that *pirlirrpa* that establishes the effectiveness of the ritual or ritual performer in the maintenance of the Dreaming.

Kurruwalpa conception sites are just one of many narrative components found in Warlpiri Dreamtime stories. These stories represent the third facet of *Jukurrpa. Jukurrpa* narratives are found in songs, objects, designs, and dances associated with ritual, and are also proffered in non-ceremonial contexts. This further compounds the confusion among non-Warlpiri regarding the term. Within a single conversation, the Warlpiri may invoke *Jukurrpa* to refer to the Rain Ancestral Being, the story of the Rain Ancestral Being, or the time (albeit ambiguous) in which the Rain Ancestral Being traveled. Context will make the particular meaning perfectly clear—to the Warlpiri. For the anthropologist, however, precise significance is often elusive.

The third (narrative) meaning of *Jukurrpa* hides the fourth, a nuance of the cosmology rarely addressed but crucial in understanding how gender and kinship play out in ceremonial contexts. Warlpiri narratives are inventoried and divided into discrete units. A narrative is generally composed of many such units, which I shall call segments. Rights to these segments—each of which is identified with a home (*ngurrara*) composed of a specific site and its vicinity—serve as a form of ritual currency, a knowledge that can be inherited or personally acquired through a variety of channels. Such segments, conceived as both geophysical and narrative entities, can be gender- and age-specific. In a narrative, sequences of adjacent segments of a specific Dreaming and their homes (*ngurrara*) are grouped together and referred to as the "country" of the kin groups tethered to them. Additionally, each segment may be expressed in versions that are gender- and age-specific. These segments, too, are called *Jukurrpa*. Thus, the travels of an Ancestral Being (*Jukurrpa*) during the Ancestral Present (*Jukurrpa*) left narratives (*Jukurrpa*) composed of site-specific segments (*Jukurrpa*) reenacted in ceremonies.

The narrative and geospecific dimensions of this fourth meaning require further amplification. A long Dreaming itinerary, or track, composed of many segments, may traverse several distinct "countries," implicating different Warlpiri kin groups and their non-Warlpiri neighbors. It is important to understand the distinctions the Warlpiri make between sites (which generally bear a specific place name), homes (known generically as *ngurrara* and identified by an associated site), and countries (which are also identified as *ngurrara* and which are composed of several homes). An example more fully explored in a later portion of the book is the Fire Dreaming known as *Warlu Jukurrpa.* It begins and ends its travels in a home (*ngurrara*) that includes the Dreaming site of Ngarna; but before it completes its itinerary, it traverses many other homes (each portion of the itinerary represents a particular Dreaming segment and a particular narrative) and many other countries owned and overseen by different kin groups, including many who are not Warlpiri.

Dreaming stories may be associated with whole itineraries in their most general rendition, but along with these itineraries there exist other sets of narratives, connective in nature, identified with sites and their related segments. These segment narratives may be gender- and age-specific in nature (though such a circumstance is much less common than various older ethnographies might suggest; see, for example, Meggitt 1962). For example, the segment of the particular Fire Dreaming that is associated with the site of Ngarna has a common narrative, open to men and women of all ages, and a more restricted narrative, limited to the ritually mature of both genders.[5] Another segment, associated with the site of Yampirri-Panturnu, generates narratives with further restrictions that exclude even ritually mature women (see Dussart 1997; Anderson and Dussart 1988). Other narratives implicating the same site, however, allow women to invoke the Dreaming site specifically through various forms of *yawulyu.*

Finally, there are nocturnal dreams that provide much of the mythological knowledge the Warlpiri possess, and these, too, are known as *Jukurrpa.*[6] It is often in these nocturnal events that overlooked or forgotten nuances of the Dreaming narratives may resurface. In chapter 4 I explore the important process by which dreams become Dreamings—that is, the manner in which ritual material is remade.

A group of Ngaanyatjarra, Pitjantjatjara, and Yankunytjatjara women from the Murtitjulu community near Ayers Rock touched on the multiplicity of the meanings buried in the single word *Jukurrpa* (in the orthography of that community, *Tjukurrpa*) in the following way:

> *Tjukurrpa* is existence itself, in the past, present and future. It is also the explanation of existence. And it is the Law which governs behavior. *Tjukurrpa* is expressed in two facts of existence. It is the land—creek, hills, claypans, rockholes, soaks, mountains and other natural features. And it is people—their

actions of hunting, marrying, ceremony and daily life. The *Tjukurrpa* has always been. It does not refer to the time of creation of all things, it is still unfolding, alongside present events, and it is being re-created and celebrated by Anangu people today. (Women's Council Report 1990:35)

THE TRANSFORMATIONAL AND TEMPORAL CONUNDRUMS OF THE *JUKURRPA*

Given the numerous meanings the Warlpiri attach to *Jukurrpa,* it should come as no surprise that anthropologists' interpretations about the nature of the Dreaming may conflict, to say nothing of the dissonance between indigenous declarations and the discourse of external observers. One of the debates central to Aboriginalist literature touches on whether the *Jukurrpa* is immutable (a fact regularly asserted by the indigenous population) or dynamic and changing, a conclusion sustained by long-term anthropological research.[7] The apparent conflict can be at least partially resolved if we specify which aspect of *Jukurrpa* we are talking about—nocturnal dream, Dreaming site, or narrative segment. The indigenous view expressed by the Anangu women in the quotation above is nicely amplified by Tonkinson in his larger analysis of the Mardu. He writes:

The Dreamtime is of fundamental importance because it set for all time the parameters of a way of life which in its essence is held to be unchanging. In the Aboriginal view, none of these essential elements changes because the Law is followed and the founding patterns are thus perpetuated. Nowhere does their ideology admit structural change as a possibility. On the contrary, the emphasis throughout Australia is on continuity of present and future with past and the notion of progress does not exist. (Tonkinson 1978:112)

This description fairly represents the Warlpiri perspective on the nature of the Dreaming's immutability. The Warlpiri evoke the eternal nature of this force in the term *tarnnga.* A common explanation of the Dreaming is "*Jukurrpa ka tarnngalku nyina,*" meaning "The Dreaming is always here." When describing their ritual responsibility, businesswomen and businessmen liken their performances (in all media) to the act of copying (*miirn-yarrarni*) schoolwork written on a blackboard.[8] The analogy suggests knowledge of a rote nature. But as Tonkinson goes on to point out, changes in the manifestation of this Dreaming are possible, and in fact prevalent among the Mardu (1978:114). This "flexibility" is also the case among the Pintupi, whose cosmology, Myers explains, manifests tremendous flux (1986a:51, 53, 67).

If one asks the Warlpiri whether the *Jukurrpa* (in this context referring to the temporal aspects) is susceptible to change, they will say, point blank, that it is not. If, however, they are asked whether a specific Dreaming segment (which, as noted earlier, is also referred to as *Jukurrpa*) can be forgotten, they will readily admit that such amnesia is quite common. These responses do not, for the Warlpiri, constitute inconsistency; while the segments may be forgotten temporarily (say, through the demise of a kin group or various speech taboos associated with an individual's death), they never are irretrievably lost. Those dreams that are indefinitely *wajawaja-manu* (loosely translated as "misplaced" or "lost") are part of the larger cosmological *Jukurrpa* that can and will be reclaimed through ceremonial action and nocturnal dreams. In this sense, certain distinct components of the *Jukurrpa* can change while others remain immutable.

Further superficial contradictions associated with *Jukurrpa* require clarification before any social analysis of ritual can be undertaken. The Warlpiri state that the Dreaming has always existed, but that before the Ancestral Beings originally emerged, the land was flat and shapeless. The appearance of these mythical Beings and the travels they undertook in the distant past—travels registered in the segmented narratives in both secular and religious contexts—are what transformed an indistinct terrain into the totemically charged geography of watercourses, trees, hills, and other features. Beyond that, it was these travels, in conjunction with the social organization and living habits of the Ancestral Beings, that provided to the Aboriginal people with whom they cohabited the patterns of obligation that were (are) simultaneously distant and contemporary (Stanner 1966:226). The Warlpiri living at Yuendumu today (or twenty years ago) do not dichotomize the Ancestral Times and the present, nor do they characterize the temporal dimension of their cosmological universe in linear terms (see Munn 1964:91). Ancestral Beings continue to occupy the land from which they sprang and through which they travel(ed). The terms *Jukurrpa* and *yijardu* (the latter meaning "true, actual") are not contrasted. As one business leader told me: "The *Jukurrpa* is *yijardu*." She meant this in at least two ways: in the sense of "true" or "truthful" (as having actually happened in the past) and in the sense of being part of Munn's definition of *yijardu,* "a waking reality" or "ongoing present." In other words, the heretofore merges, or is simultaneous with, the here and now. The Warlpiri are quite explicit in their statements that the past is "true" today.[9] The Warlpiri regularly claim that the Ancestral Beings are *jalangu-warnu,* which Hale et al. (1982–1988) identify as meaning "new," "recent," "modern."[10] I would add to that list "ever-present," marking that which has always been. With a mixture of humor and earnestness, Warlpiri businesspeople often apply to the Ancestral Beings the same term they use for themselves, *pensioner,* to mark their long-term presence. When the Warlpiri at Yuendumu survey their land, the markers in the terrain—creeks, stones, trees left by Ancestral Beings—all offer proof that the *Jukurrpa,* in all its manifestations, is both true (*yijardu*) and ever-present (*jalangu-warnu*) (see also Munn 1964:96). That is not to say that the Ancestral Beings or their Dreaming itineraries are themselves new or changing; it is, rather, that the life forces imbuing the markers are ever-present, existing in a timeless environment encompassing what non-Aboriginal observers would call both "past" and "present." Transformation of terrain confirms the Ancestral Beings' capacity to enact change. As such, Warlpiri myth can be granted the classic "operational value" Lévi-Strauss observed, which allows for a "sequence of past happenings, a non-reversible series of events the remote consequences of which may still be felt at present" (Myers 1986a:209). The *Jukurrpa* adds to this nonreversible series of events a flexibility that enables the repertoire of dreams to be reworked and revivified.

Myers, in his exploration of temporal ambiguity in Central Desert cosmology, proposes the following explanation: "Erasing the specific past, the Dreaming pursues continuities between current human action and a realm of order transcending human affairs" (Myers 1986a:70). This transcendent realm of order is perhaps as close as standard Western philosophy can come to addressing the *Jukurrpa*'s temporal and transformational conundrums. The Dreaming is an Ancestral Present, a distinct component of which is situated in a distant and distinguishable (if not distinct) past. It is a cosmology that is both unchanging and ever-changing. And the principal structure that sustains this cosmology in all its "contradictory" complexities is a special form of kinship, a pattern of relatedness that the Warlpiri argue replicates (and has its origins in) the relationships of the Ancestral Beings who created the sites, homes, and countries of Warlpiri terrain, and who created the manner by which Warlpiri relate to the *Jukurrpa* in all its aspects.

WARLPIRI SOCIAL ORGANIZATION

The complexity of the *Jukurrpa* yields concomitant complexity in the kinship relations that reproduce and maintain it. *Jukurrpa* and its sustaining rituals tie the Warlpiri both to the land and to each other in specific patterns of kinship—patterns that have been modified by the social reorganization that occurred following sedentarization. As such, both the theoretical model according to which the Warlpiri arrange and identify themselves and the changes brought by forced settlement must be discussed prior to any assessments of gender or personal prestige in the ritual enactment of the Dreaming.

Before sedentarization, the Warlpiri lived in small groups (five to thirty-five individuals) composed of siblings and their spouses, their parents, and their offspring. Residence was bilocal, with family units sustaining both virilocal and uxorilocal habitation. This model, flexible even prior to sedentarization, changed significantly with forced settlement. As we shall see, the change profoundly transformed the patterns of ritual expression, and with it the manner by which the Warlpiri manifested social identity.[11] Traditionally, during the hot, windy, dry season, known as *jurrkarra* or *yuntayunta,* small groups consisting of a husband and one or two wives, their children, and a widowed mother-in-law or father-in-law hunted and gathered at various waterholes, which served as focal points of economic, political, and spiritual activities. In the wet season, these small groups would congregate with other Central Desert Aborigines, often in assemblies of as many as four hundred people, to perform religious ceremonies that maintained social relations (Meggitt 1962:55). Geospecific Dreaming sites in the aforementioned *ngurrara* served as focal points of Warlpiri cosmology and informed both settlement patterns and domestic organization. It was only at these sites, owned and managed along complex lines of kinship association, that ritual activity such as initiation and betrothal could take place.

Generally speaking, men were fifteen years older than the women to whom they were betrothed. A man could marry as many as three women, and the couple could reside with the family of the husband or that of the wife. Separation was possible but rare, and those who were widowed generally remarried (Dussart 1992b). While this description provides certain basic, crude delineations of Warlpiri social organization, it neglects the rigorous forms of engagement that link all Warlpiri on a daily basis to each other in both ritual and nonritual contexts.

Known among experts for the complexity of their domestic patterns, the Warlpiri follow an Arandic system of kin classification first fully delineated by Meggitt (1962) and amplified by Laughren two decades later (1982). The Warlpiri divide the world into kin and nonkin, the former group incorporating all Warlpiri, though not all Aboriginal peoples. The nature of these kin relationships can be "actual" (that is, one in which both parents are shared), "close" (a bond through some other relative, say, a grandparent), or "classificatory." The last relationship is the most pervasive and the one serving as a social mastic binding the Warlpiri to one another. Classificatory kinship, as Myers notes, is a multigenerational system of relationships that extends ties "beyond the immediate family in the production of individuals as full, social adults" (1986a:180).

There are three principal components of the Warlpiri kinship system. (1) Four terminological lines of descent are distinguished in the second ascending generation (that is, the parents of ego's parents). (2) The Warlpiri usually refer to only five generational levels: grandchildren, children, one's own generation, parents, and grandparents. (3) There exists a rule of preferred marriage.[12]

The protocols of spousal arrangement pressure members to marry one of four classificatory relatives in an opposing subsection. In the template of preferred marriage, a woman should marry either a mother's mother's brother's daughter's son, a father's father's sister's son's son, a father's mother's brother's son's son, or a mother's father's sister's daughter's son. Men are reciprocally bound by the same classificatory subsection links. Two acceptable alternatives—described by the Warlpiri as "second choice" or "not promised" marriages—exist outside this schema of preference. Spousal relationships for both men and women may be formed with a mother's brother's child. Alternatively, men may marry a mother's mother or a mother's mother's brother's son's daughter, while a woman may choose from a more restricted pool of mother's mother's brothers.[13] (The reason for this gender limitation, the Warlpiri explain, is the ideal fifteen-year spousal age difference; it would be highly unlikely for a mother's mother's brother's son's son to be old enough to be a husband.)

Men traditionally could be married to more than one woman at the same time—a pattern still practiced today—while women could be spousally linked to only one man, though serial unions for females were acceptable (Bell 1980). Men who did not choose a spouse from the preferred category in a first marriage often satisfied this protocol in a subsequent liaison.

Preferred marriage extends and solidifies ritual territory and ceremonial authority along lines of kinship by establishing unions between spouses from opposite patrimoieties. This social pattern, which summarizes and simplifies more complicated kinship relations, is part of a system of subsection relations that further coordinates ritual life. All Warlpiri residents at Yuendumu belong to one of eight subsections that give individuals forms of address and reference used both in daily interaction and in formal ritual activity. In the nomenclature of subsectionship, the gender of an individual is easily identified. Women's subsection names all begin with the letter *N*, while those of their male counterparts start with the letter *J*; to wit, a Nangala and Jangala belong to the same subsection, and bear either a sibling or alternate-generation patrilineal relationship that implies complex social, ritual, and financial obligations. The eight subsections are (1) Jangala/Nangala, (2) Jungarrayi/Nungarrayi,

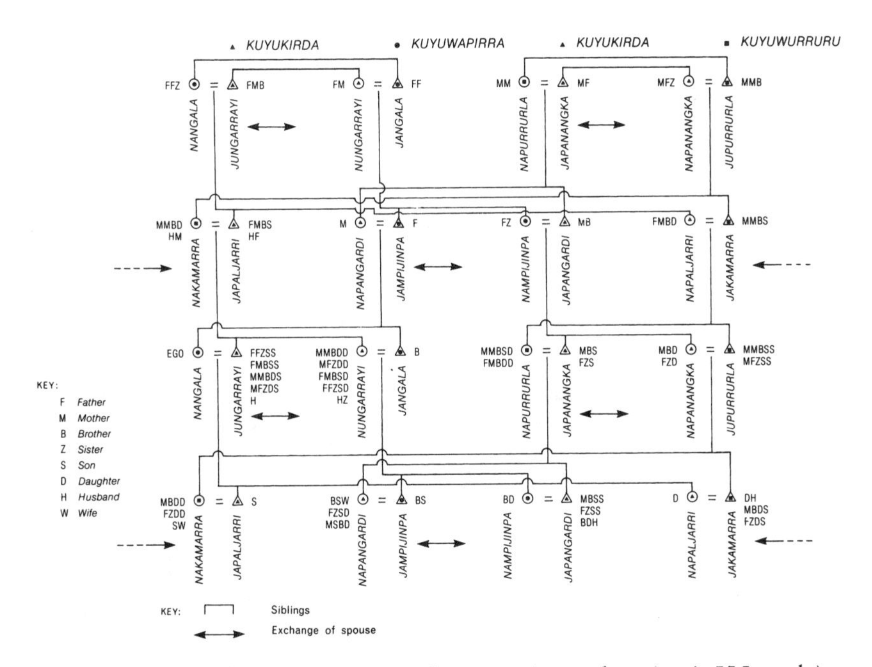

Figure 1. Distribution of kin among subsections (ego subsection is J/Nangala) (*Source:* research, F. Dussart; del. J. R. Goodrum, Australian National University, 1988)

(3) Japangardi/Napangardi, (4) Jampijinpa/Nampijinpa, (5) Jupurrurla/Napurrurla, (6) Japanangka/Napanangka, (7) Japaljarri/Napaljarri, and (8) Jakamarra/Nakamarra.

Following the conventional Arandic kinship chart, Figure 1 exemplifies the terminological kin relationships and preferred marriage pattern of one individual—a Nangala—and establishes how the Warlpiri merge an egocentric kinship system with a sociocentric subsection system. Thus, a Nangala enters into egocentric (that is, kin) relations with members of all subsections.[14] What the chart does not explain is that these larger subsection groupings are arranged into matrilineal, patrilineal, and generational moieties.

KIRDA AND *KURDUNGURLU*

On the basis of the ethnographic record and contemporary life stories, it seems that the Warlpiri of Yuendumu have always placed primary emphasis on patrilineal descent rights for the maintenance of their ritual identity.[15] Despite the suggestion embedded in the prefix *patri-*, patrilineality does not restrict transmission of ritual knowledge to a single gender. Patrilineality involves both men and women on the father's side. As such, this system in no way weakens the role of women in the process of ritual inheritance. A close analysis of how patrilineality is constructed and conceived by the Warlpiri can dispel much of the inequity implicit in the term. While it might be tempting to dismiss outright such vocabulary, doing so denies a viable, even crucial organizational construct that the Warlpiri themselves employ subtly and with rigor. In all their discussions of land, land ownership, *Jukurrpa,* ritual, ceremonial responsibility, and ceremonial rights, the Warlpiri use kin terms that articulate patterns of patrilineal descent. Though such patrilineality characterizes one of the chief transmission lines by which both men and women obtain and pass on ritual knowledge, it in no way restricts the role of women in the performance or inheritance of that ritual knowledge.[16]

The Warlpiri system of ritual activity, land ownership, and inheritance cleaves individuals into two interrelated patrimoieties.[17] One's patrimoiety is referred to as *kirda,* while the opposite patrimoiety is referred to as *kurdungurlu*—terms crucial in comprehending how the Warlpiri construct and negotiate their ritual universe, marriage rules, and other forms of social and economic obligation. In the most basic sense, a *kirda* is the "owner" of a Dreaming and its associated sites. As owner, one must maintain the well-being of the land and its people by reenacting the Dreaming stories associated with that land in ceremonial contexts. *Kirda* status, traditionally constituted, also confers the right to live on that land and to use its resources. It is important to recognize that the nature of *kirda*-ship is age- and gender-specific. While men and women may be identified as *kirda* for the same segments and sites and share certain versions of the Dreamings associated with that site, there are also segments of that Dreaming that are the exclusive performative province of either men or women.

The *kurdungurlu* is a "manager" of a *kirda*'s Dreamings and sites.[18] Reenactment of a Dreaming, in rituals that involve singing, dancing, and painting by a *kirda,* requires the surveillance and advice of a *kurdungurlu.* No visits to major ritual sites or decisions about ceremonial performance associated with a given country can be made without both *kirda* and *kurdungurlu* being present or consulted. Their relationship is, at least in theory, reciprocal. As David Nash points out in his richly detailed linguistic analysis of the paired terms, "If one is related as *kurdungurlu* to a Dreaming ancestor [and associated lands], then it follows that the particular Dreaming ancestor is in the opposite patrimoiety, and thus uses terms based on *kirda* to refer to the Dreaming with a *kirda* as reference point."[19] The two moieties that divide owners and managers are each further divided into two patricouples corresponding to the four grandparental terminological lines of descent. It is through these patricouples that the ritual expression of the land ownership is inherited, divided, and maintained. The individuals in these four patricouples form the eight subsections previously cited. While one can share land with any member of one's patrimoiety, inheritance is generally transmitted through the specific patricouples within this patrimoiety. In other words, land inheritance is transmitted between the two subsections that form a patricouple. There are two generational levels through which one can inherit land. At the parental level, land and associated ritual knowledge are acquired from the subsection of one's father, father's brothers, and father's sisters, which forms the other half of one's patricouple. At the grandparental level, one inherits rights from one's father's father, his brothers, and his sisters, all of whom are members of one's own subsection. For example, if ego is a Nangala, she inherits her *kirda* status from her father (Jampijinpa) and his siblings (Jampijinpa and Nampijinpa), and from her father's father and his siblings, who all belong to the J/Nangala subsection.

The chart in Figure 2 delineates the reciprocal relationships of owners (*kirda*) of the J/Nangala subsection and the ritual assistance of their

Ego's Patrimoiety *(Kirda)*	**Opposite Patrimoiety** *(Kurdungurlu)*
1. Father's father's descent *(Kuyuwapirra)*	3. Mother's father's descent *(Kuyukirda)*
a. Jangala/Nangala	e. Japangardi/Napangardi
b. Jampijinpa/Nampijinpa	f. Japanangka/Napanangka
2. Mother's mother descent *(Kuyuwurruru)*	4. Father's mother descent *(Kuyukirda)*
c. Jakamarra/Nakamarra	g. Japaljarri/Napaljarri
d. Jupurrurla/Napurrurla	h. Jungarrayi/Nungarrayi

Figure 2. Patrimoietal, patricouple, and subsection relationships (ego subsection is J/Nangala). Four patricouples terminological lines of descent (sets 1–4) and eight subsections (sets a–h)

managers (*kurdungurlu*) who belong to the opposite patrimoiety. To further explicate the simplified grid, it is necessary to know that the term *kuyuwapirra* refers to one's own patricouple. One's mother's mother's patricouple—with whom the patrimoiety is shared—is called *kuyuwurruru.* The two patricouples in the opposite patrimoiety (the mother's father's and father's mother's) are both referred to as *kuyukirda.* These terms are regularly used in the expression of social relations at the settlement.

While Figure 2 shows the pattern of inheritance of ritual owners (*kirda*) and their connection to their managers (*kurdungurlu*), it does not indicate how these "managers" themselves inherit their rights, which are transmitted through their mother's patriline (again in theory, but one must consider the impact of forced settlement on the template of intersecting lines of descent). What Figure 2 identifies is the existence of a reciprocal dynamic between two patrilines linked by roles of ownership and obligatory ritual assistance. That dynamic touches on the complex patterns of land tenure and of ceremonial enactment.

I wish to bolster the delineation of this link between *kirda* owners and *kurdungurlu* managers before addressing the effects of forced settlement on this relationship. In the ideal structure charted above, a *kirda* is an individual with a patrilineally ascribed interest in territory and the ritual material associated with that interest, while the reciprocally related *kurdungurlu* is responsible for monitoring the propriety of the enactment of the ceremonies and, by implication, the protection of its territorial estate. It needs to be restated that ritual inheritance of ownership passes patrilineally, while rights of protection and maintenance (*kurdungurlu*) are transmitted through the mother's patriline. The basic structure of land ownership, and by implication ritual transmission and social organization, is constituted along these lines of patrilineal descent.

Up to this point, I have restricted myself to general descriptions of the nature of the rights of land ownership, but these must now be spelled out more explicitly. The template presented in Figure 2 indicated that a J/Nangala inherits rights for the countries and Dreaming segments from his or her father (Jampijinpa), father's sister (Nampijinpa), father's father (Jangala), and father's father's sister (Nangala). When a Warlpiri businessperson is asked who in theory "owns" a certain land or Dreaming, the answer may be articulated in terms of the patricouple, employing the term *kuyuwapirra*. However, follow-up questions generally prompt informants to mention by name specific individuals within those subsections. Given the structure of the patricouple affiliation, an individual inherits rights as *kirda* to countries and Dreaming segments from two sources: one's father and his siblings, and one's father's father and his siblings. The lands and related Dreamings from these two sources would in ideal circumstances be the same; however, even in patterns of inheritance prior to sedentarization, as described by older Warlpiri, the template was modified by individual circumstances, such as conception site, birthplace, patrilineal links, death, and personal closeness to specific kin.

It is important to note that the pattern of ownership of the land is not exclusive to a particular patricouple. It is possible for the other patricouple in a patrimoiety (*kuyuwurruru*) to hold rights over the same territory and associated myths, though members of each patricouple inherit those rights through their own fathers and father's fathers. If a patricouple dies out, its rights tend to be taken over by another group whose subsection constitutes an identical classificatory patricouple composition. If no such patricouple can take over these rights, then a group representing the other patricouple within the patrimoiety (*kuyuwurruru*) tends to negotiate the rights of the patricouple that is dying out, thus sustaining patriliny in contexts of change (see also Young 1987:156).

Which particular individuals inherit *kirda* rights to the lands and rituals of a dispersed patricouple depends on territorial components more specifically discussed in the analysis of the realities of Warlpiri ritual activity after sedentarization. Still, it is important to note here that there are elements outside the template suggested by Figure 2 that strengthen an individual's claim on uninherited land rights. One's conception site, one's birthplace, a parent's birthplace, a parent's locus of decease, and overlapping territorial rights can all affect how land and ritual move from one patricouple to another within the patrimoiety.

There is another component of *kirda*-ship that warrants note, a nuance of ownership in a context exclusive to ceremony (see Bern and Labarlestier 1985). The term *kirda* is, as mentioned earlier, most commonly applied to ownership of Dreamings and their associated sites and rituals. But another use of the term is also employed. One can be identified as *kirda* for a particular kind of ceremony. Ceremonial ownership and ownership of Dreamings differ in fundamental ways. Claims to Dreamings carry with them claims to the land through which those Dreamings travel. Ceremonial ownership carries no such land rights. Also, to be *kirda* for a ceremony provides rights for only the material within that ceremony that implicates one's patricouple. Other Dreaming material in the ceremony for which an individual lacks such patricouple association is not considered to be owned. And whereas those individuals who own a Dreaming are also considered owners of all ceremonies that invoke that Dreaming, such proprietary extensions are not granted to the *kirda* of a particular ceremony.

The origins of ceremonial *kirda*-ship are difficult to pinpoint. I can, however, trace the roots of expression in at least one event, that of *Jardiwanpa.* According to older residents of Yuendumu, the conflict resolution ceremony's ownership has its roots in an exchange event between Warlpiri, Warrumungu, and Mudbura, one that significantly predates settlement. (Dates are predictably unreliable; however, this took place roughly in the first decades of the twentieth century.) Although the Warlpiri already had Dreamings and ceremonies associated with the lands implicated in the *Jardiwanpa,* that specific ceremony had not been part of Warlpiri ritual repertoire until it was performed by the Mudbura. When it was exchanged, ownership of the ceremony was bestowed both on the Warlpiri participants in that exchange and on all the Warlpiri already linked by preexisting ties to Dreaming tracks implicated in the *Jardiwanpa* (for example, the Ancestral Emu track or the Ancestral Snake track). As such, the ritual (though not the lands) was shared among ceremonial performers and landowners, groups in this case with distinct patrilineal identities. Prior to settlement, rights to perform all subsequent *Jardiwanpa* were passed on to descendants of landowners and the ritual participants along the patriline. With the advent of sedentarization, the generational patterns of transmission further complicated these parallel ownership rights by adding the influence of residential association. Ownership of *Jardiwanpa* events performed after settlement implicated many more individuals than those with patrilineal connection, whether the association was restricted to the ceremony or included broader rights to the land. The parallel notions of *kirda*-ship that existed prior to settlement were maintained, but the pool was enlarged to include individuals who had ties based on residential proximity but who often came from different patrilineal descent groups.

So much for *kirda* rights. The basic template of management, or *kurdungurlu*-ship, must also be delineated. As Figure 2 implies, a J/Nangala's Dreamings are overseen and managed by an individual from one of the two opposite patricouples (in the figure, Sets 3 and 4), both of which are referred to by ego (in this case a J/Nangala) as *kuyukirda.* Relationships between *kirda* and *kurdungurlu,* however, tend to be established along more specific lines, with the ego's manager being found within the father's mother's patricouple (Set 4).[20] This does not clarify, however, how inheritance of managerial rights can follow a different path, one that combines elements of patrilines on both the maternal and paternal sides.

As Figure 3 shows, a Nangala can and does inherit managerial rights over the Dreamings for which her father's mother (and her siblings) and her own mother (and her siblings) are *kirda.* It is the latter matrifilial line that serves as the focal point of such inheritance paths. Though less common, patrilineal inheritance of managerial roles is also a component of Warlpiri ritual transmission. When patrilineal succession of *kurdungurlu* does take place, the Warlpiri employ the verb *rdankurr-mani,* which indicates the union of such rights with patrilineally acquired *kirda* rights. What this term does not indicate is the reason for such inheritance. Because of the structure of preferred marriages, patrilineal succession of *kurdungurlu* rights enables spouses to be "managers" for each other's Dreamings and associated lands.[21]

Combining the preferred marriage and inheritance rights, the following conclusions can be drawn about *kurdungurlu* rights. At one's own generational level, the *ideal* manager is a mother's brother's child (also known as a cross-cousin). Same-sex siblings of one's spouse are also classified as important *kurdungurlu.* A woman often expects to rely on

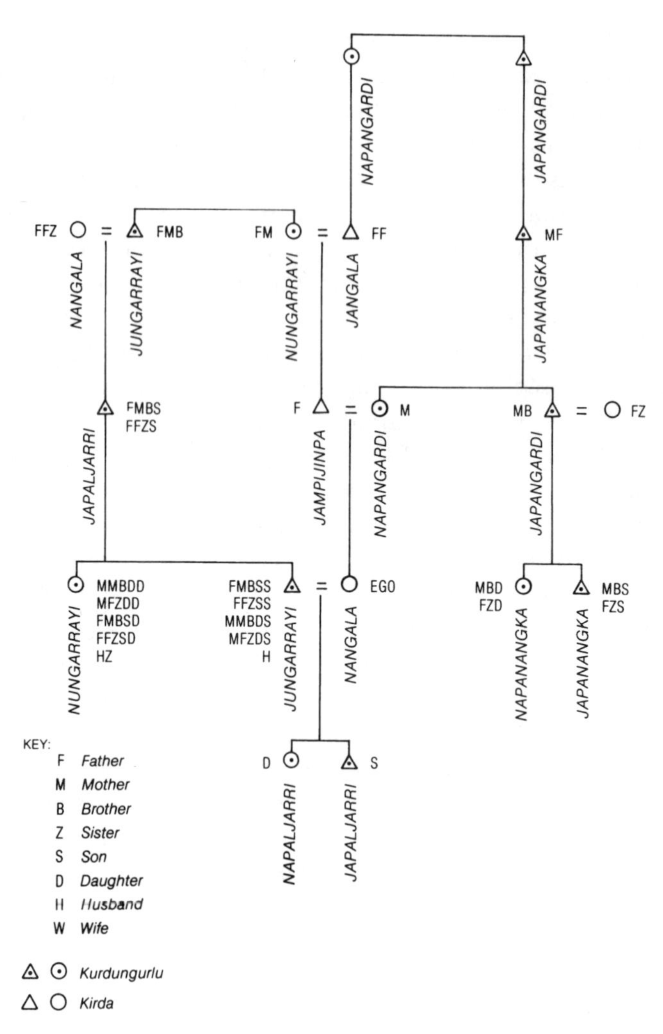

Figure 3. Patterns of inherited *kurdungurlu*-ship (*Source:* research, F. Dussart; del. J. R. Goodrum, Australian National University, 1988)

her sisters-in-law as *kurdungurlu* during ceremonial performances; however, she also relies on the assistance of her husband and his brothers in less overt ritual display (see chapters 4 and 5). One level above, it is one's mother and her siblings, as well as the father's mother's brother's children, who will serve this function. One level below, it is children (one's own children for women, a sister's children for men) who inherit managerial rights. If, for example, a sixty-year-old Nangala performs one of her Dreamings (for which she is *kirda*), her actions could be monitored by her female cross-cousin(s), her sisters-in-law, her mother and her mother's sisters (if alive), and her own daughters.[22] While Figure 3 schematizes certain key characteristics of how Dreamings are managed and inherited through multigenerational levels, it obscures at least one path to managerial control that does not involve the standard classified patterns. *Kurdungurlu*-ship can be claimed by the rights associated with the site at which one is "conceived."[23] While claims on the basis of conception site may coincide with inherited rights, there are ample examples of managerial positions being claimed by people whose ties to the associated Dreaming are only classificatory.[24]

Though an understanding of ideal relations is necessary to comprehend the basic vocabulary in which the Warlpiri delineate their ritual relations, it would be wrong to assume that such model relations are reified in postsedentary Yuendumu. While these ideal relationships are still found at the roots of ritual organization, they have been modified in the wake of sedentarization.

RITUAL AT YUENDUMU: A BRIEF HISTORY

Because of the isolation and inhospitability (by Western standards) of the Central Australian Desert, knowledge of the circumstances surrounding the region's Aboriginal ritual life prior to forced settlement in the 1940s is extremely limited, with literature on the Warlpiri proving especially thin. The early transcontinental ethnographies—Spencer and Gillen's in 1899, to name the best-known—make little mention of the Warlpiri.[25] Having said this, it is important to note that precontact data—in the form of rock art and stone implements, for example—suggest a flourishing ritual life dating back at least five thousand years (see, e.g., Smith et al. 1998). Further insight into the nature of the ritual these designs register is speculative at best—unless, of course, one applies a Warlpiri conception of the past and "data" to the history of the Warlpiri.

For the residents of Yuendumu, the *Jukurrpa*—and here I invoke the narrative aspect of the term—provides the most rigorously "factual" evidence of life as it has been lived since the distant and undatable past. The stories of the Honey Ant Being, of the Water Being, and of the Fire Being, to name just three, constitute a chronicle of the Ancestral Present more stable and enduring than the history that postdates contact. For the Aborigines of the Northern Territory, regular and sustained contact with Europeans began in the early twentieth century, when mining sites and cattle stations started to pepper the region. By the 1940s, most groups in the Central Desert were denied their migratory movements and forced to settle at various ration stations dotting the landscape. Until that time, the Warlpiri generally hunted and gathered in small groups of close relatives, undertaking hydrocentric migrations over a vast and arid land. As is common among hunter-gatherers, relatively little time was spent questing after food and water (Peterson 1974; Lee 1979). Using spears and boomerangs, Warlpiri men concentrated on tracking larger animals such as kangaroo and emu; women, employing digging sticks and smaller implements, hunted goanna and snake, and gathered honey ants and witchetty grubs. Women also collected yams, bush tomatoes, and other desert foods. The names of Ancestral Beings—Kangaroo, Bush Tomato, Goanna, Rain, and so on—and their associated sites provide, among other things, a short list of the region's principal food and water resources. The distribution of these assets followed the kinship obligations central to all Warlpiri exchange—obligations of a decidedly egalitarian tenor within the presedentary groups. Distribution, however, must be distinguished from collection. Until the 1940s, women provided between 60 and 80 percent by bulk of the diet, prepared most of the food, and collected much of the firewood and water (Peterson 1974).

The ethnographic literature on Warlpiri political organization prior to sedentarization rightly stresses the egalitarian tendencies of ceremonial encounters, noting that the structure of land tenure and management—the reciprocal relationship of *kirda* and *kurdungurlu* described earlier—provided a series of checks and balances on the individual accumulation of political authority. The migratory nature of the Warlpiri and the lability of group formation also tended to discourage nonegalitarian patterns of social and ritual engagement (Tonkinson 1988). Although there were distinct differences in the expression and function of ritual in the life of Warlpiri men and women (the specifics having subsequently stimulated rancorous dispute among specialists concerned with, among other things, the gender-specific nature of so-called secret and sacred authority), both Warlpiri men and women were able to obtain some measure of status as ritual participants through the reenactment of the *Jukurrpa* (see chapter 2).

The settlers' policy toward Aborigines was one of acculturation and suppression. Early in the twentieth century, after the Warlpiri were classified as "wards of the state," the Aboriginal economic base and ritual life, and indeed their whole social structure, changed dramatically. Many Warlpiri were obligated to pursue subsistence jobs connected to the cattle stations and mines of the region. Terrible droughts in 1924 and 1928 prompted numerous Warlpiri to abandon their traditional lands and congregate near those cattle stations and mines, as well as the small towns that had sprung up along the telegraph line between Alice Springs and Tennant Creek.

Various governmental initiatives to obliterate "Aboriginality" in all its incarnations began in earnest at midcentury with the policy of forced sedentarization. The Warlpiri were specifically implicated in this process in 1946, when a ration depot some 300 kilometers (about 185 miles) northwest of Alice Springs was established and named after the nearby soakage, Yuendumu. The depot, situated near several Warlpiri ceremonial sites (including Wakulpu, Mijilparnta, and Ramarra-Kujurnu), was used as a settlement area principally for the Warlpiri, though Pintupi and Anmatyerre of the area were also relocated there. Brought from Alice Springs, from the mining camps of the Tanami and the Granites, and from cattle stations, the indigenous populations very quickly became dependent on state social policies, a circumstance that the Land Rights Movement of the 1970s only partially overturned. As wards of the state, the indigenous populations of the Central Desert had every aspect of their lives controlled by the director of social welfare and his proxies. Alcohol consumption, sexual liaisons with non-Aboriginal peoples, and nominal economic compensation in the form of rations (in lieu of cash) all contributed to the accelerated transformation of precontact Warlpiri social structure. Ritual life came under particular scrutiny, with several missionary interventions attempting to suppress ceremonial patterns so elemental to Aboriginal life. Though these overt efforts met with only limited success, the new conditions of life took their toll. Because travel was restricted by the constraints of new work schedules, visits to Dreaming sites became all but impossible. And the bonds between kin so necessary for the reproduction of the Dreaming—the *kirda-kurdungurlu* reciprocity found between individuals—were often severed by relocation policies blind to Aboriginal notions of ritual assistance. To this day, older residents of the settlement recall vividly the loss of ceremonial collaborators in the wake of sedentarization. Furthermore, denied their nomadism, the Warlpiri had to pursue what ritual activity was possible under the scrutiny of censorious non-Warlpiri overseers. Two- and three-week-long rituals were increasingly difficult to undertake, since the indigenous population was forced to keep to strict work schedules and remain on settlement grounds.[26] One Yuendumu woman who served as a housekeeper for missionaries during the 1950s remembered the rebukes she and her sister received if they arrived at their jobs wearing the ceremonial body paints used during rituals performed after work or on weekends.[27] As the housekeeper's account of her job suggests, the Warlpiri were encouraged to follow the gender-specific mores of their overseers. Warlpiri women took on work as housegirls and laundresses, while men were given jobs as homestead hands and miners (Bell 1983; Bradley 1987:145, 150). In such a context, there was little room for ritual as it had been performed in precontact times.

In 1952, 130 Yuendumu Warlpiri were relocated to another depot 600 kilometers (about 375 miles) to the north at Catfish Waterhole, named at the time Hooker Creek.[28] The displacement of the Warlpiri people from the ritually charged environs of Warlpiri territory to Kurintji land to the north proved traumatic both for the former residents of Yuendumu and for their Kurintji hosts. In fact, the uprooted Warlpiri on several occasions returned on foot to Yuendumu, only to be brought back to Hooker Creek by governmental authorities. These desperate attempts to return to their ritual countries and to their kin—conceptualized as overlapping—clarified their spiritual and familial connections to territories inhabited by predominantly Warlpiri Ancestral Beings. Whatever semblance of ritual life the Warlpiri were able to maintain in the wake of these external assaults was aided by settlement on traditional lands. That Yuendumu came to be inhabited principally by Warlpiri with strong ties to the environs did much to sustain ritual transmission. Many other groups were not so fortunate. The Pintupi, for example, were collectively relocated in various settlements, none of which was part of their traditional country.

In 1971, uranium mining tests were initiated near Yampirri-Panturnu, the important Warlpiri sacred site mentioned earlier in the discussion of *Jukurrpa* segments. The site, implicating men and women in a number of rituals that reenacted the Fire Dreaming, was (and continues to be) a focal point of both public and restricted ceremonial business. To declare their connection to and ownership of the land—an ownership at the time unrecognized by the Australian government—the male and female *kirda* and *kurdungurlu* for the Fire Dreaming gathered and decided to present a men's public ritual (*purlapa*) for the benefit of white miners. The ceremony highlighted the segment of the Fire Dreaming that transected

Yampirri-Panturnu, where some preliminary mineral samplings had been taken. The Warlpiri hoped that by dancing, singing, and showing ritual designs, they could stop the tests that threatened to desecrate the sacred. Soon after the ritual performance, the prospectors ceased their testing. Whereas the miners attributed this stoppage to the poor yield of the test samples, the Warlpiri were convinced that it was the ritual performance that abbreviated the incursion. The Warlpiri came to view public presentations of the *Jukurrpa* as a means to counter non-Aboriginal assault, a response mechanism that the last chapter of this book shall explore in greater detail.[29] By declaring their rights over Dreamings and the sites with which those Dreaming stories were associated in a ceremonial context, the Warlpiri established a pattern by which future land claims would be pursued, one that conjoined Western-style advocacy with traditional ritual performance.[30]

Though a nationwide referendum in 1967 officially declared the indigenous populations of Australia—including the Warlpiri—to be "Australian," this legislative "legitimacy" in no way returned to the Aborigines even the smallest measure of their territorial sovereignty. It was only with the passage of the 1976 Aboriginal Land Rights Act (Northern Territory)—the end result of a push for "self-determination" initiated after the Labour Party came to power in 1972—that the Warlpiri could begin to regain (partial) control over the lands of their Ancestral Beings.[31] The act had a direct impact on ritual performance. Claims for vacant Crown land necessitated providing proof of direct genealogical connection to the territories under review. For the Warlpiri as well as other Central Desert Aborigines, such proof was frequently proffered through displays of knowledge of the site-specific Dreamings that implied direct genealogical connection between the claimant and the Ancestral Being. Proof of such links, as often as not, precipitated ceremonial performance, which quickly emerged as a powerful, if unconventional, legal tool. Song, dance, and design—the media of traditional ritual—served as property deeds in the juridical struggles to regain long-lost lands. In this way, the Land Rights Movement was advanced by physical movements of body, voice, and brush. Ritual showed itself to be as responsive and dynamic in cross-cultural contestations as it was in indigenous ones.

Today, much of the country the Warlpiri traveled prior to contact is once again held by them. The process of reclamation, however, has not been so successful in other domains. Traditional Central Desert food sources such as goanna and yam constitute less than 5 percent of the

Warlpiri diet (Young 1981). What remnant of precontact culture does survive is found principally in certain aspects of social organization, in the system of kinship (modified by the impact of residency), and in the circulation of ritual knowledge this book attempts to analyze.

The Warlpiri, most of whom now reside in the settlements of Yuendumu, Lajamanu/Hooker Creek, Warrabri/Ali-curong, Willowra, and Nyirrpi (and associated outstations, or satellite villages), represent the most populous Aboriginal group in the Northern Territory.[32] This numerical superiority among indigenous groups of the center, coupled with their residency on the actual lands traditionally associated with the Warlpiri patrimony, accounts in large measure for the vigor of Warlpiri ritual life as it is undertaken at Yuendumu, compared to that of other groups and other settlements.

The link between physical habitation and the ownership of ritual territory is crucial. One of the striking components of contemporary Warlpiri ritual life at Yuendumu is the capacity of the ceremonial leaders to nurture the Dreaming in situ. The distinctive relationship of residence and ritual is one reason to treat gingerly any model of "Central Desert ritual" that conflates different Aboriginal groups residing in different settlements. Contradictory data gathered from other settlements on matters of gender division and notions of secrecy, to name just two subjects central to regional debate, confirm the liabilities of assessments of pan-Aboriginal sedentarized ritual life. Even the notion of Yuendumu itself as a "community" might best be avoided (Rowse 1990:1). The local population within the settlement sees itself not along convenient linguistic lines of "the Warlpiri" or "the Pintupi," but as belonging to smaller social units within each of the groups, formed through residency and the bonds of kinship, some of which reconfirm the ideal patterns described earlier, others of which reflect dramatic postsedentary social realignment.[33]

PATTERNS OF RESIDENCY AND THEIR RITUAL IMPLICATIONS

The formal entrance to the settlement of Yuendumu opens onto a grid of cement houses, a large schoolyard, and paved streets laid out in casually rectilinear fashion. The concrete structures of the town, however, belie the true social loci of the settlement. The Warlpiri, scattered throughout the area, associate themselves religiously, financially, politically, socially,

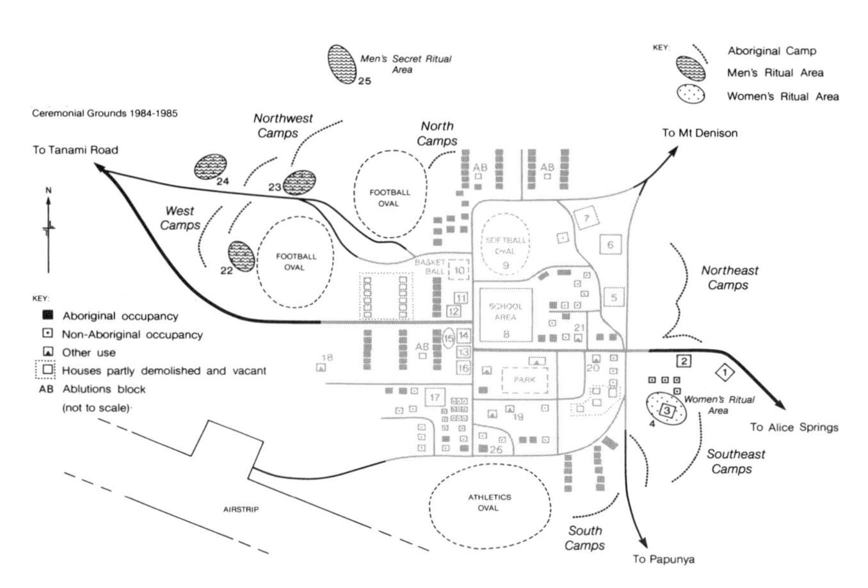

Map 2. Yuendumu (*Source:* updated from E. Young 1981:67 and *Junga Yimi* 1983; research: F. Dussart, 1983–85, del. J. R. Goodrum, Australian National University, 1988)

KEY
1. Men's Museum
2. Police station
3. Women's Museum
4. Women's ritual ground
5. Council depot and workshop
6. Power house
7. Housing office and depot
8. School area
9. Softball oval
10. Basketball court
11. Yuendumu community store and post office
12. Hall
13. Video–television station building (in progress)
14. Baptist church
15. Church corroboree ground
16. Recreation and youth center
17. Clinic
18. Morgue
19. Mining company office, store, and garage
20. Adult education and art center
21. Council office
22–24. Joint ceremonial grounds
25. Men's secret ritual ground
26. House in which author lived

and ritually with one of six "camps." Wherever one lives, and despite what government lodging is provided, the true "home" (*ngurra*) of each resident, the place where comfort, food, money, bedding, and ritual knowledge tend to be exchanged, is in one of the six outlying camps.[34] These camps have no formal place names; they are generally invoked by their directional locations: West Camp, Northwest Camp, North Camp, Northeast Camp, Southeast Camp, and South Camp.[35] Though an aerial view might suggest to a nonresident that these camps are peripheral to the physical center of town, they are in fact the primary nodes of social interaction and the primary loci of social identity.

The Warlpiri of Yuendumu and the surrounding outstations organize themselves within these camps in relatively discrete residential units of close kin. These units—which can be identified as "residential kin groups"—are composed of close agnates who may belong to different patrilineal descent groups and their affines, and vary in number between twenty and a hundred adults. Given the mobility of the Warlpiri—many move between Yuendumu, various outstations, and other Warlpiri settlements—the size of any kin group in the settlement varies greatly over time. Less susceptible to fluctuation, but still by no means static, is the number of kin groups in the settlement. During the time I conducted fieldwork (between 1983 and 1992), there were as many as seven such residential kin groups at Yuendumu, of which five were Warlpiri, one was Pintupi, and one was part Anmatyerre and part Warlpiri.

To understand kinship and gender, one must fully understand how the precontact template of social relations described above has been modified in the wake of the land rights movement. Moreover, to understand that, one must more scrupulously analyze how place fits into the formation of Warlpiri social identity. Though patrilineality is a chief component of the residential kin structure, the links extend beyond actual ties of kinship to connect individuals to each other via classificatory association. And while actual agnation is still the main locus of camp identity, classificatory relationships are increasingly woven into the kinship patterns traditionally employed to negotiate ritual authority. Clusters of non-actual agnates coming from different patrilineal descent groups form, along with their affines, a large part of this newly constituted social unit. Residential kin groups within camps tend to be established in the relative direction of the kin groups' Dreamings and their countries. Residents of West Camp, for example, tend to hold rights over many countries located to the west and northwest of the settlement.[36]

Though ritual allegiance runs along lines of residential connection, the ceremonial performance of that allegiance is not geospecific to all the camps. Only the most powerful camps tend to undertake ritual performance in close proximity to where they reside. In particular, the Northwest and West Camps oversee the majority of ceremonial grounds used during men's public events and joint rituals. (Men's secret ceremonies tend to be performed outside the settlement.) As for women's ceremonies, these are almost always held at the Women's Museum, a neutral spot in the charged geography of the settlement (see map 2). Certain infrequently performed rituals that do not involve dance can be performed in the *ji-*

limi, the unmarried women's quarters that move around the settlement, but for the most part the core environment in which the rituals of women find enactment is on the grounds surrounding the Women's Museum, which often serves as a repository of women's ritual objects.

It is possible, and in fact common, in the residential context to establish *kirda-kurdungurlu* relationships based on classificatory relations when close or actual relatives do not reside nearby. Shared location thus becomes a motive force in ritual and economic transactions. In fact, patrilineal ties to actual kin who reside outside of the settlement may be weaker than residential kin ties that may be only classificatory. As such, an individual can claim rights to Dreamings over which only classificatory connections may exist. How and who specifically can make such claims combines nonstructural elements of personal prestige and complex patterns of residential negotiation. Camp life has, in fact, extended the managerial rights previously passed on through inheritance, reconstituting them on the basis of residential allegiance. When this happens, the Warlpiri identify *kurdungurlu*-ship with the relative rather than the relative's Dreamings. This personal association yields a sense of nurturance that extends beyond ritual and its enactment.

Within each of these six camps various forms of living arrangements may be found. There are *yampirri,* or the living quarters of unmarried men; *jilimi,* or unmarried women's living quarters; and *yupukarra,* living quarters occupied principally by married couples. All of these habitations tend to be temporary in nature. The mobility of the living quarters is compounded by the movements of the residents within those habitations. In other words, an individual may relocate from an unmarried women's camp (*jilimi*) to her children's married camp or to another *jilimi,* but this does not imply a change of residential kin association.

The case of the *jilimi* at Yuendumu warrants deeper analysis because of how it differs from the widows' quarters found at other Central Desert settlements where Warlpiri reside. The descriptions of the *jilimi* that Bell provides, which are based on her work with the Kaytej and Warlpiri at Warrabri, suggest a picture at odds with the residential configurations found at Yuendumu. At Warrabri, a large measure of ritual power initially lost through settlement has been reconstituted, according to Bell, in permanent unmarried women's quarters that are mainly inhabited by widows. It is in these camps that the "ritually powerful and respected leaders" (*yamparrupatu*) reside, and it is from these camps that ritual is sustained.[37] Separated from men, the women at Warrabri possess an authority that extends to ritual and nonritual domains.[38] As I mentioned earlier, the situation at Yuendumu is significantly different from the one Bell describes, and is more complex. The distinctions between the two settlements are multiple. Yuendumu's *jilimi* are not permanent, nor is the constituency of these mobile quarters stable. The Warlpiri women in the *jilimi* of Yuendumu do not oversee ritual with the kind of authority Bell found at Warrabri, nor are the widows' quarters the locus of "ritual authority." And in order to identify gender-specific authority over ritual, it is necessary, at Yuendumu in any case, to specify the nature of the ritual in question and the individuals who may participate in it. As chapter 6 shall show, even in domains of "men's" or "women's" rituals there is the potential for cross-gender authority and ritual identification. In short, Bell finds widows controlling a large portion of the ritual universe at Warrabri. No such declaration can be made with regard to the Warlpiri widows of Yuendumu (Bell 1983:81). It is not marital status but residential kin affiliation that tends to mark the locus of ritual authority.[39] Furthermore, the widows at Yuendumu who possess the kind of ritual authority described by Bell often inhabit the camps of their married children.[40] While a great deal of ritual negotiation does take place in the *jilimi,* performance of the ritual overseen by these women transpires not in the camps themselves, but on ceremonial grounds that abut Yuendumu's Women's Museum, an area that is visible to men, if not generally open to them.

The emphasis on camp or residentiality requires further explication if one wishes to approach a fuller sense of group identity as it is expressed by the Warlpiri. "My mob"—a phrase common to all speakers of Aboriginal English—means very different things in different settlements and contexts. When, for example, the Pintupi speak of "my mob," they tend to be referring to all Pintupi, including those outside the particular settlement of the speaker (Myers 1986a). The phrase is used in a similar fashion by the Kuku-Yalanji people in Cape York (Anderson 1984, 1988). When the Warlpiri at Yuendumu speak of "my mob," however, the phrase is generally used to establish collective association with the residential kin group related to the speaker. This boundary is present in other collective terms employed at Yuendumu. *Warlaja,* the word the Warlpiri employ for "family," is not restricted to one's actual relatives but extends, in the same way that all ritual life extends, to residential kin. Not that such group identity is completely obvious in oral declarations. Take, for example, the observation of a senior woman enumerating the social obligations that make up settlement life: "Now we worry for our family [*warlaja*]. We worry for our country. We worry for our children, our brothers and sisters. We worry for their children. We worry for our brothers' wives. We worry for our sisters' husbands." To appreciate the collective resonance of the woman's fears, one must know that the specific family members she mentions include classificatory, close, and actual kin. What they all have in common is their association in the residential kin group.

In circumstances that bring the residents of Yuendumu into contact with other groups, whether or not these groups are indigenous, "my mob" generally refers not to some notional construct of "the Warlpiri," but to the inhabitants of the settlement. It must be noted that Warlpiri living in smaller settlements and outstations do not necessarily perceive their connections in such terms. The senses of place posited in the frameworks of residency and of "Yuendumu" are privileged by the Warlpiri at the settlement over other forms of indigenous connectedness.

Whether called mob or residential unit, family or camp, sedentarized groups have modified, if not diluted, the patterns of ritual inheritance. The templates so neatly provided earlier are in fact mitigated by numerous classificatory pressures.[41] An extended example may provide insights into how residential negotiation has entered into the dynamic of ceremonial life. One of the principal materials used in a number of Warlpiri rituals is red ochre, a substance generally employed on the bodies and ritual objects of both male and female ritual performers and in their ground paintings. The chief mine for this pigment, located near Nyirrpi, is part of land saturated with Dreamings central to maintenance of Warlpiri ritual life.[42] The ceremonies that protect and nurture this mine are overseen by senior men.

Sometime in the mid-1980s it was clear that the various *kirda* for this country were dying out, and that rights of succession to the mine and its associated Dreamings and rituals had to be determined. One individual, a senior man named Kumanjayi Jupurrurla,[43] clearly demonstrated the strongest and most direct connection to the dying *kirda*.[44] His efforts to take control of the mine and its associated rituals, however, were unsuccessful, not because of any direct challenge to the legitimacy of his claim or because of competing claims by men with similar status but because Kumanjayi Jupurrurla lacked a network of kin support, specifically among agnates, either actual or classificatory. He could find no one in his residential kin group willing to be trained for the managerial role (*kurdungurlu*), nor could he find any younger agnates interested in learning the ownership rules.[45] Senior men from other, more powerful residential kin groups were thus able to ignore his claims. Without the assistance of other senior men, he was unable to perform the ceremonies for the mine. None of the powerful groups laid claim to the mine, but each one in turn rebuffed Kumanjayi Jupurrurla's efforts to have his claim legitimated through ritual action. This decade-long struggle (which continues to this day) sheds light on various components of personal and collective negotiations of identity and their relationship to ritual, a leitmotif of this book.

The brief example of Kumanjayi Jupurrurla's struggle to acquire ceremonial control raises numerous questions. Was his inability to secure the Dreamings and rituals surrounding the ochre mine indicative of a personal weakness, characteristic of his whole kin group's numerical decline, or a display of debility restricted to men within his group? The answer to this question necessitates a substantive understanding of how different rituals are differentially constituted, and beyond that an awareness of the authority by which those events are controlled. These last two issues require a grounding in the language of ritual and its repertoire (the subject of the next chapter) and of the individuals who oversee it (which will be the focus of chapter 3).

2.

FROM TERMS TO TIMELINES

A Lexical and Chronological Assessment of Warlpiri Ritual

However categorized or lexically straitjacketed, the ritual act is an all-pervasive component of the Warlpiri universe. This was true prior to sedentarization, and it is true today. Long before they are born and long after they die, the Warlpiri of Yuendumu are directly and inexorably implicated in a complex repertoire of ceremonial activity. Moments of conception, birth, initiation, and death—to name a few English glosses attached to some of the more easily identifiable benchmarks of Warlpiri life—are each made manifest in ritual. Likewise, the resolution of conflicts (for example, matters of sexual transgression, kinship neglect, or violation of ritual Law), appeals for a lover, and declarations of longing can all precipitate ceremonial action. In less traditionally "Aboriginal" contexts—land claims and art openings, to mention two phenomena of so-called postcolonial life—performance also finds utility. Yet this list only begins to hint at the force of ceremony. In reenacting a Dreaming, ritual performers follow in the footsteps (spiritually and physically) of their *Jukurrpa* Ancestral Beings.[1] When those footsteps are properly tracked, a ceremony can quiet barking dogs, calm crying children, and suppress the rage of drunks. It can replenish food supplies, nourish the landscape, heal the sick, and strengthen the social bonds of the living.

So then how to approach acts so permeated with simultaneously invoked meanings? What vocabulary should be used to scrutinize the complex process by which, and in which, a large measure of Warlpiri social identity is made manifest? Is the language of the anthropologist suitable to the Aboriginal ritual participant? Is the participant's terminology sufficiently pliant to satisfy the researcher? And which researcher's language shall be chosen? Which ritual participant's? The two groups, observer and observed, are in point of fact composed of many more voices, often wielding vocabularies expressing different levels of knowledge and insight into the subject that unites them. Alternatively, the same vocabularies are at times used in different ways.

For the Warlpiri, age, gender (of both interlocutor and speaker), and settlement location all shape the meanings attached to the words used to discuss rituals and their performance. Even within Yuendumu, among those who share the same ritual access and gender, the problem of reconciling different perceptual systems exists. The result: Exploring categorical constructs variously defined can at times appear less a piece of fieldwork than some *ficciones* composed by Jorge Luis Borges, the Argentine writer whose explorations of classificatory "ambiguity, redundancies, and deficiencies" in "The Analytical Language of John Wilkins" were invoked in the prefatory material of Foucault's *The Order of Things*.[2] The problems Borges recognized attend any classification and the language(s) marshaled to describe it. And whether undertaken by the fiction writer or fieldworker (and some might question that distinction), all attempts to taxonomize the ritual repertoire of the others are quite obviously bound to reproduce the paradigms of the taxonomist.[3]

To repeat: Terminological contradictions, inconsistencies, and overlappings, so rife in the various vocabularies associated with ritual, can easily undermine the business of representing the actual social dynamics of settlement ceremony. What are we to make of "men-only" secret sacred ceremonies that involve and are influenced by women?[4] What of the "women-only" events that may include the pre- and postceremonial involvement of men? And what of those crucial interdependent "joint" events that can be performed simultaneously on separate grounds by men and women—or interactively in the same arena—but which lack a general term in Warlpiri?

Lexical problems are by no means restricted to the language of gender. Terms of ritual restriction related to access also raise these problems. "Secret" knowledge is often legitimately known by those not formally sanctioned to know it; ritual knowledge that is termed "cheap" in Aboriginal English may have tremendous value despite the vaguely pejorative label by which it is categorized. The translations of other terms denoting ritual function must be reviewed with similar caution.

Consider the ritual of *kurdiji*. Often translated simply as "circumcision ceremony" or "circumcision rite" (see Munn 1973:22), it is in fact a complex cycle of ritual activities in which the act of circumcision is only one component. The same set of ritual events also announces the betrothal of the young and marks a woman's integration into the ceremonial life of the settlement (see also Bell 1983:205–9). *Kurdiji* is as much a woman's "rite of passage" as it is a man's, though less formally declared, to be sure. Clearly there is a liability in attempting to privilege a single social function (especially when it is gender-bound) in assessing complex ritual cycles. Certain rites of passage—a term that is itself of patently Western construction—may serve many more purposes than any label implies.

Take the Warlpiri term *yilpinji,* translated into English as "love songs," "love rituals," and "love magic." As Diane Bell has noted, with justifiable outrage, the language is grossly reductive, and worse. Of *yilpinji* as "love magic" undertaken by women she writes:

> It is a translation which feeds the Northern Territory male's notion of what women ought rightly to be about. For white itinerant road gangers and station hands with whom some Aboriginal women have had sexual liaisons, "love magic" has been a smutty joke. It was something for which one could pay and then reap the results. It marked women clearly as sex objects.
>
> Acting with the support of some Aboriginal converts, the missionaries at Philip Creek banned "love magic" and labeled the practitioners "witches." Women continued to perform *yilpinji* but connotations of love magic as the devil's work are still current at Warrabri today. For Aboriginal men these debasements of *yilpinji* as "love magic" and classification of women as sex objects allowed them an avenue by which *yilpinji* could be defused. (Bell 1983:162)[5]

The problems are not restricted to glosses, however. The actual function and social value of *yilpinji* seem to change greatly over time and terrain. For example, the women's *yilpinji* Bell describes to bolster her gender-based assessments of Warrabri social engagement were restricted to men when Munn conducted her work at Yuendumu. Furthermore, the thematic and performative expressions of *yilpinji* manifest contemporaneous differences between the settlements of Warrabri and Yuendumu. This may be attributable to differences in the indigenous pluralism of two settlements—Warrabri has a significantly less homogeneous constituency—or to the fact that Bell focused principally on the Kaytej of the settlement in which she worked, and was less involved in the actions of the Warlpiri who resided there (Bell 1983:27ff.). Be that as it may, the thematic and performative aspects of *yilpinji* clearly vary significantly in practice and function from one settlement to another and through time.

Bell, linking *yilpinji* to women's *yawulyu* rituals, observes: "If the focus of the *yawulyu* is emotional management, then powerful *yilpinji* designs, songs and gesture will be used" (1983:130). At Yuendumu, designs, songs, and gesture undertaken during a *yawulyu* performance are never referred to as *yilpinji*. Indeed, at Yuendumu, *yilpinji* tend to be performed privately and informally, away from the ceremonial grounds where most rituals take place. This means not that aspects of *yawulyu* ceremonies do not deal with *yilpinji* themes identified by Bell as "emotional management," but that the issues are not connected to the set of rituals Bell privileges in her analysis. Other crucial differences must be noted. Bell details two interrelated Dreaming myths and associated sites evoked in the women's performance of *yilpinji* at Warrabri. At Yuendumu, the *yilpinji* of women lack any direct connection to myths and sites, and are regularly characterized as weak in the essence (*pirlirrpa*) of the Dreaming. The absence of direct site and myth association diminishes the forces by which kinship connections to the *yilpinji* are maintained. Though it is cross-cousins who usually sing *yilpinji* songs for one another, women are also able to undertake such performances unaided and alone. The solitary potential further diminishes kinship obligation. Again, this differs from the circumstance at Warrabri, where Bell notes the *yilpinji* of women are owned by the patricouples overseeing the Dreamings to which the songs are tethered (see Bell 1983:205–9).

Ritual themes and ritual value are dramatically transformed even by small geographic and temporal shifts. It is not surprising, therefore, that European vocabularies are not the only ones susceptible to perceiving them wrongly. The Warlpiri language is also capable of contradiction—at least as perceived by the Western ear. Yet if the dominant language of Yuendumu—which is still Warlpiri, despite the multimedia incursions of Australian English—subverts or defies our own definitional expectations, it may be that this very dissonance can help us clarify the world we endeavor to understand. Perhaps nuances of verbal and social construction can emerge if we attend to the inevitable static generated when the Same meets (and studies) the Other. All categories (whether Warlpiri or Western) are just that, categories, and as such, they require careful manipulation to open up and reveal their meanings.

One more proviso must be noted—one that is special, though by no means unique, to the Warlpiri. In addition to the spoken ambiguities that exist between the researcher and researched, there is a nonverbal dimension to the fieldwork undertaken. Warlpiri communication in matters of ritual—especially when women are the ones communicating and the matters discussed are taboo—can often take place in near silence. Speech restrictions triggered by secrecy rules over certain gender-specific acts (for example, penile subincision and circumcision) tend to orbit, and be orbited by, ritual. As such, many of the most telling observations about gender, kinship, and ceremony inhabit the silent realm of the signed. Because a great deal of the Warlpiri "discourse" (a term particularly inappropriate in this context) is undertaken without words, fieldwork is complicated that much more.[6]

So the list of liabilities grows. Speech taboos, gender distinctions, participatory status in ritual activity, the relationship of inquirer to informant and informant to ritual—all not only affect how much may be said (or signed) about ritual, but may shape the very terms used. Add to this geographic differences (for example, one settlement's "cheap" women's ritual is considered "dear" by women further north), as well as the historical factors that inevitably mutate meaning, and the Borgesian "deficiency" is made that much greater. Certain terms may conspire to suggest inconsistency; other terms may hide it. This is why lengthy explication is needed. While I have struggled in what follows to give voice to the language the Warlpiri themselves use, it has been necessary at times to resort to Western terms, occasionally nestled in quotation marks, to clarify when and where consequential distinctions lack categorical equivalents in Warlpiri.

The residents of Yuendumu tend to conceptualize their ceremonies by the gender of the participants, by the kind of access allowed to ritual currency, by the Dreamings the ritual invokes, or by the purpose of the ceremony that invokes the Dreaming. The Warlpiri terms circling the first two issues—of gender and restriction—are generally those that anthropologists rely upon in their discussions of secrecy, since no single term, synonymously constituted, can be found in indigenous ritual discourse for that specific form of exclusion.

Some of the Warlpiri terms used to characterize ritual are spoken in Warlpiri, while others emerge in Aboriginal English. Sometimes, as in the case of the ritual that calls forth the ancestral conception spirit known as *kurruwalpa,* no name at all is given for the ceremony, context making clear the ritual nature of the *kurruwalpa*'s evocation. To call it a "conception ceremony," handy though that might be, implies a procedural dimension to the actions that distorts the unpredictable nature of the ritual activities associated with the *kurruwalpa* essence.

To amplify, if not exactly match, Warlpiri constructs, I have grouped the terms defining Yuendumu's ceremonial life into four sets. The first set offers up terms in the Warlpiri language that distinguish the gender of ritual performers and observers. The three terms constituting the second set (*cheap, dear,* and *halfway* [dear]) are of Aboriginal English origin and used by the Warlpiri at Yuendumu. The terms of the third set (*tarruku, maralypi, juju, wiri,* and *warraja*) are Warlpiri. The second and third sets both touch upon overlapping notions of access, restriction, distribution, and value. The fourth and longest set of terms is composed of Warlpiri and English-language vocabulary identifying ceremonial functions of ritual. This final set is split in two, with the first subset of functional terms providing a chronologically arranged description of the so-called rites of passage undertaken by the Warlpiri, and the second subset enumerating those rituals enacted outside the ritual life cycle.

As each of the terminological sets is defined, certain ethnographic issues that their connotation or arrangement provokes are addressed in ways intended to soften, if not quell, the Borgesian uproar. Only then can one begin to understand the forces motivating the businesspeople who so value the rituals in which transacted ritual currency designated by these terms acquires meaning.

WATIKIRLANGU AND *KARNTAKURLANGU*, *WATIMIPA* AND *KARNTAMIPA*

The first two terms—*watikirlangu* and *karntakurlangu*—are easy enough to define, referring as they do to the gender of ritual performers. Those ceremonies that are *watikirlangu* are undertaken exclusively by men (*wati*); those that are *karntakurlangu* are realized by women (*karnta*) alone. The second two terms in the set—*watimipa* and *karntamipa*—add observational restrictions based on gender, thus limiting both enactment and viewing of that enactment to men alone (*watimipa*) or women alone (*karntamipa*). Though *watikirlangu* and *karntakurlangu* events may be open to all, *watimipa* and *karntamipa* events are restricted to those sanctioned to participate in ceremonial activity. This sanction, for both men and women, generally begins at the age of thirty.

On the face of it, these gender-based ritual terms appear quite straightforward. However, missing from this set is a term identifying a crucial third form of gender engagement—namely, the interdependent or "joint" event, in which the actions of men and women are required for the completion of the ritual act. Such events are identified by the Warlpiri as *wiri-kirlangu* or *wirirlangu,* which means "belonging to business-people." The term always implies the involvement of both genders, though the nature of the interdependence may vary greatly. Men and women may render such joint actions on shared ceremonial ground or separately in arenas circumscribed by gender (see map 2). Separately performed events that are joint require careful orchestration between the genders to enhance the success of the enactment. Joint rituals can have businessmen and businesswomen performing simultaneously or in an alternating fashion, in contexts restricted to themselves (and, in certain cases, their initiands) or open to the public. The portions of joint events undertaken separately are identified as *watimipa* or *karntamipa.*

In the joint initiation cycle of *kurdiji,* for example, that portion of the event given over to circumcision, and performed on men-only grounds, is deemed *watimipa*—the province of ritually active men and their male initiands. But the obligatory events both preceding and following the surgery—also part of *kurdiji*—necessitate the involvement of women and are decidedly not *watimipa.* In another initiation event known as *Kajirri,* women perform portions of the ritual separately and their acts are deemed *karntamipa.*[7]

The absence of an inclusive Warlpiri term for the connection between men and women in no way debases the value of these shared events. In fact, many of the most important ritual engagements at Yuendumu are those that bring men and women together. However, the absence of an inclusive term may explain why so many of these collaborative acts are seen as independent and why, beyond this, the less declarative—but no less obligatory—activities of women are overwhelmed by descriptions that privilege the male domain. Hence the liabilities of identifying *kurdiji*—a cycle of rituals crucial to both genders and jointly undertaken—as a "circumcision ceremony."

Though the four Warlpiri terms in this set touch on issues of restriction (for the performer vis-à-vis the audience), they do not address the values associated with those restrictions. The values, and their ties to gender, begin to emerge in the next two sets of terms, one of which is expressed in Aboriginal English, the other in Warlpiri.

"CHEAP," "DEAR," AND "HALFWAY"

Warlpiri ritual, and more specifically the danger its performance generates, is often inventoried at Yuendumu by the use of three value-laden Aboriginal English terms. For starters, there is that knowledge deemed "cheap," generally perceived as being without risk and thus usually—though not always—considered public and unrestricted. Then there is that which is "halfway," possessing a performative value dangerous enough to limit participation and observation to the ritually active of both genders (whether in joint performance or only among women). And finally there is that which is considered "dear"—knowledge so dangerous that it can be performed only by men. (The latter two terms—*halfway* and *dear*—stem from the British English for "costly" or "expensive.") These thumbnail translations are true as far as they go. However, it must be noted that, at Yuendumu, while that which is "dear" is always restricted to men, that which is specific to men is not always "dear." These differences suggest not the relative power of each gender, but rather how the value of the ritual material within that gender's ceremonial activity is determined by its ease of distribution. Though it is incumbent upon men wishing to be ritual leaders to acquire and control knowledge of all three types, the "dear" material is, as the word connotes, the most sought after, at least among men. For women wishing to be business leaders, ritual effort is devoted to the acquisition and control of "halfway" material, performed alone and with men. Women recognize the value "dear" material has for men and for the *Jukurrpa* but recognize, too, its attendant dangers. Because of those dangers, women express little interest in acquiring or manipulating that which is "dear."[8] That the women of Yuendumu express little interest in controlling what is the exclusive province of men in no way diminishes their relative authority in the ritual life of the settlement. For both men and women, it is the degree to which they control and transmit knowledge in the ceremonial sphere in which they are sanctioned to operate that grants them their authority. The gender-specific vocabularies may indicate gender-specific ceremonial activity and cross-gender notions of danger inhabiting those separate spheres, but they do not imply superiority or enhance ceremonial power. Broader access to material does not translate into some palpable authority of men over women, simply because the latter do not participate in rituals that employ "dear" material. The control of various "halfway" and "cheap" events enables women to constitute relative authority in their domains of activity, just as men do in theirs. Though the circumstances in which men are ritually implicated may be wider and more dangerous, the authority derived from this width and risk does not grant them greater authority than their female counterparts over the reproduction and nurturance of the Dreaming. Indeed, as the final chapter of the book will show, there are now domains of Warlpiri ritual life that men have, at the performative level, relinquished.

While all "dear" rituals are restricted, it does not follow that all "cheap" events are not. At Yuendumu, love rituals (*yilpinji*), performed covertly and in gender-specific fashion among businesspeople, contain narratives jealously guarded by their performers; yet these songs contain little in the way of dangerous content and are for that reason generally considered "cheap." While the songs have undeniable aphrodisiac effects, their risks, as well as the potency of their *pirlirrpa,* are nominal. On the other hand, certain public, unrestricted events—*yawulyu warrajanyani,* for instance—deemed "cheap" might contain large quantities of *pirlirrpa.* In short, the reasons for the labels applied to ritual, and the meanings those labels have, shift from one form of ritual activity to another.

The fact that potency can be dangerous is clearly the principal quality distinguishing the three Aboriginal English terms the Warlpiri use to triage their ritual currency; there is also a component of negotiative value buried in the terms. In those events that bring men and women together, it is very clear that "halfway" rituals are generally valued over "public" ones, but there are enough exceptions to cancel out the utility of any severe definitional distinctions. Furthermore, intersettlement exchange involving larger social networks points to the settlement-specific and group-specific nature of the terminology herein described. What is deemed "dear" by the Warlpiri of Warrabri can be considered "cheap" by the Warlpiri of Yuendumu.

The descriptive melding of issues of access, danger, potency, and exchange value that confuse the "cheap" and "dear" are even more complicated in the last term of the set. "Halfway" applies both to ceremonial activities jointly undertaken by businessmen and businesswomen and to those events performed by ritually active women alone. Although this subject will be revisited in greater detail later, it must be explicitly restated here that the ritually active, both men and women, believe that men, and men alone, oversee material that is "dear" or *watimipa.* Even the most restricted women's events (*karntamipa*) are deemed "halfway."

Confusion arises easily, however. If the ritually inactive of either gender are interrogated, their lack of knowledge can often legitimate a view that women undertake "dear" ritual activity, much as men do. Alternatively, the uninformed may deem certain "halfway" events "dear" because they are unaware of the specific relationship men have in the ritual. The uninitiated can misrepresent or misconstrue the scope of ritual access (and related terminology). But among the ritually active of both sexes, it is agreed that the ceremonies in which only women participate are never "dear."

Danger, and the language it prompts, is not necessarily (or fully) indicated by the descriptive term attached to ritual events. It is possible for "halfway" material to be insinuated into "public" events, which only adds to the problem of ascribing relative levels of danger (and negotiative value) to whole events, when segments of performance (and related prohibitions) can be judged separately. For the Warlpiri, value is often in the eye of the distributor, but the eye must be trained through ritual experience.

TARRUKU, MARALYPI, *WIRI, JUJU,* AND *WARRAJA*

The terms in the third set associated with ritual—constituted by the Warlpiri in the words *tarruku, maralypi, juju, wiri,* and *warraja*—have meanings that change in specific ways depending on the gender and ritual involvement of those interrogated, and their relationship to the events described. As such, these terms, more than most, tend to overlap and find only partial correlation with the Aboriginal English terms just defined. Take *tarruku;* the word is generally used to identify danger, power, and potency much as *dear* is. And, in fact, men's ceremonies are referred to, interchangeably, as "dear" and *tarruku*. However, *tarruku* is also applied to joint events, ones in which men and women perform, a circumstance also termed "halfway." As such, all "dear" events are *tarruku,* and some *tarruku* events are "halfway." This is not a direct result of men's presence in those events that bear the name, for women describe their portion of joint ceremony using the same term. The term generally is invoked to identify ritual secrecy, ritual power, potency, or danger, the nature of which is amplified by context. Describing an event as *tarruku* in itself does not indicate the gender of the ritual participants, nor does it characterize whether the event takes place interdependently or in a single-gender context. However, the term does exclude the ceremonies of initiated women dissociated from men's events; such women-only performances are not labeled *tarruku,* or the nearly synonymous *maralypi*. Does this mean that women's ceremonies, undertaken without men, lack potency? It does not. That power is communicated in the terms *wiri* and *juju*, terms men often use in like fashion to describe male *tarruku* events. Further complicating the distinction is the fact that men and women will use different gender-specific vocabularies in different contexts to describe the same events. For example, when men discuss *parnpa* ceremonies in the presence of women, they may refer to those events as *tarruku*. Women, however, will not use the word in that context for that ceremony. They will describe *parnpa* as *juju* or *maralypi* among themselves. However, they will invoke the term *tarruku* for other events to which they have access.

Warraja, the last term in this set, is described as meaning "open" or "unrestricted" on the basis of either age or gender. *Warraja* events are accessible to all: Warlpiri, non-Warlpiri Aboriginal, and non-Aboriginal. They are also, in certain contexts, termed "public," "cheap," and "free." The terms generally denote access, not ritual potency, but that is not always the case. As in all transmissions of ritual information that take place at Yuendumu, the layered understandings of the Dreaming are a key criterion for the terms employed. For the anthropologist to be told a certain myth is *tarruku* does not in itself communicate the nature of the restriction. But for the Warlpiri fluent in the Dreamings associated with the *tarruku* event, no confusion would arise. It would be understood instantly whether the restriction was one based on age alone or the additional component of gender.

There is one more use of the term *tarruku*. More loosely applied, it can be used to indicate generic prohibition or reluctance in matters of ritual. Thus *tarruku* becomes a handy "explanation" to be used to silence the queries of the young or simply uninformed (and here we must include the anthropologist). *Tarruku* can announce some ill-defined secrecy, danger, or potency, with its specific nature (whether or not related to a matter of gender) purposely masked.

THE NATURE OF RITUAL SECRECY: A THEORETICAL EXTRAPOLATION

Is it any surprise that a language radically dependent on active ritual participation, and the knowledge that emerges from it, should trigger descriptive fluctuations in the work of the researchers removed from those enactments? After all, if a large portion of the Warlpiri population receives and dispenses simplified descriptions of restricted portions of ceremonial life, should it not be expected that research would replicate the terminological disjunction? Questions about what is or is not "dear" or *tarruku* or men-only reveal contradictions that have less to do with inconsistency among the knowledgeable than they do with the schism between those who have the right to distribute and perform such knowledge and those who do not.

I mention this as a means of segueing into a discussion of a crucial theoretical issue tangled up in the multiplicity of terms upon which researchers rely to assess gender-specificity in matters of ceremonial life. This issue is the relationship of gender to ritual knowledge and its performance. I noted earlier that only men possess knowledge that is considered "dear." This might be taken to mean that what is "dear" is secret. No such assumption can be made, however. To know if gender-based secrecy exists—and how it enters the ritual lives of men and women—one must first be very clear about what constitutes secrecy.

Among the Warlpiri, it is not the possession of ritual knowledge that determines what is dear so much as its distribution—and more precisely its distribution in the context of ritual performance. It is the performative act that establishes the value of ritual knowledge as a currency of social exchange. Indeed, without ritual, the value of such material as social currency cannot be established or maintained. It is not the gender-specific knowledge per se that is considered "dear" (or *wiri,* et cetera), but rather that knowledge made manifest in performance. Knowledge requires acknowledgment for its value to be assayed, and that acknowledgment generally takes place in ritual. This is true for men and women alike.

It is sometimes assumed that because the methods for evoking the Dreaming in ritual performance (songs, designs, dances) are gender-specific, the ritual material is itself gender-specific and thus secret to the gender that performs it. Such an assumption should not be made. If one defines secrecy in terms of the performance of Dreaming segments—as distinct from the methods of the performance—then it must be stated that women do not possess any secret knowledge constituted as inaccessible by men.[9] Women may employ songs or designs or dances that men do not use when evoking Ancestral Beings, but the segments allied to those songs, dances, and designs are all well known and performed by men either in their own rituals or in rituals that are jointly undertaken. However, men possess Dreaming segments (and associated sites) and ritual repertoires that are off-limits to women who reproduce the Dreaming. Still, we should not take this fact to mean that men have a flourishing secret life that keeps women at bay. A large majority of the Dreaming segments deemed important for the maintenance of the *Jukurrpa* are shared by ritual leaders of both genders, arguing for an analysis of ritual politics that is concerned less with the exclusionary language than with terminologies that clarify connections.

In stating that women do not have performative rights over "dear" knowledge, that which is commonly identified as secret, I enter one of the more heated debates in Aboriginalist literature, though the conclusions to be drawn from this gender-specific observation (and its corollary) should be reserved until analysis is complete.[10] Do I mean to suggest women have a weak or inferior position because they lack performative rights over dangerous, gender-restricted events? Quite the contrary. In fact, I intend instead to chip away barriers built around "men's" and "women's" ritual knowledge and the walls of the "secret" and the "open." In doing so I wish to argue that women know about what is not proprietarily (in a ritual sense) "theirs," and that while much of this knowledge cannot be performed by women formally, they nevertheless exert influence in performative domains technically off-limits to them. I would argue that there is a surprising migration of knowledge and assistance between men and women even in gender-specific ritual events, and that the help is often constituted along lines of cross-gender residential kinship.

My research with ritually active women, who (if one accepts much of the traditional literature) might be thought to lack any understanding whatsoever of men's secret ceremonies, suggests instead that these women have a substantive familiarity with the *tarruku* ceremonial life of businessmen, a familiarity rooted in various forms of social exchange based along lines of kinship. This insight became quite clear one evening in 1983 when a businesswomen, a Nampijinpa, expressed interest in perusing Munn's 1973 work *Walbiri Iconography*. In particular, the woman wanted to look at the photographic reproductions of women's body paintings. She looked at the ritual designs and, unable to read the text, began to interrogate me. She asked for a summary of the content of Munn's design descriptions. She confirmed the content, and then amplified some of the narratives associated with the designs. At a certain point I asked her if she was familiar with a set of designs, amply illustrated in the book, that I knew to be the "secret" property of men (see Munn 1973:125). She immediately identified them as rock paintings (and thus by the nature of the medium the exclusive property of men). She went further, mentioning that they were drawings evoking a Dreaming itinerary that included a secret men's cave located to the west of Yuendumu. Her knowledge of men's secret designs ran counter to what Munn had described, and what I had expected.[11] Much to my surprise, she was thoroughly versed in the ceremonial content of numerous male domains of *Jukurrpa*. She very clearly was quite knowledgeable about the myths and the performances of those myths even though she had not been present at their ritual enactment.[12]

She eventually lapsed into sign language, indicating she did not have the rights to perform the knowledge and that further specific description (especially spoken description) would be dangerous because of the nature of the material. Her final signed response—an outstretched hand, palm down, moving back and forth at chest level, accompanied by a heavy inhalation—made it clear that additional invocation of such Ancestral Powers would constitute serious ritual transgression for which she might be forced to submit to *yarda,* a life-threatening "sorcery" performed by the men who rightfully owned the segment. The Nampijinpa knew a great deal about the ceremonies associated with the secret cave—she made manifest much more than an awareness of her own ignorance—but because of her gender, she was prevented from communicating that knowledge.[13] "This is men's business," she told me. She then mentioned that one of her sons, a Japanangka, managed the site as *kurdungurlu* and could legitimately provide an account (albeit more censored) of the site and its *Jukurrpa* narrative. Only much later did I learn that the Nampijinpa's filial invocation hinted at the force of kinship in mitigating the cleavages of gender in matters deemed secret.

On the face of it, the woman's comment—"this is men's business"—endorses a gender-specific view. But while the declaration identifies the prohibition on the basis of gender, it does not restrict prohibitions to that single criterion. The same woman (and indeed all other female ritual leaders) regularly expressed similar reservations about rituals for which she lacked ownership rights. Whether the material in question was part of women's repertoire or men's did not diminish her caution.

The Nampijinpa's familiarity with men's secret knowledge was by no means unique. When asked about "dear" ceremonies, businesswomen at Yuendumu often state, "We know about their [men's] different ways." But the women always add the proviso they have no right to use it. Transgression of this kind, they say, may carry a sentence of death.[14] Secret information may be received; transmission, however, follows a different set of rules, and requires a different status, one determined by various social forces including those of gender. The right to know, the right to own, the right to perform: Each of these verbal constructs implies a different status determined by age, gender, inheritance rights, and authority configured in various ways. A businesswomen, for example, may know of a cave that is *watimipa*—that is, men's alone—and can even own it in the sense of having been granted, through patrilineal inheritance, rights over the Dreaming on which the cave is located. She cannot, however, perform the segments associated with that cave. A woman may even own ritual knowledge via patrilineal inheritance but not "know" how it is performed. Similar distinctions exist among men. The right to possess does not imply possession, and possession does not imply performative rights. And while knowledge may be inherited, its control must be earned.

Women (and men) who have achieved a level of ritual leadership in the settlement are in a position to know a great deal about ceremonies for which they may lack performative rights; their knowledge, therefore, rarely finds expression. Secrecy, or the related notions of *tarruku* and *maralypi,* has less to do with what one knows than what one can say or do, especially in the context of ritual. This fact requires one of the basic assumptions about ritual to be reformulated. Instead of asking whether women (or men) have secret knowledge, the subject of Warlpiri ritual life is better served by posing this query: Do women and men have ritual knowledge with a performative expression that is gender-specific? The answer to the second question is yes.

Though ceremonial dances and songs, as well as certain designs, tend to be gender-specific, the segments they proclaim are often shared. But whereas the Dreaming segments declared in restricted women-only rituals can be constituent elements of men's ceremonies, the opposite use of men-only segments in women's business is not found. Even the most secret segments of women's ritual are found in men's ceremonial activity. The businesswomen of Yuendumu argue that the whole content of their ritual repertoire is known to those senior men with whom they share ownership and managerial rights, and that various aspects of restricted women-only ceremonies regularly migrate into the ceremonies of their male counterparts performed in contexts that may or may not exclude women.

In light of certain recent Central Desert ethnography—and by "recent" I mean work that postdates the research of Meggitt and Munn—on matters of gender, such statements are, I will admit, controversial, but again conclusions should be resisted before the fuller implications of this absence of "dear" or secret material in women's ritual are articulated, for it would be ill conceived to assume that secret performance is the sole criterion of authority. Nor is it terribly useful to construct a simplistic push-me-pull-you of power that pits men against women simply because certain forms of ritual activity happen to be gender-bound and favor (if that is the right word) men.

Does granting the male sphere of ritual a measure of secret performance that is deemed potent, "dear," or powerful in ways absent from the events in which women participate diminish the authority of women? Not necessarily, for no direct connection can be presumed between the control of ritually powerful events and social control outside that specific enactment. In other words, exclusionary rights over "dear" rituals do not on the face of it diminish the ritual status of women, for the size of the repertoire or the danger of the material in it does not translate into superior ritual authority, despite what some Aboriginalist literature might suggest (see, for example, Meggitt 1962; Bell 1983). Women wishing to establish their ritual authority at Yuendumu—authority acknowledged by both men and women—may do so without control over the secret material of men. In fact, powerful female ritual leaders can manifest their authority even though they lack access to certain kinds of powerful events. At all times it is necessary to distinguish ritual power from powerful ritual. Lack of access to the latter does not preclude having the former.

In this regard, Hamilton's observations are worth noting:

> [T]he "status of women" in any society cannot be conceptualized as a see-saw balanced on a central fulcrum, with women sitting on one end and men on the other. Debates about "oppression," "subordination," "asymmetry" and so on are basically concerned with questions of power; the implicit question is, which sex is the more powerful, in which contexts, and how is the pattern of those power relations maintained, reproduced and sometimes transcended? (Hamilton 1981:74)

This strikes a tone that differs from one found in an earlier discussion on the Pitjantjatjara, wherein she says:

> Existence of women's secret ceremonies is necessary in order to constitute women as subjects independently of men's definitions in Aboriginal social for-

mations, and in order to maintain the possibility of a dual social order based on the Law of men and the Law of women. (Hamilton 1979:297)

It would seem that Hamilton herself sits upon the seesaw. She is not alone. Bell, too, undertakes a "balancing act," one that moves between interdependence and autonomy. In *Daughters of the Dreaming,* a study that focuses on the Kaytej at Warrabri, she exhaustively explores the secret ritual domain of Central Desert Aboriginal women, a domain that is profoundly separate, autonomous, closed, and exclusionary.[15] And yet, while presenting this exclusionary model, she also notes that "the body of knowledge and beliefs about the ancestral travels was shared jointly as a sacred trust" (1983:34) by men and women, further noting, "Women and men do know much of each other's ritual business" (1983:36). How the "closed" ritual life is reconciled with this shared knowledge is never explained, and Bell takes pains to note that communication of secret material is greatly discouraged on the basis of gender, a circumstance that differs from the cautionary provisos of Yuendumu's ritual leaders—provisos that include, but are not restricted to, matters of gender. If one recognizes a distinction between the knowledge of ritual and its performance, then the schism between interdependence and separation can be understood and even reconciled. Ritual undertaken in a closed arena suggests that the transmission of secret material across gender lines is greatly discouraged, but this in no way denies the epicene elements of ceremonies that exist beyond the boundaries where the activities take place. Indeed, it is not enough to acknowledge interdependence of the genders in ritual without endeavoring to explain the nature of the cross-gender connection and the domains in which that connection is made manifest.

What to make of an Aboriginal settlement such as Yuendumu, where women lack secret ritual but possess exactly the authority that should be, according to Hamilton, concomitantly absent? The short answer is that Hamilton's cautionary flag needs to be waved all the more vigorously. A woman's lack of performative rights in "dear" ceremonies or a ritual repertoire unknown to men does not establish her inferior relationship to the opposite gender. The transcendence Hamilton alludes to does in fact take place, though through subtle communication in ritual rather than separation during it.

Take the case of a women-only *yawulyu* event that evoked a segment of the Flying Ant Dreaming known as *Pamapardu Jukurrpa.* Performance of the ritual segment had been suspended for nearly a decade. When the businesswomen gathered to perform, they suddenly realized that an appropriate female manager could not be found among the ritual participants. The owner, a senior Nangala, called out to her husband, whose spousal and patrilineal association gave him managerial rights to the Flying Ant Dreaming and thus to the segment being performed. The man stepped into the women's ceremonial ground and monitored a ceremonial dance "restricted" to women.[16]

I witnessed similar cross-gender assistance a few years later. A Warlpiri man standing near the fence that bordered the women's ceremonial ground called out to a sister leading a reenactment of another *yawulyu,* this one evoking the Fire Dreaming. Not only was he completely knowledgeable about the event undertaken, he even provided his sister with a song previously restricted to men's ceremonies. Material that was *watimipa* thus entered *karntamipa* domain, where it could be used in subsequent events. Admittedly, such modifications of actual ritual procedure during ritual are rare, but rarity should not squelch the message transmitted in the exception, namely, that cross-gender communication in matters of ritual exists (as chapter 5 shall show, such synergy inhabits other domains as well) and that its existence preserves and strengthens ritual performance.

In both examples cited above, the connections of kinship superseded the barriers of gender. On the basis of extensive interviews with older residents of Yuendumu, it would appear that such assistance and donation were, if anything, more common prior to sedentarization, though not necessarily provided to sustain the coherence of the residential kin group as it is constituted today.

Men may possess performative rights to ritual knowledge that are denied to women. And men additionally may be able to adapt women's ritual performance to their own gender-specific ceremonies. But the absence of performative rights and exclusion from the rituals of men do not weaken the voice or effect of women in the ritual. Rather, they point to the inadequacy of a vocabulary that denies informal and nonstructural influence. Terminology notwithstanding, businesswomen are crucial to almost all ritual acts, even those at which they are not present—those considered the exclusive domain of men. So great is the pressure of residential kinship that tethers men to women that it is impossible for men to avoid the censure of their spouses and other female kin, even in events that are putatively their own.

In the domain of the *watimipa,* far from being marginalized, women exert their presence through the nexus of residential negotiation that hovers around events circumscribed by restrictions of gender. Participation may at times be gender-specific, but the decisions emerging from those encounters, often involving lengthy preparations and postceremonial negotiation, implicate men and women.

Take, by way of example, the *kurdiji* cycle already mentioned. Even in those segments from which women are banned entirely, their influence is palpable. The night before the act of male circumcision (a portion of the cycle deemed *watimipa*) the mothers of the initiands present a charred stick (*nginji*) to specific potential mothers-in-law—and by implication spouses for their sons. The presentation of this stick gives cues to the male relatives responsible for choosing the circumciser (generally the husband of the ember's recipient)—a choice that then determines the specific preferred marriage for the initiand. In short, women establish the pool of future spouses for their sons, and it is from this pool that male relatives are supposed to make their selection, via the choice of the circumciser. The ceremony linked to circumcision, an event from which women are banned, thus contains a process of spousal selection influenced by the actions of these women. Following the surgery, the brothers of the mothers of the initiands inform their sisters of the identity of the circumciser to alert them of newly established taboo relationships—prohibitions emerging from the betrothal patterns established by the selection of the circumciser. When the procedure is not followed, the influence of women can be felt ex post facto. I was present at one *kurdiji* cycle when a senior woman provided a charred stick to three potential mothers-in-law for her son. Immediately after the circumcision of her child, she learned that the selection of a circumciser had ignored her wishes. The man chosen lacked the appropriate kinship ties to the women the initiand's mother had selected, thus negating the marital aspirations she had for the son. She felt the selection of this circumciser, a choice made by her male relatives, carried unacceptable martial obligations, since the preferred spouse came from a distant settlement with little political or ritual connection to Yuendumu.

The businesswoman expressed outrage and demanded that the preferred marriage, as constituted by the circumcision, be ignored so that her son could form an alliance respecting "proper" kin patterns, a union that would enhance the cohesion of the settlement. For the next three years she confronted her male relatives. Ultimately she managed to betroth her son to a daughter from the pool of women to whom she originally handed the charred stick. The circumciser whose rights were circumvented received compensation in the form of male ritual objects and money.

The wishes of female relatives are regularly factored into the determinations that take place during male ritual activity. Though not necessarily present, female relatives exert a pressure. This example, by no means exceptional, not only highlights the limitations of certain gender-bound assessments of gender-specific ritual performance (pointing as it does to the migration of knowledge and influence along lines of kinship), but further elucidates the guardianship women often demonstrate, and the intervention they undertake when ritual procedure, as they perceive it, is neglected.

When earlier I cited the Nampijinpa's access to certain ritual knowledge that Munn suggested was the exclusive province of men, I did so to note the distinction between what is known and what is distributed. There is, however, another issue that the example raises. Did Munn get the conceptual framework of genderized ritual knowledge "wrong"? I would argue she did not; rather, the nature of that framework has probably undergone some change. The cross-gender diffusion of ritual material that makes its way into performance has steadily increased with sedentarization. The knowledge itself, however, may or may not have been accessible to businesswomen regardless of gender even when Munn was conducting her fieldwork. Older women at Yuendumu, and ritual leaders in particular, are quite adamant in declaring (if not showing) their awareness of men's business, an awareness they insist female ritual leaders have "always" possessed. These women do not accept the premise that the possession of ritual knowledge per se has undergone modification any more than they accept that the Dreaming itself has.

As I have stated repeatedly, the Warlpiri are vigorous in their declarations of the *Jukurrpa*'s unchanging nature. The Dreaming does not modulate, nor does the obligation to enact it through ritual. What does undergo transformation is the repertoire of that ritual, the ceremonies themselves. Some of these, so exactingly described by Meggitt in the 1950s, are very rarely performed at Yuendumu today.

Among women's ceremonies, for example, so-called birth rituals have been suspended (see Meggitt 1962:274–78). Babies are almost never "smoked"—a traditional health procedure that requires both mother and newborn to be placed near hot coals covered with green eucalyptus leaves—since births are now primarily performed in hospital settings.[17] Western medical practice has also reduced the frequency of curing rituals such as *nyurnu-kurlangu*. The knowledge required to perform these rituals is rarely transmitted to the younger members of the settlement. This is true of love rituals (*yilpinji*) as well.

Still, some of the traditional imperatives associated with suspended events do surface in nonritual contexts. Ever since rumors suggested that the afterbirth of women was being fed to dogs by the staff at the Alice Springs hospital, the Warlpiri—men and women alike—have vigorously attempted to reclaim the afterbirth (*makarra*) for proper ritual burial by the newborn's maternal grandmother. And though these attempts have yet to yield the afterbirth itself, the efforts have prompted widespread ritual discussion about the ceremony's reestablishment.

As for men's ceremonies, here, too, there has been a marked reduction in the performance of *yilpinji* love rituals. Also less frequently undertaken are so-called increasing ceremonies (*parnpa*), intended to precipitate an abundance of rain, vegetation (yams in particular), and game (Kangaroo, Emu, Goanna, and Bush Turkey are among the Ancestral Beings most often invoked). Men's revenge events, such as bone pointing (*yarda*)—generally termed "sorcery"—have, if one believes the women of Yuendumu, greatly diminished, though the threat is often felt (men are silent on this matter when approached by a female researcher). All these changes, however, should not be taken as suggesting a diminution of ritual activity or of a concomitant reduction in the significance of ritual in settlement life. For while the particular ceremonies just cited may be less frequently performed, other rituals have been added to the repertoire of ceremonial life. Newly established, creolized activities such as "Church *Purlapa*," which blend elements of Christian narrative with the rhythms of Warlpiri ritual, are undertaken at the settlement, though almost exclusively by members of two particular residential kin groups. As such, these events have little impact on settlement ritual life as a whole. However, recently established intergroup ceremonial cycles, wholly banned from public discourse, have seen a marked increase in both enactment and significance at Yuendumu. Among those long-standing events that may be defined as "traditional," the repertoire may be slightly smaller and the duration of events shorter, but the frequency has increased, as has the size of the gatherings.[18] The rituals that the Warlpiri consider the most consequential—the ones that touch on matters of initiation and conflict resolution—generally take place at times that maximize settlement-wide participation, that is, during school breaks and often right after Sports Weekend in July, when Yuendumu's population swells substantially.[19] Broad-based enactment is thought to compound the value of ritual.

However, regardless of the size of the event—or the gender of its participants, for that matter—the kin patterns that define so much of Warlpiri social identity are regularly maintained in the performance (see also Meggitt 1962:309). In so doing, ceremonies bring together relatives—mothers with daughters, nephews with uncles, cross-cousins, brothers-in-law, sisters-in-law—in patterns that sustain the *kirda-kurdungurlu* dynamic found at the core of settlement life.

TERMS OF THE RITUAL REPERTOIRE

I would like to end this chapter with the fourth set of terms—a descriptive list of the ceremonies themselves—and inject wherever possible the earlier terminologies hovering around the issues of restriction and their ties to gender. Two points require clarification. First, I have cleaved the list into two subsets. The first subset traces the rites of passage marked by ritual: ceremonies orbiting birth, initiation, and death. The second subset of terms encompasses those ceremonies outside the obligatory ones connected to the cosmological construction of identity. Events in this second subset have been grouped, with provisional caveats, by the gender of the participants. But to reiterate a point already made, one that shall be explored in subsequent chapters: Some rituals bring men and women together and other rituals very clearly keep them apart, but present even in gender-specific events is the force of kin connectedness. True, there are events deemed too dangerous for women, but prohibition from such dangerous activity does not impinge upon either the status or the social utility of women in the overall ritual life of the settlement. Indeed, as we shall see, the presence of women is increasingly felt in Yuendumu's ritual life (especially in the public manifestations explored in the final chapter of this work). Yet again it must be stressed that in the same way many men's events must often represent the interests of women, women's events are obligated to respond to the concerns of men, and in particular their specific residential kin. Actual performance may implicate only one gender, but collaborative negotiations often precede and follow gender-specific action in both formal and informal ways.

One final note: Where the terms employed in the following catalog of ritual are the result of ethnographic invention or the indigenous embrace of English, I have resorted to the application of a common rhetorical device of distantiation, quotation marks.

Subset One: Ceremonies Punctuating the Life Cycle of the Warlpiri

KURRUWALPA. Performed by male relatives of a pre- or neonatal being (male or female), the ceremony that invokes the "child-spirit" known as *kurruwalpa* is undertaken to establish connections between the locus of conception and a newborn. The event, principally relying on men's songs, is considered "dear" and *tarruku*. However, the event is often stimulated by nocturnal visitations of the "child-spirit" in the dreams of the pregnant woman or relatives principally situated in the child's matriline. No term exists in Warlpiri for the ceremony per se, or rather none that either Warlpiri men or the literature on Warlpiri men provides. The "conception-site ceremony" establishes ritual rights and responsibilities of *kirda-* or *kurdungurlu*-ship that may exist outside formal patrilineal inheritance. In the past, individuals received personal names associated with their conception site, but this practice is now rare (Meggitt 1962:208; Dussart 1989a; Glowczewski 1991:41).

"BIRTH CEREMONIES." Like the ritual performance mentioned above, no name is attached to the rituals surrounding birth, and like "conception events," "birth ceremonies" are now rarely undertaken. Women old enough to remember describe a strict procedure attending the delivery of children prior to sedentarization, the details of which are kept among mothers.[20] Variously classified by senior women as *karntamipa* or "halfway" (but never *wiri*), these birth rituals were performed to strengthen babies (male and female) so that they could avoid crying (*yulamiwangu*) and grow up healthy.[21] These rituals also declared the child's gender through song. The women's ceremony did not exclude men entirely. In fact, a pregnant woman's first contractions necessitated ritual singing by men—specifically the husband and the mother's brother of the pregnant woman—an act performed in isolation. This *watimipa* component of a *karntamipa* ceremony was then followed by a series of acts restricted to women. These included being "smoked" near eucalyptus-covered embers, the cleansing with warm ashes of both mother and child, the ritual burial of the afterbirth, and the making of a birth necklace. The necklace, formed from hair string (*wirriji*) and fitted with a small section of the umbilical cord, was placed around the child's neck in gender-specific fashion. A few days after the birth, the baby would be rubbed with kangaroo fat to ensure growth and health.

KURDIJI. This joint ceremony, variously identified as *wiri, tarruku,* and *maralypi,* can more accurately be described as a cycle of gender-restricted ritual events with plural motives. The most notable is the recognition of the first stage of a young man's ritual initiation through the act of circumcision, an obligatory surgical intervention that takes place during adolescence, usually between the ages of twelve and fifteen. Those components of the cycle that are restricted to men (for example, participation in the circumcision itself) are deemed "dear" and *watimipa,* whereas other portions that require the intervention of women are considered "halfway." Both components of the *kurdiji* that implicate women and those that do not are considered *tarruku* or *maralypi.*

The rituals in *kurdiji* that require both men and women are performed together on shared ceremonial ground. In addition to declaring the male adolescent's entrance into the ritual domain (though not yet as an active participant), these joint undertakings are imbued with consequence for women. It is in these events that a marital association between the initiand and his preferred spouse is declared, as previously described. This declaration has direct, albeit nonformalized, impact on the ritual life of women. It is also generally during the *kurdiji* that the mothers of initiands begin in earnest their careers as "businesswomen." A shift takes place in their lives whereby the physical nurturance of the child is supplanted by a spiritual responsibility over the Dreaming. This new responsibility necessitates a willingness to be educated in matters of ritual performance by senior relatives, both male and female. It is also during these events that female siblings of male initiands begin to learn of their ritual responsibilities. (Sisters dance at their brothers' *kurdiji* to help them "become men." Such assistance will be reciprocated; brothers will provide ongoing assistance to their sisters in their ritual career.) In short, though much of the performance of *kurdiji* is focused on the circumcision of young men, it is no less crucial for their sisters, mothers, mothers-in-law, and (future) wives.[22] It has the added cross-gender importance of defining, through spousal identification, taboo relationships that will have an impact on social interaction in both the ritual and nonritual spheres.[23]

MARDUKUJA-KURLANGU. This term, literally meaning "belonging to women," is invoked to identify a complex ceremonial cycle that has as its purpose "female initiation." No longer (or at least not currently) practiced, *mardukuja-kurlangu* events were restricted to women. This cycle was, according to senior women, "their" version of the *kurdiji.* The events required girls between the ages of eight and twelve to learn the ritualized actions that attended menstruation and birth, as well as the social obligations of kinship, in particular the manner by which female initiands should interact with their mothers-in-law in such matters as food redistribution and ritual assistance. The Warlpiri vocabulary specific to this material "belonging to women" is now rarely employed, with one exception. A remnant of the breast-enhancing portion of the event, a ceremony called *lampanu-kurlangu,* continues to find reenactment in certain public *yawulyu* ceremonies. Unlike the event in which young men are circumcised, the female breast enhancement ritual is not obligatory. No reference of value (for example, "halfway" or "dear") has been recorded with regard to this suspended cycle of female-specific rituals.

KAJIRRI AND KANKARLU. The second stage of male initiation bears two names, distinguishing the Dreaming itineraries evoked in the separate ceremonies, which serve an equivalent function. Young men may be initiated by undertaking one or both of these events. Participation depends on the individual's association with the Dreaming sites and the timing of the events. Performed only once every few years and targeted at young men between the ages of fifteen and seventeen, the *Kajirri* and *Kankarlu* are performed to further advance the initiation of young men in their ritual responsibilities (for example, Dreaming narratives, designs, song), as well as in the skills associated with hunting. The events are likened to high school by senior men familiar with the restricted teachings.

Like the *kurdiji,* these rituals have moments that are undertaken by men alone and those performed in conjunction with women. The nature of the joint activities, however, differs from the first set of initiation activities. Unlike *kurdiji* initiation events, the joint ritual at this stage is undertaken separately, requiring a coordination of *watimipa* and *karntamipa* rituals that keep the genders separate. Only very brief ceremonies are performed on ritual grounds shared by men and women at the beginning and the end of the ceremonial cycle.

Young men who have undergone the initiation ceremonies of *kurdiji* and *Kajirri* (or the variant of the latter, *Kankarlu*) can be subincised, a highly restricted surgical intervention that precipitates correlative dances by women (specifically the mothers of the initiands) near the secluded ceremonial grounds of men. Older female informants note that these ceremonies once triggered sympathetic scarification on the part of the mothers, though this practice is no longer performed.

The joint ceremonial cycles of *Kajirri* and *Kankarlu* are variously identified as "dear" and *tarruku* and *wiri, karntamipa* and *watimipa*. Though the performance of a women's restricted event, especially in the context of a joint ceremony, might justify the employment of the term *halfway*, that term is never used, perhaps because the women's dancing is conducted away from the "dear" events of men.

MALAMALA. Undertaken by all relatives of the deceased, regardless of gender or age, *malamala* is the first of two formal ceremonies associated with death.

In advance of the *malamala*'s actual ritual performance, certain female relatives of the deceased establish gender-restricted mourning camps, also known as "sorry camps." Which women enter these camps is determined by kin relations to the deceased, with widows, mothers, and mothers-in-law usually taking occupancy. Once they are in these camps, the women wail, cover their bodies with pipe clay, singe and cut their hair, and fall under a speech taboo that has been known to go on as long as three or four years. (It is now more common for such restrictions to last a matter of weeks or months [Kendon 1988].)

Men, for their part, conduct "sorry business" in a less formally circumscribed fashion, but also along lines of kinship, with the mother's brothers, fathers, brothers-in-law, and husband of the deceased all painting designs on their bodies: semicircles on the forehead and two lines rising in parallel fashion from the umbilicus to the sternum, where they diverge, tracing the pectorals like the handles of canes.

The formal ritual of *malamala* begins with self-inflicted mutilation by relatives of the deceased. Fathers, cross-cousins, and mother's brothers gash their thighs, while widows, mothers, and mothers-in-law shed blood by wounding themselves on the top of the head. Other relatives who feel extreme sorrow may, if they wish, join in these acts, though no kinship obligation necessitates it.

At no point in the ritual is the name of the deceased ever mentioned. In fact, the name in any context is placed under a speech taboo. All individuals sharing the name of the deceased are subsequently identified as *kumanjayi*, or "no name."[24] Additionally, all performance of Dreaming segments strongly associated with the deceased are suspended, and marriage restrictions on the spouses of the deceased are imposed until proper "finishing-time" rituals are conducted to lift the various bans. With death, the essence of the individual ceases, temporarily, to be called *pirlirrpa,* entering a liminal state identified as *yama* or *marnparrpa.*

The next stage of the event is undertaken by men alone. Without dance or song, in flamboyantly ritualized fashion, the men ritually accuse various individuals of neglectful or outright vengeful action. Among the Warlpiri, there is no such thing as death by natural causes. The accusation of murder is commonly cried out in these events even in the case of an old person's death. This performance by men is generally unilateral, with those accused remaining silent throughout.

At this juncture, the audience and performers scatter. Women related to the deceased use tree branches to sweep the ground associated with their dead relative, so that his or her personal essence (*pirlirrpa*) may return to the ancestral country. Usually men watch this portion of the event, offering no assistance.[25] The sweeping is followed by a non-Aboriginal (Baptist) service, with attendance constituted along lines of kinship. The relatives sanctioned to mutilate themselves do not attend any subsequent *malamala* events, including the actual burial. Though there are portions of *malamala* that are gender-bound, control over the activities is located among close kin, both male and female. No gender-specific or value-laden terms are invoked when death rituals are discussed. The ceremony has no negotiative value in domains of ritual exchange. While it may be viewed by outsiders to be jointly and publicly performed with kin restrictions, the *malamala* avoids the standardized vocabulary mentioned above. The Warlpiri explain that discussion of the deceased, especially in close temporal proximity to actual death, may jeopardize the reintegration of the deceased's spirit into the ancestral country whence it came. The "unnatural" and even murderous nature of death weakens all around it. This, the Warlpiri explain, prevents any ritual activity except *malamala* from taking place. If, say, an individual dies of a heart attack during a *kurdiji* (as happened once during my fieldwork), all ceremonial activity is instantly halted until all the funeral ritual has been completed. With sedentarization, the number of *malamala* (and accompanying "sorry business") has increased dramatically.

"FINISH-TIME." A postfunerary event for which I was unable to find a Warlpiri term, "finish-time" (the phrase is Warlpiri English) is undertaken jointly by the ritually active relatives of the deceased.[26] No gender- or value-laden terms are applied to the event. Women generally invoke the ritual in sign language, bringing together the palms of the hands so that the fingers are at right angles and then sweeping the top palm across the fingers of the bottom hand.

This ceremony lifts the marriage restrictions on widows and widowers. It also allows for the reintegration of suspended segments of the Dreaming into the ritual life. To that end, the "finish-time" tends to be performed in conjunction with those ceremonial activities in which the suspended segments of the deceased were previously invoked. The event can take place a few months or many years after the death of the individual whose country is "opened up." This process of reintegration has wide-ranging implications, offering insight into the relationship between the living, the dead, and the spiritual Ancestral Beings. Death in itself does not transfer the Warlpiri instantly into the ancestral realm. Only with the enactment of a "finish-time" event does the spirit of the deceased shift from a *yama* or *marnparrpa* essence back to *pirlirrpa*. However, the nature of this *pirlirrpa* essence is no longer individual, but instead part of the collective essence that imbues the Ancestral Beings in their ancestral homes (*ngurrara*). This fusion of the individual essence with the larger cosmological one allows for the resumption of ceremonies associated with the ancestral homes.

With the "finish-time" event transacted, not only are name restrictions lifted, but the deceased are now associated directly with the Ancestral Beings for which they were *kirda* during life. When the living subsequently refer to these Beings they consider them actual manifestations of their deceased relatives. The personal connection to that relative is not lost immediately; it erodes slowly over time. The direct connection between ancestor and Ancestral Being is rarely made once three generations separate the living from the dead. This general amnesia explains how the living parent will become *kumanjayi* upon death, become "my father the Ancestral Emu" after "finish-time" events, and eventually find identification simply as the Ancestral Emu with no actual relationship either declared or perceived. This is true for both men and women.

Subset Two

Rituals Performed by Women

NYURNU-KURLANGU. These women-only (*karntamipa*) events, also known as *yikipirrki*, are generally considered "halfway" and are no longer performed with any frequency except by the older women of Yuendumu, who know the songs and designs intended to restore health to a body jeopardized by sorcery. *Nyurnu-kurlangu* are usually performed in conjunction with *yawulyu* rituals, public or restricted. When properly undertaken, this curing ritual reestablishes the healthy spirit (*pirlirrpa*) of women by returning it to the proper position in the kidneys. The Warlpiri offer no explanation for the reduction in frequency of such curing events. It may be the diminution of sorcery, the intervention of Western medicines, or some other social force that explains the near cessation of intergenerational ritual transmission of the details of *nyurnu-kurlangu*. Depending on the constituency of the audience, the women knowledgeable about the ritual consider it "halfway," *wiri,* or *warraja,* but never "dear."

YAWULYU. An umbrella term for the most pervasive of women's rituals at Yuendumu, *yawulyu* defies easy translation because of its plural functions. *Yawulyu* events can be performed to enhance knowledge, sexuality, fertility, well-being, and growth of both a spiritual and physical nature. Warlpiri women perform both public versions of these events and ones restricted to ritually active women. As in the case of the curing rituals, the descriptors *cheap* and *halfway*, *wiri* and *warraja* are invoked depending on the social networks and initiation status of those present at the ritual.

Warlpiri women tend to identify their various *yawulyu* ceremonies by the Dreaming itinerary evoked during performance. However, because different segments, serially or individually, may be performed, a ritual bearing the same name might involve different dances, designs, and songs. For an exact understanding of which *yawulyu* has been performed, it is necessary to know both the Dreaming itinerary and the specific site or sites evoked during the event.

Rituals Performed by Men

PARNPA. These men-only *watimipa* events, identified as "increase" and "revelatory" ceremonies in the literature, are undertaken for many of the same reasons as the restricted *yawulyu* mentioned above. In fact, Warlpiri women often liken their event to the *parnpa* of men.[27] The specific function of the men's version is directed at the increase of rain, game, and flora. There is also a pedagogic component to the performance, one considered revelatory by Meggitt (1962:221). Young male initiands are educated in the manner by which to sustain the natural resources around them. Because of the ritual's educational dimension, *parnpa* is often performed as part of the *kurdiji* cycle.

Parnpa ceremonies tend to be directed at specific circumstances in need of increase (*ngarrmirni*), whereas the *yawulyu* are invoked for the more general maintenance of Warlpiri well-being.[28] The ceremonies, always "dear," and additionally described as *maralypi* and *tarruku,* are performed less often now than when Munn undertook her fieldwork at Yuendumu, but their relevance in the ritual life has in no way diminished.[29]

PURLAPA. Known often by the generic phrase "men's public ceremonies," these events, now rarely undertaken, so closely resemble both in performance and social function the *yawulyu warrajanyani* of women as to be correlates. In fact, so direct is the concomitant decrease of these men's events with the increase in the public version of *yawulyu* that detailed study of the changing roles of men and women in public enactment of ritual shall constitute the focus of the whole of chapter 6.

Meggitt described *purlapa* events as "public entertainments"—a term suggesting relatively inconsequential diversion (1962:244). However, *purlapa* now (and then, according to older residents of Yuendumu) do more than divert, as I shall show. These rarely studied public performances enable ritual leaders to manifest, in the broadest and most open context, their control over stories and sites, and the resources associated with them. The rituals are often described as *watikirlangu, warraja,* "public," and "cheap," and they are generally performed by senior men with young initiates in contexts that are unrestricted by the demands of initiation.

YARDA. Though rarely performed, "sorcery rituals"—generally invoked by the noun *yarda* (a curse)—are very much a part of Warlpiri consciousness. These highly covert events, the performance of which is restricted to senior men (though instigation, the Warlpiri note, can come from either gender), generally involve the act of bone pointing and of singing curses (*juyurdu*). To "bone" or "sing" (*jirriny-pinyi*) an individual sentences the victim to illness and, in certain extreme cases, death. Traditionally, the kin group of the "boned" tended to counter *yarda* with the female curing ritual of *nyurnu-kurlangu* and a visit from an *ngankayi,* a so-called medicine man. The existence of such events is generally denied by actual performers but cited by others, both men and women. Few details regarding *yarda* are ever offered for fear of reprisal by the performers of these revenge acts. As a consequence of this reticence, no terms of value used by the Warlpiri can be provided.

Rituals Performed by Men and Women

YILPINJI. According to senior Warlpiri residents, *yilpinji* were the exclusive province of men prior to sedentarization. However, the performance of *yilpinji* was opened up to women in the wake of forced settlement. The new population density and the accompanying social disruption stimulated a dramatic increase in the "love songs" used to find lovers. These events, rarely performed at Yuendumu today, tend to be restricted to older residents and are undertaken in gender-restricted, nonceremonial settings by both men and women. As such, they are *watimipa* and *karntamipa,* respectively.

Yilpinji have a rich history in Central Desert migration and associated ethnographic documentation. Kaberry (1939:268), Berndt (1950:28), Munn (1973:45–47), Meggitt (1962:209), and Bell (1983:145–46) all assess the social relevance of love songs used to declare sexual desire and manage gender conflict. According to various life stories at Yuendumu and the anthropological literature, *yilpinji* were regularly traded among various Central Desert groups, with particularly strong exchange ties forming among the Warlpiri, the Anmatyerre, and the Pitjantjatjara.

During female performances of *yilpinji* women rub their bodies with animal fat or, in a modern update, Johnson's baby oil, so that the skin gleams—a sign of beauty, health, and sexual potency. This is usually followed by the "singing" of certain body parts—belly, thighs, vagina—to encourage an enlargement that augments appeal. While the Warlpiri believe such rituals are powerful enough to provoke the transgression of sexual taboo—women provide accounts of mothers-in-law and sons-in-law or brothers and sisters engaging in unacceptable liaisons as a direct result of the *yilpinji*—the rituals are not deemed potent in the nurturance of the *Jukurrpa.* The *yilpinji* are never considered public. Performance of these events, generally relying on cross-cousins (for both men and women), is almost always undertaken covertly. Bell, working at Warrabri, has described the *yilpinji* of women in terms that suggest a resemblance to the performative functions of certain *nyurnu-kurlangu, yilpinji,* and *yilpinji-kari* events undertaken at Yuendumu (1983:172–73, 145–46). Such associations are not present at Yuendumu.

YILPINJI-KARI. Literally meaning "different kind of *yilpinji,*" the *yilpinji-kari* bear structural resemblance to *yilpinji* but manifest a radically different social function. Rather than being performed to promote sexual desire, these ceremonies are enacted to express sadness for relatives who are far away or to mitigate tensions among kin. *Yilpinji-kari* express feelings of longing and a desire for appeasement or mollification. No longer performed with any regularity, the ritual is not terribly valued even by those who possess the knowledge necessary to perform it.

JARDIWANPA, KURA-KURRA, NGAJIKULA, PULUWANTI. These four ceremonial cycles are distinguished by the Ancestral Beings they invoke, and thus the patrikin who perform them.[30] (For example, *Jardiwanpa* events are owned by several kin groups belonging to the same patrimoiety that includes the subsections of J/Nangala, J/Nampijinpa, J/Nakamarra, and J/Napurrurla.) The events are undertaken jointly by ritually mature men and women in predominantly restricted fashion, though the activities of the final night are obligatorily open to all. Some portions of the events are restricted to men (*watimipa*), while others are performed jointly on shared ceremonial ground. Identified by Peterson (1970) as conflict resolution rituals, their function at Yuendumu now appears to contain features beyond the resolution of transgressive acts such as disrespect toward kin and the violation of marital relations. Both transgressions (whether kin or spousal) tend to implicate relatives involved in the marriage (or remarriage) of the various *kirda* for that event. Because mother's brothers are implicated in all such activities from the very start of betrothal, problems that require conflict resolution events tend to implicate these relatives directly.

During conflict resolution rituals, various activities are suspended: Spouses halt sexual activity, and the physical manifestation of Ancestral Beings cannot be consumed by their *kirda* (for example, the owner of the Emu Dreaming cannot eat emu meat). Performance of these events allows the transgressors to atone for their violations of the Law. But beyond the resolution of such conflicts, these cycles establish alliances between widows of both genders with future spouses. By accepting ritual punishment and a variety of kinship obligations, participants of these events become ritually and physically more mature. The ceremonially stimulated maturation process, for both men and women, can be enhanced by men "singing" a restricted song that encourages the graying of hair. These songs are undertaken along lines of kinship. (To give but one example, a maternal uncle will "sing" his niece.)

Jardiwanpa are undertaken by the owners and managers of the Snake (also rendered as Python) Dreaming (*Yarripiri Jukurrpa*), Emu Dreaming (*Yankirri Jukurrpa*), and Spectacled Hare Wallaby Dreaming (*Wamparna Jukurrpa*). *Kura-kurra* coordinate the activities of the reciprocally allied kin associated with the Budgerigar Dreaming (*Ngatijirri Jukurrpa*), Bush Onion Dreaming (*Janmarda Jukurrpa*), and Brown Bird Dreaming (*Jalalapinypinypa Jukurrpa*).[31] *Ngajikula* coordinate the managers and owners of the Rat Kangaroo Dreaming (*Marlu Jukurrpa*) (Peterson 1970:201). *Puluwanti* allow for conflict resolution and marital realliance among the *kirda* and *kurdungurlu* of Dreamings for three Ancestral Beings: the Boobook Owl (*Kuurrkurrpa*), Green Parrot (*Jarrurlu-Jarrurlu*), and a Snake (*Warna*).

The interrelationship of the four ritual cycles prompts an obligatory reversal and exchange of owner/manager roles in performance from one associated cycle to the next. The *Jardiwanpa* material bears a *kirda-kurdungurlu* relationship with the other three rituals, and alternates with them in ways that enable owners and managers of opposite patrimoieties to exchange roles. And because the itineraries of all four events are lengthy and require many owners and managers to enact them, large-scale participation implicating different kin groups belonging to opposite patrimoieties is obligatory.

The resolution components of the performance necessitate ritualized acts of assault and support. Assaults come from members of ego's matrimoiety, while support emerges from the opposite patrimoiety. Who supports or attacks runs along specific lines of kinship that differ on the basis of gender and age in the following way.[32] Men are assaulted by relatives of two generations who bear alternating relationship to each other; mother's brothers and daughter's husbands are both implicated in the assaults of men. The attacked men receive support from mother's brothers' sons, brothers-in-law, fathers-in-law, and sisters' sons.

Ritual assault on women requires no such bigenerational intervention. Women tend to be assaulted by mother's brothers and find support from daughters, cross-cousins (both male and female), and sisters-in-law. Women may assault their assailants along specific kin lines. Men in such rituals may not. When joint portions of the rituals are enacted, men monitor the atonement of women along specific lines of kinship.

These events do more than resolve conflict. Through the remarriage component of the event, they also consolidate and establish new kin ties among kin groups. This realignment can itself provoke conflict that will require subsequent resolution, since ceremonies demand that widows and widowers ritually confirm new connections to individuals they may or may not wish to marry. As such, these rituals contend with the issue of conflict but do not necessarily resolve it.

These joint events contain a great deal of intra- and intersettlement importance, and their content, highly valued, is regularly exchanged inter-Aboriginally. In fact, *Jardiwanpa* material from Yuendumu was traded for covert syncretic material found in *Jurlurru* (see next section).

These rituals are generally identified as "halfway," "dear," *tarruku,* and *juju,* with the Warlpiri English terms marking the gender-specific portions of these shared activities. The final night's open activities, mandatory for all kin associated with the Dreamings invoked, are deemed *warraja.*

JURLURRU. Little discussed but regularly performed by both women and men, these syncretic "cult" events are highly valued as a form of covert, intergroup ritual exchange. According to senior ritual leaders, *Jurlurru* activities arrived at Yuendumu in the 1970s, part of exchanges with businesspeople from the northern settlement of Balgo. The initial exchange of *Jurlurru* material was transacted between various *kurdungurlu* subsections for *Jardiwanpa* and unspecified residents of the northern settlement.[33] This event celebrates ritual obligation by rejecting it. Transgressive gestures within it include women shaking the hands of their sons-in-law, and circumcisers making unspecified contact with the mothers of the circumcised. More than that cannot be said without violating the ritual restrictions that accompany participation or viewing. Both men and women describe these events as *tarruku* and *juju.* Women are given access to material that is "halfway," whereas men oversee elements deemed to be "dear." The "dear" material establishes control by senior men over their ritually active juniors.

"CHURCH PURLAPA." This is an Aboriginal English term for those creolized events, jointly and publicly performed by men and women, that merge components of long-standing Warlpiri ritual with Christian (and in particular Baptist) narrative. Traceable to the impact of long-standing missionary activity, but only formally constituted after 1977, "Church *Purlapa*"—originally identified as "Church Corroboree"—merge certain graphic and performative traditions of Warlpiri ritual with Bible stories (Swain 1988:457–59; Fleming n.d.:47). For example, the Crucifixion of Christ undertaken in these events is merged with the body decorations generally associated with the funeral practices of *malamala*. The Warlpiri say that the events are identified as *purlapa* because of their public nature, and note that certain "traditional" aspects of the events have their origins in non-Warlpiri Aboriginal sources. "Church *Purlapa*" tend to be performed only by two of the settlement's residential kin groups—one living in West Camp and another in Southeast Camp—and the enactments appear to be as much a product of long-standing personal associations with the original missionaries as a commitment to the Baptist message contained in the narratives. Beyond these two residential kin groups, "Church *Purlapa*" are never performed and rarely discussed.

CONCLUSION

What I hope this terminological survey has triggered is a suspicion, if not suspension, of those theoretical models that emphasize a "secret" ceremonial life and overemphasize differences of gender. The connections between men and women are too strong to situate the businessman in one domain and the businesswoman in another. Their ritual actions, and the languages used to describe them, are too entangled to keep them apart. Minimizing the similarities of their ceremonial aspirations on the basis of ill-defined notions of secrecy is to miss the motive force behind ceremony, whether undertaken separately or together—a motive that engenders ritual, and allows us to see parallel worlds as convergent.

My time at Yuendumu reduced rather than increased the number of gender-based secrets I acquired. That is because the more I understood of Warlpiri ritual, the fewer secrets I found existed, at least for the ritually mature. Senior women knew a great deal of what men did, and senior men knew much of what women did. They often performed separately, to be sure, but in ways that were always intended to consolidate a sense of group identity, an identity that was less gender-based than kin-based in nature. Inside and outside the ceremonial domain, spouses, cross-cousins, brothers, and sisters shared ritual insight and provided assistance that tempered the purported secrecy of a dichotomous ritual life. Did such exchanges pauperize ritual by reducing the exclusionary potency of the material? No. The exact opposite proved to be the case. Gender connectedness, supported by residential kinship, sustained rather than debilitated ceremonial life. *Juju, tarruku, maralypi,* and *wiri* all are terms marking sacred, potent knowledge. All are terms employed in the ceremonies wherein women participate. And if men own segments of the Dreaming considered too dangerous for women, that does not mean that men concomitantly hold a status that is deemed superior.

Does the discrepancy between men and women in the breadth and danger of their repertoires pit one gender against the other? Not at all. Women are only too happy to leave the dangerous business to men so that they can tend to less stressful but no less important domains of ceremonial enactment. After all, the essence of the *pirlirrpa,* the source of the *Jukurrpa*'s strength, can be found in the most public of events. And even if Yuendumu's women were to have access to secret ritual material involving Dreaming segments unknown to men—as appears to be the case in certain neighboring settlements—that does not, in itself, legitimate the construction of an autonomous ritual existence, any more than such autonomy may be said to exist among Yuendumu's men because of their ownership of segments kept away from the ceremonies of women. Furthermore, the absence of such performative control by women does not imply competition, implicit or overt, between genders. Competition in ritual does, in fact, exist at Yuendumu, but, as the following chapter shall show, it is constituted not along lines of gender, but in the confrontational dynamics of residential ceremonial display, one predicated on "winning" ritual.

Declaratively male initiation events—the *kurdiji,* for example—show that women possess a great deal of knowledge and influence, influence felt in the actual ritual undertaken and in the impact it has. True, the "female initiation" ceremony no longer exists, but that does not imply that women's engagement in matters ceremonial has decreased. In point of fact, despite the constriction of their repertoire (seen, too, in the ritual of men), women have been able to maintain, and indeed enhance, their ceremonial presence.

Ultimately, debates regarding gender primacy do a disservice to the Warlpiri, forcing upon them alien arguments that frame their social universe using notions of authority and power that are of decidedly non-Warlpiri construction. Competition and the ritual authority that coordinates it exist among men and women, not between them. How that authority is constituted, where is it situated, and how it is maintained raise questions that require substantial understanding of the role of Yuendumu's *yamparru*—a disunited group of ritual leaders, male and female, who oversee the ceremonial life of the settlement. These leaders, representing their close residential kin in ways intended to promote the broader imperatives of the Law, acquire their authority in large measure in gender-specific arenas, but they are sanctioned to do so via the collective approval of their kin. What (and who) makes a Warlpiri business leader? That is the focus of chapter 3.

3.

ON BECOMING A "BIG" BUSINESSWOMAN

Trajectories of Egalitarian Leadership

The religious life of the Warlpiri is made most manifest during frequent ritual performances, events overseen by individuals whose authority extends beyond the ceremonial grounds into social and political spheres connecting ritual to less overt forms of negotiated identity. Because of its permeating presence in settlement life, ritual must not be seen as some ancillary or dissociated evocation of moribund traditionalism, an act that retains some tenuous connection to land and lore. Ritual remains a principal means by which the prestige of certain older individuals, men as well as women, is declared. Beyond that, ritual serves as the forum in which the currency of knowledge (or rather, a specific form of that knowledge) is displayed and exchanged. As such, ritual is a tool of social empowerment and political engagement, a means by which the tensions that pit autonomy and connectedness against each other find expression, if not reconciliation. Understanding those tensions repositions issues of personal, gender-specific, residential, and intercultural identity at the fore. I say "currency of knowledge" in part because of the language the Warlpiri themselves employ—a language rich in descriptors that have their roots in value.

Undertaken by men and women jointly (both separately and together) and in single-gender events, in contexts that are restricted to the ritually active or open to all, the ceremonies of the Warlpiri are performed to reenact the itineraries of the *Jukurrpa,* a procedure intended in the most general terms to maintain the equilibrium of the Ancestral Present. But in realizing those connections, the Warlpiri engage in a subtle (and sometimes less-than-subtle) struggle for social power. By whom and in what manner ritual material is ceremonially presented points to the existence of a core elite of ritual leaders known as *yamparru,* a disunited group composed of older men and women who manage to combine vigorous ritual education and personal charisma with the support networks of close residential kin and subsection. In doing so, *yamparru* oversee how, when, and to what end ritual is undertaken. The attainment of the status of *yamparru* is highly competitive, and one that demands ongoing, widespread affirmation for its maintenance, thus mitigating the very nature of the control. For this reason and many others, *yamparru*-ship is highly stressful, requiring the individuals in that role to balance an ever-present sense of competition—identifiable, if not reducible, to what the Warlpiri call *jijami,* or "winning"—with the responsibilities of nurturance so central to Central Desert life. Indeed, the predicament of the business leader at Yuendumu is one evoked by two very different vocabularies. There is the language of care and of watchful attention (a language easily allied to the ethos of egalitarianism) and there is the talk of competition and victory. Only by exploring the relationship of these two sensibilities can the fuller functions of ceremony be understood. The principal paradox of ritual is this: The expression of harmony is the locus of competition, and the expression of that competition is the means by which harmony is often maintained. As such, it is this far-from-subtle irony of leadership that serves as the focus of this chapter.

Do male *yamparru* have more ritual authority than their female counterparts? Any attempt to answer that question throws the researcher into a maelstrom of ethnographic dispute (one of many). There is a preponderance of fieldwork among Aboriginal groups throughout Australia arguing for a diminished or inferior status ascribed to women, especially in matters of ritual. Even among female researchers there is a general sentiment that leadership, identified by Anderson as "boss-ness," is not sought by women in the same fashion as men (see, for example, Berndt 1970; Kaberry 1939; White 1970).[1] The circumstances at Yuendumu between 1983 and 1991, however, argue against gender-specific exclusion from the competition in matters of ritual leadership, though the arenas of that competition tend to be gender-specific. The language of leadership and of winning, whether expressed in Warlpiri or English, permeates the ritual spheres of women's ceremony much as it does that of men. Though it is undeniable that men have broader ritual authority than women in the performance of ritual, it is an authority that requires the acceptance of women. Women may, and indeed do, regulate excesses or abuses of ritual display manifested by their male counterparts. And lest we conclude from that statement that women have only a marginal role in either ritual or its leadership, it is necessary to underline that arguments about relative gender-based authority obscure the ongoing obligatory reciprocity that links men and women, and in particular male and female *yamparru* within residential kin groups, though the connection may be maintained outside ceremony. Such cross-gender assistance within residential kin groups tends to be minimized or left unmentioned in debates on the relative value of male and female leadership.

Important as these gender differences are, my analysis of leadership has less to do with the constitution of such authority between genders than with its expression within a single gender, that of women. To cast the issue of leadership along lines of gender opposition miscalculates the true locus of competition, one situated within genders. Beyond that, the division in this context muddies the kin-based commitments and allegiances between men and women who together compete against *yamparru* from other residential kin groups for control over the expression of the settlement's ritual life.

The ritual enactment of myth, whether undertaken by women or men, always serves a larger ungendered function: the linking of all Warlpiri to each other and to the lands from which they came, to which they will go, and of which they are. Associations expressed in ritual are simultaneously territorial, social, and religious. A Napanangka who sings the Honey Ant Dreaming establishes the place she owns, which also owns her. Such links to the land are inalienable, and though they may at times be neglected, they can never be denied. As *kirda* for the *Yurrampi Jukurrpa,* she can, in consort with the myth's manager (*kurdungurlu*), ritually reenact lands inherited from her father and her father's father. However, the same Napanangka, though having inherited the claim to this ritual patrilineally, may nevertheless fail to control its performance. She may have to endorse a *yamparru* version of the Dreaming she owns, a version sanctioned by other ritual participants. Possession implies expressive rights, but the manner and locus of that expression will always be controlled—"edited" is the apt metaphor Anderson introduces—by a few individuals with the authority to orchestrate, interpret, and edit ritual (Anderson 1988:519). To repeat an earlier dictum: *Kirda* ownership is often inherited, but control is always earned. Performative authority is acquired, never ascribed, and so is the status of business leader, a status forever susceptible to (and indeed requiring) challenge and change.

Ownership, as distinguished from control, legitimates the claim to the ritual content of a Dreaming and participation in its expression, but the decision to express it in ritual context requires more than *kirda*-ship patrilineally or personally obtained. Such enactment requires the efforts of a leader. For small-scale events restricted to one's residential kin group (aptly called "small" by the Warlpiri), the leader need only mobilize other ritually active kin members. In multigroup ("big") events, such acceptance and participation require the engagement of other residential kin groups whose performances are overseen by their leaders. And in the same way that the internal status of leadership can be tested, so, too, can the control between residential kin groups. In all forms of engagement, the status of ritual control is impermanent, contested, dynamic. Control of a Dreaming performance, like the Dreaming itself, requires constant attention, ongoing nurturance, and the approval of all those implicated in its material presentation. Absence of such nurturance can result in the loss of a leader's status or the material he oversees. The negative results have an impact not just on the leader but on the leader's kin as well.

Perhaps an example is in order. Much of my fieldwork coincided with the so-called outstation movement, an offshoot of wide-scale land rights reforms. The movement had as its premise the reestablishment of small Aboriginal communities in ritually and physically fecund sites beyond the permanent settlements that had been established, often at the whim of erstwhile white authorities. One of the outstation locales chosen for development, located north of Yuendumu, was situated along the itinerary of the *Ngapa Jukurrpa,* or Rain Dreaming. The location, rich in precious soaks, springs, and rock holes, was selected after receiving the approval of the ritually active men and women who were *kirda* for the site. All together, some eighty individuals, divided between the settlements of Yuendumu and Lajamanu, were consulted before drilling began. With that approval, non-Aboriginal geologists began to look for water. After repeated surveys and drilling attempts, the specialists gave up, unable to find water deemed suitable for drinking. A bitter dispute then ensued. At first, the *kirda* and *kurdungurlu* for the Rain Dreaming blamed the team of white experts, but the anger quickly shifted to two individuals from Yuendumu, the *yamparru* men responsible for overseeing the site-specific *parnpa* ceremonies targeted at sustaining the water supply and general "health" of the area. The accusations came from both men and women, *kirda* and *kurdungurlu* alike, from Lajamanu and Yuendumu. The accusations were never direct—such confrontational behavior runs counter to the sensibility of kin nurturance. However, in triangulated fashion the owners of the land agreed that the two men had been *warungka*—that is, ritually "forgetful" or "unthoughtful"—and that it was excessive alcohol consumption that had caused them to neglect their duties as *yamparru*. Proof of this neglect was obvious to all: The paucity of potable water at a sacred site that had yielded fine water prior to sedentarization meant the appropriate rituals had not been performed in the proper manner. The saltiness discovered by the geologists, which rendered the bore water undrinkable, was conceived as a direct result of ceremonial inattention.

What was the outcome of this crisis? Did the two *yamparru* hastily organize a performance of the appropriate *parnpa?* No. It was deemed a tardy and inappropriate intervention by all those implicated in such an event. The neglect ultimately led to a shift in control over the "increasing" ceremony. The two Yuendumu *yamparru* had no choice but to suspend their authority over the ceremony associated with the site and over the site associated with the ceremony. That authority was immediately claimed by three male *kirda* for the Rain Dreaming who resided at Lajamanu. These men, already *yamparru* for other activities at their settlement, extended their ceremonial authority over the *parnpa* linked to the troubled site. The Lajamanu Warlpiri thus garnered the controlling, if not exclusive, performance rights over the Dreaming segment previously overseen by the Yuendumu group, much to the disappointment of the former *yamparru* and the other owners and managers of the site. In fact, so troubled were the men that nearly a decade after the incident they had yet to organize ceremonies in which that Rain Dreaming segment was performed. Beyond that, their ritual status was weakened in other ceremonies. For example, when they performed the Fire Dreaming during a subsequent *kurdiji* event, their efforts were met with diminished interest. The malfeasance in the matter of the Rain Dreaming had jeopardized their control over other material. The episode attenuated, albeit temporarily, the status of their male kin, and it fell to their female *kirda* counterparts, two *yamparru* in particular, to buoy if not sustain the group's overall standing in the ceremonial life of the settlement. The authority of the two men, and with it the authority of their male kin, was reestablished only after their control over a *Jardiwanpa* ceremony was disputed unsuccessfully by the very same Lajamanu men who had claimed authority over the Rain Dreaming.

The Lajamanu "winners" of ritual authority over that Rain Dreaming declared their control over not only the site's ceremonial performance but, by implication, any potential resources that the site associated with it might someday provide—that is, if their nurturance of the Dreaming was maintained in the appropriate fashion, namely, through the oversight of ritual and the social behavior that attends such control. To be sure, claims of this sort are never all-encompassing. Inherited rights to the land cannot be denied wholesale, and as such, there is often a discrepancy between acquired rights of *yamparru*-ship and inherited rights of *kirda*-ship. One individual may own a Dreaming, while another one may control its performance. No *kirda* can be denied a territorial claim legitimated through patrilineal inheritance. Such claim requires no ceremonial engagement.[2] However, there is a general correlation between ritual control and control of land implicated in ritual. I was told directly that those who came to control the ritual of the Rain Dreaming that was associated with the outstation could allocate resources related to the development of an outstation if (and this is an important conditional nuance of authority) water was found during their control. Their allocations, however, would be subject to the inherited rights of all those associated with the site.

Although loss of ritual control because of extraceremonial circumstance (for example, the discovery of salty water) is exceptional, fear of such loss is not. It is in fact that very worry that prompts the enactment of many rituals at Yuendumu. Ritual often functions as a preventative act intended to quash accusations of neglect by businesspeople both within and outside the settlement. It also reduces the more ominous risks of sorcery. This does not mean that all ritual neglect generates the tensions that attended the Rain Dreaming narrative. When, for example, men responsible for undertaking another *parnpa*—this one celebrating a Possum Dreaming (*Janganpa Jukurrpa*) traveling through Ramarra-Kujurnu—did so only irregularly, the result, according to Warlpiri businesspeople of both genders, was the diminution of the possum population in the area associated with the "increasing" ritual. This faunal absence, noted casually by many, was not a source of much consternation to the settlement's ritual participants, though certain white environmentalists did express predictable concern.

"WINNING"

When the Lajamanu Warlpiri, and in particular their *yamparru,* acquired control of the Rain Dreaming segment from their Yuendumu counterparts, their mandate was declared by numerous Warlpiri leaders from both settlements in the following way: "The Lajamanu mob won." The verb *win* (and its Warlpiri equivalent, *jijami*) is more regularly employed now than it was in the days before settlement life, according to older residents of Yuendumu. They note that the overlapping *kirda* rights and the large sedentarized population have meant that the shared ritual domain and the resources dependent on it are more frequently contested. To give a sense of the frequency of ritual and the competition it inspires, take the case of the most commonly performed ritual, the women's event called *yawulyu.* During the first two years of my fieldwork, between 1983 and 1985, I recorded no fewer than ninety-two gatherings of *yawulyu* throughout the settlement. Of these, more than half (fifty-six) were full-scale undertakings involving dance. And of these fifty-six, most implicated multiple residential kin groups struggling for confirmation and control. At each of these events, the issue of winning was a palpable presence.

What exactly is meant by "winning"? And, more basically, what is the nature of the ceremonial competition by which such victory is achieved? Answers to both questions tend to be elusive. A basic fact must be acknowledged from the start: Though competition permeates the discourse of ritual, its specific contours escape easy detection. Viewed by the non-Aboriginal eye, a large public ceremony involving *kirda* and *kurdungurlu* from many different kin groups may appear highly collaborative (as indeed it is), with the Dreamings seemingly performed in unison. But below that surface harmony exists the stressful declaration of ritual competence, personally and residentially conceptualized, that will inevitably be collectively judged. Not all events result in a verbal declaration of victory, but the possibility of such an announcement is an implicit part of ceremony.

The winning of a ritual, or a part thereof, by a group or by its leader usually emerges on the day following completion of the performance and is determined by the *kurdungurlu* who oversee the actions of the owners. In women's events, it is the female managers who make this determination. In male events, it is the men. In joint events, men determine which *kirda* win. However, when women perceive error or misjudgment by their male relatives in assessing the virtues of individuals and groups during such joint ceremonies, they will contest the determination. Such intergender confrontation is exceedingly rare. I have witnessed only one such dispute, which occurred immediately following a jointly performed conflict resolution ceremony of *Kura-kurra*. The female *yamparru* who were *kurdungurlu* disagreed with the decision made by their male counterparts. During the requisite financial payments that owners provide to their managers, a process known as *kunari,* various *yamparru* women, owners and managers alike, decried the decision. They maintained that the *kurdungurlu* men had disproportionately valued the male portions of the joint ceremonies and had overlooked the flawless performance of women who performed with a group of men who had failed to be identified as winners. (I avoid the term *losers* because such status is never acknowledged in, and is indeed alien to, the discourse of Warlpiri ritual life.) After days of discussion, the decision was modified with Solomonic adjudication. The women of the group earlier denied the win were granted the status of winners along with the men who had already received that title. No mention was made of the women allied to the original group of male winners, but it was made clear that the men whose female relatives had been granted elevated status did not share that victory with them.

Winning in joint contexts sheds light on the scope of gender interdependence. During one cycle of conflict resolution ceremonies (*Jardiwanpa*) that necessitates the enactment of the Spectacled Hare Wallaby, Snake, and Emu Dreamings, a *yamparru* male, a ceremonial *kirda* for the Emu portion of the *Jardiwanpa,* attempted to postpone a portion of the event when he discovered that one of his sisters, a *yamparru* who was an important *kirda* for the ceremony, and upon whom he relied, could not attend. Because his group's representation was weak to begin with, he worried that the woman's absence might lead to a win situated among other performers. His residential kin group—associated with West Camp—had long been recognized as "big winners" of the event, and so the pressures he felt were particularly intense. In particular, he worried that the Snake *kirda* who resided in Northwest Camp might earn the praise of the ritual participants. Because his status as *yamparru* had been achieved by default (he was the oldest representative of a group of men poorly represented in ritual, agnates of powerful *yamparru* women with affinal associations that were also very strong), his efforts at postponement were rebuffed. The ceremony was conducted despite his request. This disappointed him bitterly, for the underrepresentation of the Emu Dreaming he owned along with his residential kin from West Camp led to the victory he predicted the dominant Snake performers would achieve. It must be noted that though the victory was identified by the Dreaming undertaken (Snake), the performers themselves were all localized within Northwest Camp, who, to the further chagrin of the male *yamparru* from West Camp and his kin, earned the title of "big winners." The injection of the adjective *big* marked the flawless performance of both the men and women who reenacted the Snake Dreaming.[3] In addition to the confirmation of the group as a "big winner," a *yamparru* by the name of Long Maggie Nakamarra was singled out and granted that title personally. She responded as all good *yamparru* must, savoring the collective recognition in silence. No Warlpiri ever *claims* victory. Such achievement can only be bestowed. At the personal level, the label of "big winner" is granted only to *yamparru,* though of course not all *yamparru* receive such acclaim.

Sometimes the title of "big winner" has less to do with cross-gender performance than with the announcement of a significant change (and improvement) in ritual circumstance previously eroded through transgression. For example, the dramatic and uncharacteristic declaration of victory during an intersettlement *kurdiji* cycle at Mt. Liebig was made to announce that Yuendumu men could once again undertake initiation ceremonies they had been forced to suspend after violating certain secrecy taboos. The actual announcement was silent: A *kurdungurlu* man rushed onto the joint grounds holding up a stick marked "Yuendumu" during the *witi* portion of the cycle (which formally presents the circumcisers). After the event was complete, various *yamparru* informed me that the gesture declared two things: that the Yuendumu men were big winners and that these winners could, and indeed were obligated to, resume initiation events at their settlement.

Winning is generally declared when a performance is deemed both particularly challenging and proper. The challenge may be physical. Inordinate heat, lengthy performance (some events can last from sunset to sunup), pain that is sanctioned as part of the ritual and which is to be dutifully endured—all are crucial for the title of winner to be attached to a particular group of performers or individual. Properness requires flawless singing, high-quality painting, and choreography fluently and fully expressed. When numerous *kirda* dance the same Dreaming during a ceremony, all eyes are drawn to the relative correctness (*jungarni*) of their efforts, to how *jukarurru* ("right" or "straight") the enactment is.[4] If a performer must stop constantly to ask advice about what to do next, if sequences are shuffled, if designs (whether applied to the body or to the ritual objects) are less than beautiful (*marrka*), if dogs start barking and thus show less than the requisite respect for the Ancestral Being invoked, then rights to perform a Dreaming can be placed in jeopardy. If too much or too little material is presented, if the sequences appear to be attenuated or abrupt, leaders, performers, and viewers can all be placed at risk. Each of these impediments can result in (or manifest already existing) weakened ties to the *Jukurrpa* and to kin responsible for its sustenance.

Contrarily, an event may sometimes be deemed so effective that the actions of the performers allow viewers to "actually see" (*nyanyi*) and "actually hear" (*purda-nyanyi*) the *Jukurrpa*. These phrases are accompanied by wails and cries that when combined establish an unambiguous connection to the Ancestral Present. Such "actuality" should not be taken to mean that ritual performers "become" the Ancestral Beings that their skillful actions invoke. Without exception, ritual performers of both genders laugh off any suggestion of such transmutation. They argue that ritual replicates myth but does not enable the replicators to become the figures in it. Ritual invokes the Ancestral Present, but performers do not inhabit it.[5] The declarations of *nyanyi* and *purda-nyanyi*, infrequent and long remembered, almost always confirm the victory of those performers who provoke the comment. During the first two years of fieldwork, these shouts attended only seven performances. The following year, they were uttered only thrice.

Each Dreaming segment emphasizes slightly different criteria by which proper performance and correlative success are determined. In events that reproduce Emu Dreaming segments, for example, theatricality of dance is highly valued by the *kurdungurlu* who pass judgment on the merits of that enactment. For the Goanna Dreaming, it is the coordination of the many *kirda* and the synchronicity of their dance steps that is the principal criterion of winning. Although that label is attached to performing owners by managers, it is one that situates victory within the particular residential kin group with which the victor is associated. The only circumstance in which the label will be attached to more than one camp is intersettlement competition, which can bestow victory upon the settlement as a whole. However, though "Yuendumu" may win an event that is presented in conjunction with the settlements of, say, Lajamanu and Willowra, it is only those residential kin groups who prompt that victory who are seen at Yuendumu as winners.

To be sure, winning reinvigorates the cosmology and all Warlpiri, but generally the status it bestows is restricted to the victors, a single residential kin group. Such status, like the spiritual nourishment recognized by the declaration, is temporary. Knowledge must regularly be reenacted and acknowledged as proper for a *yamparru* and a residential kin group to retain control over the Dreaming segment and ceremony in which that segment is performed. Control in the ritual sphere requires constant vigilance and repeated performance—or, in some exceptional cases, actively determined *non*performance. It is possible to establish control by gaining the support of other leaders to ban the enactment of a Dreaming segment deemed too dangerous for the well-being of the settlement. Such was the case with the suspension from all ceremonial events of a segment of a particular Possum Dreaming traveling through Yaturlu Yaturlu. That segment, which told of a sexually transgressive relationship between brother and sister Possum Beings, had been regularly performed in various male and female events (*yawulyu* and *purlapa,* to name just two) until the late 1960s. However, when two *kirda,* classificatory siblings, for that Dreaming transformed ritual enactment into secular action and ran away to reenact the transgressions not far from Yuendumu, the benefits of the segment were called into question. The ritual overseers, male and female, proposed to suspend reenactment, and after much negotiation, other *yamparru* ceded to this anomalous control through nonperformance.

The two cases invoked, that of the Rain Dreaming segment and that of the Possum Dreaming segment, show how leadership was lost or retained through nonperformance. These are, as noted earlier, exceptions. Usually it is through ritual activity and subsequent assessment that control over Dreamings is retained or ceded, thus sustaining, strengthening, or weakening the status of the "big" businesswoman or the "big" businessman.

The lack of congruence between the vocabulary of victory and the egalitarian ethos that prompts the event is not restricted to the notion of winning. In fact, a whole set of functional terms adhering to ritual clearly forces reconsideration of assumptions about an all-encompassing egalitarianism. Patently hierarchic language must be reconciled with an ethos of diffusionary social control. Consider the connotations of these key English-language nouns central to the speech of Warlpiri ceremonial life: *business, boss, manager, worker, leader,* and *hard work*. All are organizational terms related to production.[6] And though the goal of all ritual may be nothing less than broad-based maintenance of the well-being of the land, lore, kin, and country, this in no way reduces the competition that attends attainment of that goal. It is only through the active display and exchange of knowledge—the circulation of ceremonial currency—that the industry of ritual is sustained. Indeed, circulation augments, rather than diminishes or debases, the value of ritual, a dynamic that offers up a dramatic counterexample to the place of ritual in, say, certain Melanesian cultures.[7] One of the superficial paradoxes of Warlpiri ritual is the discrepancy between the motives for ritual—a sense of nurturance, harmony, and so on—and the context of overt competition in which they emerge.

Yamparru, "business leader," "big businesswoman," "big businessman"—each of these, and related terms, declares a large measure of authority in ritual. However named, the individuals possessing such authority are the ones who determine ceremonial accessibility ("dear," "cheap," "halfway") and related restrictions associated with ritual knowledge and its enactment. It is these individuals who determine when events take place, and they see to it that the events take place properly, thus enhancing the spiritual well-being of participants and related kin. Though these leaders are often called "bosses," that is a term I shall avoid throughout this book because of its multiple and conflicting applications both outside ritual (where it can be invoked to identify Aboriginal village councilors, as well as whites in various positions of authority) and within ritual (where its use is more complex).[8]

This is not to argue, however, that the multiple meanings of *boss,* especially with regard to ritual, do not warrant brief investigation. As Nash, invoking the work by Hale, points out, the terms *kirda* and *kurdungurlu*—commonly glossed as "owner" and "worker"—are both identified as "bosses" by the Warlpiri, a conflation with interesting lexical and social significance.[9] After all, how can a Dreaming's "owner" and "worker" both be considered to be "boss"?

In earlier portions of this book I purposely avoided translating *kurdungurlu* as "worker" (though the Warlpiri at times do use it) for just this reason; instead I chose "manager." The seemingly incompatible association of a single hierarchic title to two very distinct hierarchic terms is an incompatibility that the Warlpiri readily clarify. They never perceive the role of *kurdungurlu* as one of subservience, inferiority, or dependency vis-à-vis the *kirda.* In fact, such notions of personal dominance or control are counter to the interdependent connection of the owner and manager. Nash's exploration of the term makes this point indirectly when he notes that control of country is marked by the phrase *pawuju-jarri nguruku,* which the Warlpiri dictionary renders as "to be big boss for country." One can be boss over land but never over people. The closest the Warlpiri come to such personalized control is when they identify their authority over other groups within settlement life by announcing themselves to be "big boss" for Yuendumu. The terms *worker* and *boss* thus muddle the collaborative manner by which the Warlpiri undertake performance (Morphy and Morphy 1984). What the terms do suggest is the seriousness of ritual activity. And the fact that the Warlpiri use *boss* for the ritual leadership of both men and women argues additionally against certain models of ceremonial authority that deny female ritual actors a measure of significant control.

In lieu of *boss* I rely instead on the phrases *yamparru,* "big businesswoman," and "big businessman" when identifying ritual leaders. This must be distinguished from the unqualified terms *businesswoman* and *businessman,* which identify only active engagement in ritual activity, not a higher degree of status within that activity. The glosses do not circumvent or destabilize hierarchic assumptions, nor should they, as I shall show later. But they do temper the titular crudeness of *boss,* a crudeness that runs counter to the subtle nature of competition and exchange, which rely on collaboration to establish an individual's ritual authority.

The same kind of terminological static attaches itself to *ownership,* a term I do employ, although with certain qualifications. Indeed, the nature of "ownership" requires much the same clarification that "secrecy" demanded in the previous chapter. Whereas many individuals may claim ownership of a particular Dreaming and associated sites, performative control over that Dreaming in ritual (which is also often termed "ownership" and thus a source of considerable confusion in matters of intergroup analysis) is limited and sanctioned.

THE BUSINESS OF RITUAL AND THE LOCUS OF ITS LEADERSHIP

"Business" implicates the Warlpiri from an early age. However, the youthful obligatory participation of boys and girls in a variety of initiation ceremonies does not mark their formal entry into ritual as active participants. Generally speaking, businesspeople are those ritually engaged adults—married, in the case of men; mothers whose first sons have been circumcised, in the case of women—willing and able to participate in ceremonial life, if only to corroborate the actions of other members of their residential kin group. Between the time they assist in the circumcision of their first son and the onset of menopause, women who choose to participate in ritual usually restrict their activities to initiation ceremonies of younger relatives. During two counts of women in the settlement, taken in 1985 and again in 1991, I found that on both occasions exactly 70 percent of those over the age of forty-two actively participated in ceremony. The 30 percent of older women who chose not to engage in ritual declared a lack of interest and usually lacked elder sisters with strong connections to ritual activity. (The chronological categories did not precisely replicate the categories of menopausal status.) At the time I defined as "active" those who regularly attended rituals outside the obligatory rites of passage identified in chapter 2. Though this selective use of statistics might suggest stability in patterns of ritual involvement, the detrimental effects of alcohol and active resettlement patterns require such data to be treated skeptically. The figures regarding numbers of active participants vary greatly from year to year. In 1987 there were, by my count, ninety-two active businesswomen at Yuendumu, of whom fourteen were regularly identified as *yamparru*. By way of comparison, four years later the number of active businesswomen had dropped to seventy-six, overseen by nine *yamparru*. In 1992 principal performers within two of the most powerful residential kin groups dispersed to Alice Springs. Roughly half the *yamparru* women were married, and half were widows in 1984. None were never married. But again, that ratio between widowed and married *yamparru* turned out to be highly fluid. Three years later, a wave of remarriages in a West and Northwest Camp *jilimi* completely changed the figures. Age, however, was a constant. During my tenure, all leaders were over fifty and had entered menopause, which is often described as a peak time of ritual engagement. In fact, terms for that physiological status—*muturna* and *wurlkumanu*—are often employed to identify intense ritual energy. (The male equivalent—*ngarrka* or *purlka*—invokes the graying of the hair.)

Women who became business leaders generally showed long-standing interest in ritual life and kin relatedness, an interest encouraged by family members, male and female. Anderson, in his taxonomy of those attributes required of "bosses," a taxonomy that is restricted to men and does not directly implicate ritual, isolates four related features:

(i) a willingness and ability to gauge opinion, to be able to make decisions based on these and, most importantly, to take responsibility for those decisions; (ii) a capacity (beyond that stemming from structural position) to make people dependent upon one, so that they let one make decisions or have opinions for them; (iii) instantiation or embodiment of the group in the individual; (iv) an ability to "look after" people in a variety of ways including membership of a mob, as well as providing access to "spiritual" protection through intermediary action. (Anderson 1988:518)[10]

To be sure, these general criteria identify certain prerequisites of leadership at Yuendumu, but they provide only a partial explication of the scope and nature of the role, and the means by which it is attained.

For a woman to become a business leader she must be in possession of a vast cache of ritual knowledge. Only when she "knows all the ceremonies" (*juju-ngarliya*) will she have the potential of being identified as a *yamparru.*[11] This knowledge must include a capacity to perform, in tremendous detail, those Dreaming segments for which she holds *kirda* and *kurdungurlu* rights. This detail must be rendered faithfully in song, dance, narrative, and design. Additionally, a *yamparru* must have a participatory (if not authoritative) familiarity with those myths for which she possesses no patrilineal or personally acquired claim. She must know, furthermore, which version of which Dreaming segment is appropriate for each performative context: joint or gender-specific, public or restricted. For instance, when a *yamparru* is involved in the exchange of *yawulyu* with another settlement, she must make sure that certain "halfway" segments are not performed in public contexts unless a formal exchange of those segments has been discussed and collectively authorized.

Business leaders must display extraordinary mnemonic skills (visual, verbal, spatial, and historical) that extend beyond their own repertoires to the material owned by other members of the settlement. They are the primary repositories of ritual knowledge, the ones to whom all ritually active individuals turn when news of unattended ceremonies must be obtained or confusions in performance must find clarification.

Such knowledge, however, is not enough. A ritual leader must be able to display (or restrict) that ritual currency diplomatically. The achievement of this demeanor tends to be recognized by other ritual performers in the absence of various negative qualities the Warlpiri are quick to detect. *Jalpi, kurlpukurlpu,* and *mimayi* are common accusations that can be glossed as "selfish," "stingy," and "jealous," and are often targeted at those who fail to sustain qualities required of a leader.[12] The line between control, which is proper, and domination, which is not, is a thin one. And since leaders must rely on other *kirda* and *kurdungurlu* for ritual enactment, they must conduct themselves in a manner that distinguishes the manipulation of performance from the manipulation of performers. There is a difference between the leader who controls and the one who is controlling. When *yamparru* are perceived to overstep or misrepresent their task as orchestrators of ritual, they can lose the participatory willingness of the people they expect to monitor and direct. One couple arranging for the *kurdiji* initiation events of a son informed me they were taking their child to another settlement, where the *yamparru* orchestrating the event was knowledgeable and not "selfish," implying not authoritarian. The local *yamparru* was guilty, they said, of *ngamarr-karrimi,* of "bossing around."

Education, too, is an important component of leadership, one shared with other senior *kirda* who may not direct ritual events. All *muturna,* but leaders in particular, count among their many ritually specific obligations the education of younger and less knowledgeable close *kirda* (sisters' and brothers' daughters) and close *kurdungurlu* (daughters, cross-cousins, and sisters-in-law). Added to the various educational and diplomatic imperatives, there are also countless aesthetic criteria by which leadership is attained and reconfirmed. A *yamparru* must dance, sing, and paint skillfully, or, if disabled, must be able to monitor the skillful dancing, singing, and painting of relatives who undertake the ritual at her behest. Leaders must correct imprecision in the design, song, or dance of other performers whose actions they monitor.

Beyond their performative responsibilities, leaders must determine repertoire. When the events are "small" (restricted to a single residential kin group), the negotiation of repertoire does not necessarily involve other *yamparru.* However, during "big" events, ones that implicate more than one camp, the needs of various *yamparru* must be satisfied to determine the scope and order of a ritual repertoire. In such intergroup presentation of ritual, not only must leaders properly display what they control, but they must be willing to attend, and thus give spiritual credence to, those events (or portions thereof) to which they may have only an indirect connection or interest. For example, one female *yamparru* from South Camp, a Napaljarri, felt compelled to attend a *Jardiwanpa* ceremony for which she had no *kirda* or *kurdungurlu* responsibilities. She did so, she explained, to placate the female *yamparru,* who believed her presence would enhance the importance of the event in the eyes of all ritually active residents of the settlement. In this case, attendance was all that was required to establish the social value of the ceremony. However, in other rituals, *yamparru* may be called upon to help, though their formal obligations or connections are limited. Unless asked by the *yamparru* in control, invited business leaders who are not owners or managers will not dance or otherwise participate. Refusal to attend when asked declares an indifference that is recognized by all as hostile. Acts of avoidance publicly declared are not quickly forgotten.

In short, a leader must perform elegantly, advise cautiously, appear to participate willingly, educate unfailingly, and always be careful to teach by example rather than command. Part-time performer, ever-ready participant, part-time pedagogue, full-time diplomat, the Warlpiri ritual leader is—in conjunction with other *yamparru*—responsible for nothing less than the preservation of social cohesion. However, since the social cohesion each *yamparru* attempts to promote is often residentially circumscribed, leaders from different groups must frequently undertake the stress of competition with each other to establish or maintain the role through which that group-specific harmony and strength is affirmed.

And what benefits does all this stressful effort provide? In material terms, not very much. The better cut of kangaroo that a ritual leader may receive is given to him or to her not because of ritual prestige but because of kin relations and age, social circumstance that may be confirmed by leadership but is not established because of it. Older individuals lacking such ceremonial status will be given the better cuts as well. In fact, since leaders, by virtue of their age, tend to emerge from the ranks of the pensioned and are thus recipients of supplemental governmental subsidies ("sit-down money"), they often find themselves enduring the headaches of obligatory redistribution of their fortnightly funds to a kin network that grows larger with *yamparru*-ship. The one reward such forced generosity provides is the knowledge that close kin will respond quickly to a *yamparru*'s social and economic demands. Still, material compensations for the stresses that accompany the title of *yamparru* are extremely limited. Indeed, the strains of leadership are more readily identified by the leaders than the benefits that come with the role.

What stresses must leaders endure? The principal ones arise from conflicts between kin group and settlement obligation. As has been implied, *yamparru*-ship identifies more than the simple status of leadership; it marks leadership within a particular residential kin group. For example, Judy, whose ascendancy in the ritual life of the settlement is described in the second half of this chapter, was seen as a *yamparru* not for Yuendumu or even for the Warlpiri, but for the people with whom she lived, her male and female residential kin residing in West Camp. The broad-based template of kinship would argue that Judy projected her leadership role to a vast network of relatives, and so she did. No fewer than eight close sisters and four close father's sisters (all of whom were *kirda* over some of the same Dreamings as Judy), six close or classificatory daughters, three close sisters-in-law, and two close mothers (all of whom were connected by the dynamic of *kurdungurlu*-ship) sought Judy's advice and assistance when the Dreamings that connected them were performed. The same overlapping connections of kinship existed among her male relatives. Three close brothers, one classificatory father (each of whom shared *kirda*-ship with Judy), five close brothers-in-law, two classificatory cross-cousins, and three mother's brothers (two actual and one close, all of whom were connected by *kurdungurlu*-ship) considered Judy the principal overseer of Dreamings performed by the numerous female *kirda* in various women's and joint ceremonies. However, Judy's principal commitment in her role as a *yamparru* was localized in a different, albeit overlapping network, from within the kin group members just mentioned. Her allegiance was fundamentally directed at those kin with whom she lived. In particular, it was her sisters, daughters, sisters-in-law, brothers-in-law, and two of her brothers within the camp to whom she was beholden and from whom she gained support. And lest I leave the impression that such connection was limited to ceremonial matters, it should be stated explicitly that the nature of the attachment extended beyond ritual, to spheres of economic and political negotiation. This cleavage between residential and larger kin group identity is where much of the leader's diplomatic skills are called into play. While serving the smaller group, she can never ignore the larger. The leaders' various orbits of obligation—familial, residential, and kin-based—are of different diameters and different pull strengths, hence the sense of strain. Ritual events can be read as declarations of spiritual harmony that hide efforts of nonspiritual control. Ceremony is never just about ceremony. When and when not to perform, what to display and what to keep hidden, the order and duration of performance—all assert leadership intended to precipitate victory for a residential kin group that extends beyond the ritual grounds.

The notion of extending those victories beyond the ritual grounds raises an obvious question: What connection exists between ceremonial and nonceremonial leadership at Yuendumu? Does control of ritual translate into economic or political control dissociated from the reproduction of the Dreaming? Or does that valence, if indeed it exists, work in the other direction, with ritual leadership merely manifesting controls constituted in the secular dynamics of social negotiation? Before those questions can be addressed (to say nothing of the questions that those questions themselves spawn), certain assumptions have to be proven. Only after links between various forms of institutional leadership are established can the relationships of those forms be assessed. Beyond that, gender discrepancies within such leadership must be described, since by focusing on women in this chapter, there has been the presumption of parity in the structure of leadership—a presumption that runs counter to certain traditional gender-bound assessments. Indeed, the ethnographic discussion of ritual leadership in the Central Desert, minimal though it might be, now often seems to be situated within a larger discourse that is every bit as age- and gender-bound as the ceremonial life under scrutiny, with male anthropologists commonly validating the prominence of men's events and their female counterparts establishing the primacy of their own gender.

The problems raised by the question of causation between ceremonial and nonceremonial authority—if and how such connections exist—are multiple and entangled. Meggitt was perhaps the first to raise the full range of issues with regard to Central Desert hunter-gatherers, and this prompted subsequent researchers to explore those issues more selectively. Meggitt concluded that "an approximation to institutionalized leadership" existed for the Warlpiri, though only among its older men (1962: 248). Furthermore, he argued that such leadership was impermanent and had little causal connection to the secular sphere. He wrote:

> [F]requent variation in the extent of the authority that an individual [Meggitt refers only to men here] exercised from one situation to another militated against the emergence of a class of permanent leaders of community enterprises, of men who could regularly and legitimately direct group behavior in several fields of action.
>
> Moreover, there was no consistent correlation of social prestige with authority, with the accepted control over the actions of others. A man who had high prestige as a custodian of ritual knowledge was often a mere spectator in certain community activities, whereas a man of poor reputation could, because of the kinship statuses involved, be the currently active organizer. (Meggitt 1962: 249–50)

Though the circumstances now found at Yuendumu obviously differ greatly from those Meggitt discerned, his concerns summarize nicely key issues that must nevertheless be addressed in matters of leadership. They are (1) the importance of seniority, (2) gender restriction, (3) impermanence, and (4) the separation of ritual and secular authority.

SENIORITY AND THE MYTH OF THE ELDER

Maturity is perhaps the one issue that all researchers working in Central Australia agree is a prerequisite for ritual authority. This gerontocratic component should be clarified, however, since such authority does not accumulate uninterrupted until decease.[13] Men and women at Yuendumu who become ritual leaders generally attain such authority in their fifties and retain it for no more than a decade, after which the arc of their ritual power begins to decline, either by personal choice or as a result of social pressure. The ritual prestige attached to *yamparru*-ship must be reconciled with social obligation and an egalitarian ethos that resists long-term individual control of material, be it ritual in nature or not.

Suspension of such leadership can be gradual or abrupt, made by choice or by demand. It is never "decided" formally. No ceremony or announcement is made to mark that change. The transition, a process by which younger members of the leaders residential kin group take over the role of the *yamparru,* is an unspoken one that is obvious to all. Explanations for such renunciations are numerous. The onset of the state of *warungka* (senility)—perceived to be temporary or permanent—can be invoked by those who wish the leader to retire control.[14] Such claims, accompanied by accusations of "forgetfulness" in performance, are sometimes accepted immediately; at other times they are not. The dismissive label is regularly used by kin members to diminish the risk of a sorcery curse being directed at kin who display aggressive, but by no means *warungka,* behavior. Alternatively, the leader might plead exhaustion, evidencing a willingness (indeed, desire) to abandon the stressful negotiations that are part and parcel of *yamparru*-ship. Since leaders, even more than other *kirda,* are considered custodians of ritual knowledge, or rather the ceremonial expression of that knowledge, they should represent the interests of that intellectual property (and the kin who sustain it) when they endeavor to orchestrate ritual performance. Because *yamparru* derive their authority from relatives with whom they live, they are answerable to their needs and monitored closely by them. In other words, the monitors are themselves monitored. If a *yamparru*'s attentiveness is not made manifest, his or her authority can be reined in by various forms of nonresponsive behavior. An observation by James Woodburn on the !Kung and Hadza warrants quotation here. He notes, "People are well aware of the possibility that individuals or groups within their own egalitarian societies may try to acquire more wealth, to assert more power or to claim more status than other people, and are vigilant in seeking to prevent or to limit this" (Woodburn 1982:432). Such is the case at Yuendumu, though that vigilance and prevention tend to have greater success within the residential kin group than they do when assertions of power are group-wide.

Yamparru who display excesses or who are seen to orchestrate ritual events in a disharmonious or improper fashion run the risk of indirect criticism, outright ostracism, or, in extreme circumstances, sorcery that can, it is said, lead to death.[15] Businesswomen with whom I spoke regularly ran through lists of former *yamparru* who were "too much trouble" and whose powers were precipitously relinquished. Interestingly, whenever the authority of an ex-leader was called into question, the title of *yamparru* never found employment; personal or kin names were used. When criticism is repeatedly and broadly voiced, the authority of the individual erodes, forcing the leadership role to be abandoned. Such assessments by residential kin are highly effective "leveling mechanisms," to use Woodburn's phrase, a means by which abuses of leadership are limited (Woodburn 1982:436). In short, leadership is a sanction that must be regularly reviewed and renewed by those who participate in ritual. If the abuse of privilege threatens the proper enactment of the *Jukurrpa* or kin relations it established, authority can be revoked.

Take the case of two Napanangka sisters, both in their mid-fifties. When I observed them at various rituals, they were regularly identified as *warungka,* a term as I mentioned earlier that is used to suggest, among adults, "senility" and "unthoughtfulness." But when I spoke with them I discovered both to be lucid and knowledgeable about ritual in ways that clearly marked them as *yamparru.* Though they were never denied access to events, their efforts to control the Dreamings for which they had *kirda* rights were ignored. In fact, so troublesome were these two women that some *yamparru* purposely "overlooked" the two Napanangka when rounding up performers.

I inquired further about their status as *warungka* and the avoidance behavior it precipitated. Their close kin explained that the sisters had lost their status, separately constituted, as big businesswomen a few years before my arrival because of their combative behavior on the ritual ground and even—this was emphasized repeatedly—during ritual performance itself. Such behavior forced their kin to first downplay and then ignore entirely the sisters' subsequent actions. To be sure, some competition between *kirda yamparru* is acceptable; it is even to be expected. However, competition should never lead to the kind of direct confrontation these two women had displayed. That the conflict arose between sisters—sisterhood is a kinship bond upon which the Warlpiri place great value—only exacerbated matters.[16] Apparently the culmination of their improper ritual behavior and associated kinship impropriety erupted during an initiation ceremony (*Kajirri*) requiring mutual assistance. Instead of aiding each other, the two sisters fought bitterly, each disputing the leadership role of the other. Indeed, so overt was their antipathetic behavior that the younger Napanangka confronted her sister with the accusation of "inventing" Dreaming stories, a charge outrageous both for its directness and for its destabilizing effect on the presumptive immutability of the *Jukurrpa.*

It was obvious to the women who now controlled the segments performed in a variety of rituals previously monitored by the feuding Napanangka that the disputatious temperaments of the former *yamparru* and the excessive personal ambitions each displayed manifested gross "weakness" of personal essence (*pirlirrpa*) exposed to the force of Ancestral Powers during ritual. Had their *pirlirrpa* been strong, the events would have consolidated and unified their ritual authority. Relations between the two deteriorated after the *Kajirri* to the point that the older of the two left Yuendumu and resettled permanently at Lajamanu. Six years later they were still fighting on those occasions when they occupied the same ceremonial ground, and their status, even when engaged in ritual separately, had considerably eroded. It is important to note that the charge of "unthoughtfulness" emerged not from all owners and managers who shared connection to the Dreamings of the sisters, but rather from those *kirda* and *kurdungurlu* who were also close kin and with whom the sisters resided. Some of these relatives used the label of "unthoughtfulness" to diminish the risks of sorcery that can befall the ceremonially impolitic; other kin employed the term to temper the efforts of the women, whose behavior was seen as a threat to the ritual's potency.

LEADERSHIP AND GENDER

The risks of sorcery are not restricted to the Warlpiri inasmuch as anthropologists, too, possess a form of potent and manipulative incantation: the language of ideology. I should like to approach the second issue that must be isolated from Meggitt's work—the implicit gender basis of ritual leadership—by citing an anecdote that entangles the two issues. In 1984 some forty Warlpiri men and women from the settlements of Yuendumu and Willowra gathered to perform a conflict resolution ceremony known as *Kura-kurra*. For the first two days, all activity proceeded uneventfully, with the *yamparru* men deciding, as they usually do in such contexts, the order and nature of the presentation. As they sang the songs in the cycle, the women danced. On day three, conflict entered the conflict resolution ceremony. The men, deciding they were hungry, ended a segment abruptly—too abruptly, according to one particularly prominent female *yamparru* monitoring the event. Calling out to her brother, a *yamparru* who had spearheaded the suspension, she expressed her dissatisfaction, noting that another song should be sung by the men for the segment to be complete. Her brother and the other men did not respond to her mild censure verbally. However, they sat down and sang, to the contented accompaniment of women dancers, the song the female *yamparru* said was obligatory. This interaction punctures any number of assumptions regarding the gender-based exclusivity of ritual and ritual leadership and points to a cross-gender monitorial activity bringing men and women together. Are men the only ritual leaders at Yuendumu? Clearly not. And when, in those rare cases, the men and women find themselves in direct conflict during ritual activities, there is still a collaborative spirit that does not necessarily privilege the status of men.

Female authority vis-à-vis men can be observed in a contrary example as well. During another conflict resolution ceremony, a *Jardiwanpa* performed in 1985, several female *yamparru* decided they were hungry and tired of dancing. They called out this fact at a moment when men were clearly eager to continue the joint events. After a moment of silence, the men agreed to the implicit request and suspended their ritual activities so that the women could rest and eat.

I do not wish to argue that men and women leaders manifest equal control in the ceremonial domains they share. There is ample and indeed indisputable evidence that men tend to oversee these activities when gathering with women on the same ground. Even then, however, male control is always placed under the scrutiny of women leaders, who are quick to pass judgment regarding any impropriety they consider significant, which has a censoring effect. In those domains where male and female *yamparru* oversee events apart, gender autonomy, at a performative level, is nearly total, but consultation between men and women ritual performers tends to bracket activity. This discussion is undertaken by *yamparru* along lines of residential connection, and not among *yamparru* as a class.

Leadership over material is gender-specific, but that does not mean it is gender-restricted. In fact, male and female *yamparru* connected by residency rely on each other as performers—witness the increased role of certain female leaders when their male relatives proved neglectful. And in those residential kin groups where there is a paucity of male *yamparru,* the prestige of that group in joint contexts is sustained by the intensified female equivalent. I have even witnessed on one occasion several female *yamparru, kirda* for the Emu Dreaming, intervening in the actions of non-*yamparru* men, urging the male *kurdungurlu* to sing and monitor the actions of the male *kirda,* a task generally circumscribed along lines of gender. The men accepted this intervention, recognizing that the assistance of a *yamparru,* even of the opposite gender, would strengthen the effectiveness of the performance. Leaders, women and men, may be obligated to perform in gender-specific ways, but their worries and their obligations of nurturance imbue all events and individuals to which they have residentially constituted kinship ties. Though they oversee men's business and women's business, leaders do not do so to advance or protect their gender. *Yamparru* rally their *kirda* and *kurdungurlu* for the sake of the *Jukurrpa* and the connected kin who sustain it, not the individuals of a single gender who happen to be performing it. This shared motive among leaders, and the response among those they oversee, cannot be overemphasized, since it calls into question analyses that privilege a single gender, be it male or female, in the reproduction of the Dreaming.

IMPERMANENCE OF LEADERSHIP: ON DISTINGUISHING THE INDIVIDUAL FROM THE GROUP

The third issue Meggitt's brief overview of leadership raised was that of impermanence—the inability of leaders to retain their ritual authority for extended lengths of time. While, as previously noted, this is true, it overlooks certain structural components of leadership that provide a measure of stability, since the individual is a member of a particular group. Because transmission of impermanent authority always favors the patriline—

more specifically, siblings of the same sex within the residential kin group—there is a component of structural constancy. The only time transfers of leadership do not follow this pattern is when no willing and competent siblings can be found. This eventuality is rare. Among women, when it happens, a *yamparru* cedes control, still within the patricouple, to one of her male sibling's female offspring in the residential kin group. Among men, I was provided with no data about *yamparru*-ship transferred to nonsiblings. However, to extrapolate from Central Desert literature on male inheritance patterns of ritual (see Myers 1986a), transfers would privilege patricouple association but direct it to the next generation, that is, the male *yamparru*'s son if that son had attained the appropriate ritual maturity status as a *purlka* (mature man with gray hair).

While it is true that individuals tend not to hold on to authority for extended periods, their kin most certainly do. Impermanence exists on a personal level, but the paths of transmission and the associated control remain within the residential kin group over longer stretches of time. The shift of control from one group to another tends to be prompted by *yamparru* unable to find replacements who can carry on their work, but such erosion usually takes decades to play out. No such declared or undeclared shift in residential power manifested itself during the time I conducted fieldwork, though the *yamparru* from various camps did identify one minimally involved residential kin group that resided in South Camp as having once been very powerful and active.

REALMS OF SECULAR AND RELIGIOUS LEADERSHIP

Does ritual authority stretch beyond ritual? At Yuendumu it most definitely does. Bern's challenge to Meggitt's restrictive conclusions is apt. "Authority," Bern has written, "derives from the organization of religion, but its competence is extended to most social activities" (1979:121). However, Bern imposed his own restrictions, ones touching on gender. He found that only men occupied positions of prestige and leadership and "that the relevance of women's ritual is for them alone" (1979:129). Such is not the case, or no longer the case, at Yuendumu, where the influences of female *yamparru,* and indeed the actions of all ritually active women, are felt throughout the settlement in religious and secular domains. Further clarification of Bern's comment must be made, however, for when the leadership of a kin group's *yamparru* in the ritual sphere is conjoined with the authority of other members of the group in nonreligious institutions, it makes it possible for its *yamparru* to acquire a more sustained, settlement-wide influence.

How specifically do Warlpiri ritual (male and female) and Warlpiri ritual leadership (male and female) situate themselves in the context of broader social exchange? What relationship does ceremony have to the political economy of the settlement? Though the domain of Warlpiri ritual is distinct from other institutional structures found at the settlement, the influence of those individuals overseeing religious performance extends beyond it, either directly or via the actions of their residential kin.

Agendas, as acts of social exchange, by their very nature require a delicate negotiation of personal, residential, and larger kin obligations. Institutional barriers separating a religious event from a profane one in no way diminish the overriding obligations implicit in both. The tentacular nature of authority is felt at *Jardiwanpa* ceremonies, at town council meetings, and in countless informal settings of social exchange. As such, control rarely exists in one sphere; it tends to migrate, to be corroborated in other domains. This extension may or may not be undertaken explicitly by the *yamparru*. In the politico-economic realm—and by that I mean in those organizations that allocate limited financial resources to residents of the settlement—control is often situated among younger members of the *yamparru*'s kin group. Hence, this suggests some need for revision of Meggitt's exclusionary observations about personal authority.

During my time at Yuendumu, one of the strongest collective ritual voices was localized in a residential kin group within West Camp. The *yamparru* of this group, male and female, had little direct involvement in settlement politics; however, their younger kin, often at their older relatives' behest, devoted themselves to various organizations. The position of Yuendumu town council president, perhaps the most influential Aboriginally filled job in the settlement, was consistently occupied by younger Warlpiri men who shared residential kinship ties with the *yamparru* who controlled a large measure of Yuendumu's ritual life. The presidents' fluency in English, coupled with their older relatives' fluency in matters of ritual, consolidated the religious and political authority of the settlement within a single residential kin group. This fact was regularly acknowledged by other residential kin groups. All presidents had kinship obligations to the settlement's most prominent ritual leaders. Indeed, when ritual events coincided with council elections, the *yamparru* often preceded ceremonial undertakings with mentions of their younger kin's judicious efforts on behalf of all residents. The conjunction of the ritual and political was overt. In much the way that the older *yamparru* would "look after" ritual, their younger kin were said to "look after" the business of the council. And like the distribution of ritual knowledge, items controlled by council presidents tended to pass along lines of residential kinship. Housing allocations and firewood distribution routes—two council activities of particular consequence to settlement life—were systematically overseen by the kin of the West Camp *yamparru,* and their conduct was egalitarian only insofar as they allocated resources fairly among those with whom they resided.

Such group-specific equity does not go unnoticed, nor is it free of risk. Take the case of a powerful female council member, a resident of the influential West Camp residential kin group, who wished to remain anonymous. Six months into her tenure, she fell gravely ill, complaining of debilitating headaches. No biomedical cause for the blinding pain could be established, and rumor quickly spread that she had been a victim of *yarda-jangka,* that is, she had been cursed through song. I spent a good deal of time exploring the potential gender-based origins of this attack—she was at the time the only female council member of significant authority—but discovered that the reasons for the assault, according to both male and female kin, had less to do with her gender than with her residential affiliation. In the eyes of all observers, she was a victim of camp competition. To counteract the *yarda* curse imposed by unspecified senior men, the *yamparru* of her residential kin group, men and women both, took the extraordinary step of bringing in a medicine man from a distant settlement. The *ngangkayi* confirmed the diagnosis, that men on the council (men not from her camp, though never specifically identified) had had her "sung." The medicine man performed a successful curing act, and the woman eventually recovered, but the perceived application of the curse tempered subsequent inequity in the distribution of the council's limited resources.

The titular president of the council, like his kin *yamparru,* is seen as an authority, not *the* authority, and as such he is never able to acquire a large measure of power without the approval of other kin. Any perceived abuse or neglect of obligation is quickly confronted, albeit indirectly, often by the *yamparru* and other older relatives within his kin group.

The influence of ritual leaders in nonritual domains need not be indirect. When, for example, a group of woman *yamparru* traveled to

Canberra, the nation's capital, to perform a *yawulyu* ceremony at the 1984 Australia Day celebrations, they established a bond of obligation and entitlement between performers and viewers that could be revived at any time. This became clear nearly seven years after the performance, when three brand-new washing machines arrived at the Yuendumu Women's Center. The bounty was the focus of considerable discussion. Who was rightly entitled to the resource? Because the quantity of clothes and blankets that were washed far exceeded the capacity of the machines, some restrictions had to be established.

The *yamparru* who long before had danced at the nation's capital argued successfully that the equipment, purchased with government (that is, Canberra) funds, established the leader's claim. Their justification was religious. First, they argued that since it had been the *yamparru* women who had danced at Canberra, they were entitled to the resources of that site. They then refined this argument, invoking the reciprocal relationship established between the performers and the viewers—in this case the Australian government. The *yawulyu warrajanyani* ceremony had served as a moral contract that presumed dancer and spectator would take care of each other. The care was declared in the verb *jinamardarni* (meaning "to look after," "to protect," "to hold," "to keep"), which established ties that endure long after the performance is over. The washing machines ended up being controlled by the *yamparru* for the benefit of older women in general. Those women too young to be engaged in ritual were denied access. Furthermore, older women who failed to maintain their ritual activity had a difficult time gaining access to the machines.

One of the primary tasks of ritual authority is the mobilization of kin. Such mobilization, most visible in the enactment of ritual performance, is also associated with various secular endeavors that have explicit, though limited, economic implications. Success and failure in such nonritual enlistments speak to both the force of leadership within a residential kin group and the relative authority various leaders have within the settlement. Throughout the late 1970s and 1980s, non-Aboriginal funding organizations, an outgrowth of Labor government policies mandating "self-determination," encouraged the development of indigenous "arts and crafts." During my tenure at the settlement, two activities in particular were promoted and received favorably by the Yuendumu business community: batik cloth production and acrylic painting. Both enterprises adapted ritual iconography for secular ends and thus required oversight by *yamparru* in a position to assay the virtues and liabilities of presenting designs in a public context. The two media very quickly became identified with two camps, and more specifically two residential kin groups within those camps. The acrylics were undertaken by a mob residing in West Camp, the batiks by a mob associated with South Camp. At the end of a year-long initiative, the batik activities were moribund, while the acrylics flourished, soon becoming a principal, if nominal, nongovernmental financial resource for the whole of the settlement. While it might be tempting to attribute the results of the two efforts to external reaction to the media, such attribution would be ill advised. When the batik production ended, the artists producing the clothes and those producing the acrylics were compensated and encouraged in ways that were almost identical. No artist from either camp received more than $A 200 that year. Why, then, did one medium flourish while the other was allowed to wither? At Yuendumu, the explanations residents provide focus on the authority of *yamparru* from each camp. The West Camp *yamparru* were able to mobilize their residential kin to create canvases in the collaborative fashion that characterized the ritual activity they already dominated.[17] Their South Camp neighbors lacked such social authority. Indeed, soon after the batik efforts stopped, the *yamparru* of South Camp, unsuccessful in bringing together their kin for the cloth medium, joined the ranks of the acrylic painters, taking on subsidiary roles. To this day, acrylic production at Yuendumu is overseen by the *yamparru* of West Camp and their close kin, who control the medium in much the way they control major portions of the settlement's ceremonial life.

This control by a *yamparru*, sanctioned by the kin group, which monitors and limits the excessive expression of authority, demands personal prestige that is socially constituted and collectively confirmed. To reach that point of confirmation, the protoleader must undertake extensive training that itself presumes long-term forms of mutual assistance. Leaders are made, not born—made by themselves and by those with whom they reside. The path to authority and the obligations it entails—obligations that are by no means gender-bound—can be observed in fuller detail through the ascendancy of one *yamparru* with whom I lived for several years, a woman named Judy Nampijinpa. The circumstances surrounding Judy's rise to authority substantiate any number of points made in the first half of this chapter, showing as they do the influences of close kin, of both men and women, of that which is inherited, and of that which is personally claimed. Does Judy's example of ritual trajectory speak for the path of *yamparru*? Most certainly it does not, and since no parallel material of similar scope exists for male *yamparru,* the making of cross-gender parallels of a substantive nature must be granted to future researchers working more extensively with men.

JUDY: A CASE STUDY OF RITUAL LEADERSHIP

Judy Nampijinpa Granites was born "out bush" sometime in the early 1930s. Hospital records provide an exact date—1934—but this figure, like all such data of the period, is of dubious accuracy. Judy was at the peak of her ritual career when I first arrived at Yuendumu in 1983. A *yamparru* in full control of her ritual faculties, Judy was a business leader whose authority extended far beyond the residential kin group in West Camp with whom she resided and from which she derived so much of her support. Bolstered by the other *yamparru* of her residential kin group—one that dominated much of Yuendumu's ritual life as well as its secular domains—Judy vigorously pursued the strains and satisfactions of ceremonial life, diligently performing, overseeing, and competing with noteworthy virtuosity, which regularly earned her personal recognition as a "big winner."

Of course, to say she was born "out bush" is grotesquely general for the Warlpiri. Specifically, Judy was conceived at Warnipiyi, a site located due west of Yuendumu, situated on the itinerary of the Creeper Dreaming known as *Wayipi Jukurrpa.*[18] Though Judy had no patrilineally inherited rights to the Creeper Dreaming, her conception site (identified through a men's ritual that invoked the *kurruwalpa*) granted her ownership of its myth and resources. Her claim was additionally bolstered by her membership within the subsection (J/Nampijinpa and J/Nangala) associated with the Dreaming. From her father and her father's father, she inherited ownership rights as *kirda* to at least three more Dreamings: the Water Dreaming (*Ngapa Jukurrpa*) that passes through the sites of Kurlpulunu, Puyurru, and Mikanji; the Fire Dreaming (*Warlu Jukurrpa*) of Ngarna; and the Butterfly Dreaming (*Panjirti Jukurrpa*) that travels through Nyirrpi. In addition to these inherited Dreamings, Judy received from her father's father *kirda*-ship to a ceremony, specifically the *Jardiwanpa.* This ceremonial inheritance gave her rights to the Emu Dreaming evoked in the *Jardiwanpa* but not to any of the other Dreamings that the conflict resolution ritual required.

To this collective birthright Judy managed to add other forms of *kirda*-

ship, some associated with specific ceremonies, others constituted more generally. Her ownership over this material ultimately evolved into performative authority. She acquired her ownership through residential connection to individuals who themselves possessed *kirda* ties to ceremonies or Dreamings. For example, it was through a member of her residential kin group, the spouse of a close maternal uncle, that Judy learned to perform and nurture the Wattle Dreaming (*Watiya-warnu Jukurrpa*) connected to the site of Yamurrdurmu, located to the south and west of Yuendumu.[19] This nurturance led to her ownership and ultimate control of that Dreaming in various ritual events.

The first time I tried to register the scope of Judy's ritual expertise, she made no mention of her ownership of and profound fluency in the songs, dances, and designs of the Emu Dreaming enacted in *Jardiwanpa*. She did so only when the event was about to take place. Such selective demonstrations of knowledge, emerging on a need-to-know (or rather need-to-show) basis, are the norm among leaders. *Yamparru* tend to attach their claims of ritual authority to specific Dreamings that are connected to specific ceremonies enacted in specific contexts to specific ends. In this case, it was the potential honorific of "big winner" that stirred Judy to mention previously uncited ownership and performative control over the Emu Dreaming invoked during *Jardiwanpa*.

Though sedentarization facilitated and indeed multiplied opportunities for uninherited, personally negotiated ownership claims, Judy says such mechanisms of nonpatrilineal ritual acquisition were present before she and her kin were forced to settle at Yuendumu. She cites, by way of example, her acquisition of rights to the Seed Dreaming (*Lukarrara Jukurrpa*), owned by her mother's mother, a woman with whom she lived prior to sedentarization. This "proof" presents a conundrum common to any attempt at tracing the origins of ritual ownership. Judy's residence at Jila was limited to a moment in her youth—the exact age is impossible to provide, but she was certainly not yet a teenager—predating ritual activity. However, her subsequent leadership position enabled Judy to combine knowledge acquired from other *kirda* and *kurdungurlu* with her childhood associations with the maternal grandmother who "owned" the material. The knowledge was acquired from one source and legitimated by connection to another.

Close kinship ties reinforced by residentiality often serve as the basis on which nonpatrilineal claims of ownership can be established. Such claims are additionally substantiated when the source of the knowledge is a *marlpa* (*marlpa* is a term of social commitment inadequately translated as "friend"). This bond of friendship—predicated on the sharing of lodging, hunting trips, and food; indeed, upon the exchange of resources in general—can also include the gift of ritual knowledge. Whether that knowledge finds subsequent display in the ritual domain, reformulated as ceremonial currency, depends on a variety of factors. Judy explained that two of her important Dreamings had their origins in the principal *marlpa* friendships she established at different moments in her life. Early on, prior to her settlement at Yuendumu, she was granted rights to the Seed Dreaming (*Lukarrara Jukurrpa*) through a *wurruru* association with her mother's mother—an association outside the link of patricoupled subsections by which such material is formally inherited. The acquisition was substantiated not only because of residency and the friendship that grew out of it, but because of the geospecific relationships between the paths of the *wurruru*'s Seed Dreaming and the Water Dreaming Judy had properly inherited from her father. The two itineraries crisscrossed and commingled. Thus, the space the two women shared on the ground reiterated and indeed reinforced the space that their inherited Dreamings shared in the ancestral landscape, providing further confirmation that Judy was within her rights to perform and later control the myths of her mother's mother.

Judy's managerial responsibilities were also extensive. From her mother's patrilineal inheritance, she acquired *kurdungurlu* rights to the Euro Dreaming (*Kanyarla Jukurrpa*) and Red Kangaroo Dreaming (*Marlu Jukurrpa*). Marriage added the Initiated Woman Dreaming (*Karnta Jukurrpa*) to her managerial repertoire. And because many of her residential kin in the opposite patrimoiety owned the Goanna Dreaming (*Wardapi Jukurrpa*), it was natural, she said, for her to manage that Dreaming as well.

These, then, were the primary Dreamings Judy declared to be hers for the purpose of ceremonial enactment. However, other ritual knowledge, to which ownership and managerial claims were attached, emerged in nonceremonial contexts. With the acrylic art movement that began to flourish at Yuendumu in the mid-1980s, ritual leaders and their kin started to draw designs for which they held claims. The process by which the designs were selected and then executed (and sometimes later effaced or modified) clarified how much ritual knowledge is never mentioned unless utility requires it. It was only by the acrylic designs Judy applied to canvas that she recognized long-dormant connections to the aforementioned Butterfly Dreaming, an activity also taken up by the other female patrikin who had inherited the designs. When I asked why the ritual material never found ritual expression, Judy explained that though she possessed all the necessary knowledge as *kirda,* she lacked the requisite support from other knowledgeable owners. I mentioned the other female *kirda,* and she said that they were too inexperienced to handle the burdens of performance properly executed. She said that despite repeated attempts to train them, she had never been able to reestablish that Dreaming in the ceremonial repertoire. The Butterfly Dreaming now existed only on the nonceremonial surface of acrylics. She told me this with neither regret nor remorse, but rather the presumption that all ritual, though overseen by an individual, was by its nature a collaborative act, and that absent those collaborators it was relegated—temporarily, to be sure—to the memories of the ritual leaders and to the margins of their ritual life.

When I inquired about the origins and path by which she acquired her authority, Judy was very clear about the stages that marked her ceremonial engagement. She said there was, at first, a long time of observation, during which she was directly involved only in her own initiation and in *kurdiji* events that implicated her brothers. These involvements, she said, occurred before she was forced to settle at Yuendumu in 1947 and are only vaguely recalled. Limited observation of ritual continued when Judy, as a young wife, was obliged to reside at Yuendumu. Active regular participation did not begin until her first son was ready to be circumcised; this happened in the early 1960s.[20] That *kurdiji* marked the next stage of Judy's ritual involvement, the point at which she entered the performative sphere as a businesswoman, under the oversight of senior kin and in particular of her kin *yamparru.* Only after years of such participation and the death of her husband in 1974 did Judy attain of the status of big businesswoman—of *yamparru.* This was the penultimate stage of her ritual life, one followed a decade later with relinquishment of *yamparru* status to a younger married sister. These, then, in the broadest terms, serve as the markers of Judy's ritual trajectory. Because the final transition coincided with my first years of fieldwork, I found Judy in a liminal state between leader and ex-leader that made her especially reflective about the nature of ritual and authority.

Judy's earliest memories of ritual were of sitting with her mother and her mother's mother, prior to sedentarization, during the performance of a now unpracticed initiation ceremony for girls. The ceremony was, as Judy recounts, conceived as a two-step process. The first required that her torso be painted with a ritual design taken from those Dreamings for which she was *kirda*. This application was intended to enhance her sexuality. (Remnants of this currently unpracticed ceremony regularly surface in the *yawulyu* body designs drawn to enhance the breast size of young girls.) The second stage of the event focused on educating Judy about matters of menstruation and proper kin relationship with future in-laws. After this initiation, Judy explained, she began to attend, passively and in total silence, the ceremonies of her female kin. Her activities in these events extended only so far as the reapplication of her *kirda* body designs, which Judy explained were executed to maintain her health, both spiritual and physical—a distinction less obvious to the Warlpiri. Some of these events, she explained with no small pride, were supposed to be restricted to older initiands, but she was taken under the wing of her mother and a classificatory father's sister, the latter a Nangala who was also connected to Judy through marriage. (She married Judy's actual mother's brother.) Though Judy's mother was helpful in matters of ritual, it was the Nangala, a powerful *yamparru,* whom Judy most regularly cited as the source of her ritual knowledge. The patricouple link between a father's sister and brother's daughter was amplified by friendship that precipitated a decade-long association nourished by the pleasures and challenges of ritual pedagogy. Though this woman gave her access to all manner of ritually restricted information, Judy was not allowed to display that material in ceremonial contexts.

Until her first son's *kurdiji,* Judy's involvement in these activities extended little beyond being painted up, viewing the dances and listening to the songs of others, and sitting next to her residential kin as the *Kankarlu, Kajirri, Kura-kurra,* and *yawulyu* were performed by older, more experienced women. Her active participation in ritual and the start of what, at the risk of extending the commercial metaphor, might be called her career as a businesswoman came only when Judy participated in the *kurdiji* ceremonies in which the first of her five children (all sons) was circumcised.

Circumcision of a first son is regularly cited as the most important event in the ritual life of a woman, an act that simultaneously repositions the child into the sphere of men and redefines the mother's role of nurturance. (If a woman does not have a son of her own, she may enter active ritual life by participating in the mother's role for the *kurdiji* of an actual sister's son.) Though the ceremony in no way reduces the responsibilities that bond mother and son, it enlarges the obligations of the mother to nurture not just the child (in Judy's case five children) but the larger community as well. This community extends to kin and the Dreamings associated with those kin. As such, the initiation of the son is in fact an initiation for his mother as well. Judy remembers that she greeted the *kurdiji* of her first son with great eagerness as an event that legitimated years of passive commitment to a ritual life she could now pursue with vigor.

It was during this event that Judy acquired the basic paraphernalia crucial for her involvement in ritual. From her mother's sisters (her own mother had passed away by this time) and her fathers' sisters, Judy received head- and armbands made of hair string (*wirriji*) covered with red ochre, ritual digging sticks (*karlangu*), and ritual site markers identified in Warlpiri as *kurturu* or, more regionally, *nullah nullah*.[21] Her mother's brother also provided her with ritual bounty. He cut and shaped an elliptical board of mulga (*Acacia aneura*), a wood commonly used to make boomerangs. The board, Judy explained, was provided by her maternal uncle to declare in concrete terms the transformation in the dynamic between mother and child. This "dancing board," known as a *yukurrukurru,* found service in the ritual activity Judy subsequently started to undertake actively.

The board, more than any other item, identifies entry of the initiand into the community of men (though not into active ritual participation) and marks, too, the entry of women into active ritual participation (if not the community of men.) It, along with the *kurturu,* is the primary ritual object used by women.

As Judy pursued her ritual activities, she acquired additional paraphernalia, which indicated her expanded and deepened ceremonial associations. These objects served as a measure of the regularity and virtuosity of her efforts. Some of these items, such as *nullah nullah,* dancing boards, baby carriers, and water carriers, were almost always made by male relatives, specifically mother's brothers, mother's husband, or brothers-in-law. Women, Judy included, restricted their production of ritual objects to arm- and headbands and painting sticks (*jipiji*) used to decorate the body. Exchange of these ritual objects is a regular feature of ritual preparation. Businesswomen almost never use ritual objects they themselves make. Only unexpected exigency—the absence of a needed item possessed by someone else—will prompt such use. More commonly, women exchange ritual objects to extend the bonds of caring and nurturance. Such exchanges privilege *marlpa* (friendship) connections over all others. For example, a *marlpa* tie will systematically overshadow obligations between sisters when it comes to the redistribution of paraphernalia needed to transact business.

Judy was very direct about one point when showing me her cache of objects: A woman who does not accumulate ritual paraphernalia cannot be considered a good businesswoman. But the nature of this accumulation must be understood more fully. Accumulation is undertaken with the intention of almost immediate redistribution. It is by giving others the objects they need to undertake events that one's role as a businesswoman is confirmed. The hoarding of objects is denigrated and impossible to maintain for any length of time. Accumulation and quick redistribution of objects is a defining characteristic of ritual responsibility, though not a constituent component of ritual leadership per se. Objects do not, in themselves, sanction any action or authority. And among ritual objects there is no hierarchy of value. One dancing board has the same measure of utility and value as any other (see Weiner 1992). Once a woman possesses the ritual paraphernalia necessary for her particular performance—most pervasively dancing board, *nullah nullah,* and arm- and headbands—she maintains her efforts to gather additional objects, for to do so allows her to extend her bonds of friendship broadly.[22] The act of redistribution confirms one's concern for the Dreaming of the recipient and is an acknowledgment of her nurturance of it.

The principal objects of women's ritual—dancing boards and *nullah nullah*—are typically painted with designs associated with the Dreamings of those who use them. When subsequent events requiring different designs are undertaken, the women erase previous patterns to apply the new ones. An especially old dancing board (and here I mean one that has been in use for five or ten years, not lost or discarded) will often reveal traces of previous designs and wood stained a deep red from repeated administration of ochre; such a board is a palimpsest of ritual endeavor.

The descriptions above are restricted to the exchange of ritual objects within women's business. Men's paraphernalia and the relationship men have to it differ dramatically. For starters, the palimpsestic qualities of the *yukurrukurru* (and *kurturu*)—the serial application and erasure of ritual designs on the surface of the wood at the start of events—do not saturate the equivalent objects employed in the rituals of men. In fact, the most potent men's objects, engraved stones and shells of a highly secret nature, resist the very modification that gives women's objects some of their value as objects of renewal and sustenance. Even among those men's ritual objects that could accept modification—men do indeed use items shaped from wood that are painted—most tend to be discarded at the termination of each ritual cycle.

The material differences of the objects speak to certain material differences of the rituals in which they are employed. Men guard many of their secret items in much the same way they guard the secret, dangerous, "dear" material associated with them. Women exchange theirs publicly because of the less dangerous but equally obligatory nurturance for which those objects are used. This is not to say that the women of Judy's stature do not know what those secret designs found on the stones of men are, but rather that such knowledge never finds display in performative contexts, or even acknowledgment in the discourse among senior women.

Besides those objects fashioned by men for women's ceremonies, cross-gender exchange of objects at Yuendumu is limited to the redistribution of hair string.[23] The significance of this material in ceremony must not be undervalued. Men and women exchange hair string as a means of maintaining the authority and strength of their kin group in the ritual life of the settlement. Men proffer string to women in formalized fashion at the end of both conflict resolution and initiation events. The female recipients sometime pass on the spiritually potent material to other men immediately, but more commonly the string is retained for later strategic distribution to men within their residential kin group. The abundant display of hair string in ritual is seen as a measure of vigor and prominence, and men rely on women regularly to supplement their own holdings from hidden supplies provided at the end of past events. Judy said she generally redistributed her hair string soon after ceremonies, but certain female members of her kin group often hoarded balls of the powerful material to insinuate themselves into the ritual discussions of their male kin.[24] Implicit in Judy's comment was the assertion that her strength as a leader had never required such machinations.

This points to a fact often undervalued in assessments of gender and ritual, namely, that concern and nurturance bring men and women together even though they may not perform together and that, more often than not, cross-gender bonds require membership within a residential kin group. Shared responsibility, however, is not identical responsibility. In their oversight of dangerous material, men use and distribute ritual objects, and in particular secret engraved stones, wood, and shells, in ways far different from the patterns of distribution described by Judy and corroborated by other businesswomen (see, for example, Meggitt 1962).

Soon after the circumcision of her son, Judy, recognized as a businesswoman, began to have dreamt (see Glowczewski 1991:81). By this I do not mean that previously her sleep had been unencumbered by nocturnal visitations, but rather that she now dreamt of events identified by senior residents of the settlement as allied to the *Jukurrpa.* This is an oft-mentioned symptom of entry into ritual activity, and an important means by which ceremonial life is itself reconstituted and invigorated. (A linguistic aside on *visitation,* the archaism I employ here: Though the word is commonly used to suggest a unilateral receipt of dream material from some otherworldly source, I wish to clarify that the "visitations" of the Warlpiri, and indeed all Central Desert groups, in manifesting spiritual value, propel the dreamers into the domain of the Ancestral Present, wherein Ancestral Beings interact with the *pirlirrpa* of individual Warlpiri. This and other aspects of nocturnal dreams and their ties to the Dreaming shall be amply explored in the subsequent chapter.) By themselves the dreams Judy had did not peg her as a future leader, but they did situate her among the female *yamparru* (and other senior businesswomen) of her kin group, women whose early morning analyses were instrumental in assessing the spiritual value of all visitations, and the merits of integrating their content into ritual activity.

What did mark Judy as a potential *yamparru,* however, even in her early years of ritual engagement, was her perspicacity as a ritual performer, a talent recognized by both men and women of her kin group, especially then-current and erstwhile business leaders. No one pushed Judy to involve herself in ceremony, but her efforts to acquire ritual knowledge were greeted favorably, a response that is by no means a given. The struggle to attain ritual leadership is a choice, but one that must be socially sanctioned. Consider the example of a Nangala who died in 1992, a woman whose recent death requires that she be identified as *kumanjayi.* Though she expressed, from an early age, the same ritual aspirations as Judy, her efforts to involve herself in ritual activity were discouraged. She displayed many of the skills needed to be a ritual leader, but these were regularly downplayed by the businesswomen of the settlement. The reason: familial obligation. The premature death of a daughter (in a horrific car accident) demanded that the Nangala care for a grandson whose antisocial behavior required constant vigilance. It was deemed inappropriate for the Nangala to pass the burden of the troubled child's care to younger female kin, the usual protocol for the ceremonial aspirant, and so, absent residential support, the would-be leader was discouraged from participation in Yuendumu's ritual life. The bond of kinship between mother and deceased daughter extended maternal responsibility to her daughter's difficult son. The Nangala was warned that the risks of ritual involvement, even if it meant only temporary separation from her grandchild, were far too great to be justified. Her role as a mother's mother superseded ritual responsibility. This restriction diminished somewhat when the grandson began to attend the local school. Yet while the Nangala was welcomed back into the domain of ceremonial performance, she could never elevate her standing to the *yamparru*-ship she had long sought. Caring for the grandson meant that she could engage only in *yawulyu* undertaken during school hours. Nocturnal participation in various important joint ceremonies eluded her, despite her known performative skills.

The principal context in which Judy acquired early ritual knowledge was *yawulyu* ceremonies, both "big" and "small." These women's events not only provided her with the specific segments and associated dances and songs, but reinforced the sensibility of obligation that ritual activity codifies. How she should behave with other women, and toward men in those rituals jointly undertaken—these and other protocols were provided by the older women during these gender-restricted events. While any ritually active woman can, in principle, attend *yawulyu,* participation is usually limited to senior ritual performers, specifically menopausal (*muturna*) women. Judy's precocious engagement in *yawulyu* was another indicator of her potential leadership role. During my fieldwork, no more than half a dozen premenopausal women regularly attended *yawulyu* events. Of these, only two were routinely encouraged and sought out. Encouragement of this kind, coupled with extra-ritual displays of ceremonial knowledge, is the closest the Warlpiri women come to identifying or supporting potential leadership. While she was attending the *yawulyu* of her older female kin, other women of Judy's cohort limited their ritual activities, if they undertook any at all, to joint ceremonies.

In this way, Judy acquired much of her ritual knowledge earlier than her peers. It would be wrong, however, to characterize such acquisition as "premature"; her trajectory was never perceived as such, not by Judy nor by her older relatives. Precocious engagement is, in fact, seen as common to potential *yamparru.* When I noted a young woman dancing knowledgeably in a *Kura-kurra* event generally restricted to *muturna* women, I asked Judy whether such action was unusual. Judy replied, "*Wirntijarna, nyuruwiyi, ngaju-piyajarna ngampurrpa,*" which means, "No. I danced the same way a long time ago. She's eager like me."

Judy's precocity as a ritual participant, particularly in the domain of *yawulyu,* coupled with her keen memory, kin support (principally from her father's sister), and strong personal *pirlirrpa* (which she said enabled her not only to withstand night-long joint events, but to be invigorated by them), led to a leadership role within her kin group, though not one considered as yet to express *yamparru*-ship. Whenever possible Judy attended rituals that implicated other camps within Yuendumu and other settlements within the region. She was constantly—some claimed voraciously—bolstering her knowledge of rituals owned by others, committing to memory repertoires and itineraries for which she had no genealogical responsibility but which were crucial for ultimate broad-based recognition as a leader. Encouragement by her kin intensified, especially among older businesspeople. Senior women with whom she shared *kirda* rights asked her to paint on their torsos the body designs they shared with Judy, a gesture of great trust. Such a gesture imposed significant responsibility on Judy, for the quality of a body design—a complex evaluation based on, among other things, the beauty (*marrka*) of the application—directly influences the health and performative capacities of the individual who is painted.[25] When Judy was able to display this beauty regularly, she no longer was explicitly asked to undertake the design; that role, though never formally sanctioned, became hers presumptively. Indeed, so skilled was she in matters of corporeal decoration that her *kurdungurlu* often asked that she paint them up, a pattern of engagement uncommon at Yuendumu.[26] As for the support she received from men in those early days of leadership, Judy never described this specifically, though she says such support existed.

Cross-gender assistance of women struggling for leadership in ritual is now made manifest by certain exhortations and offerings that follow lines of kinship. During events, husbands, brothers-in-law, and mother's mother's brothers can shout praise of a performer. After events, fathers, brothers, and husbands often express their satisfaction with a woman's performance by providing additional ritual information to supplement the aspirant's cache of knowledge. This information generally takes the form of a song or design and associated narrative. I was present, for example, when a woman on the path to *yamparru*-ship was shown, immediately following her performance of a Fire Dreaming she owned, a male portion of that Dreaming, one she had never before seen. The presenter of this material, her brother, told the woman that the segment marked a stretch of the Fire Dreaming's itinerary that traveled through Pitjantjatjara country. He then narrated a brief story, one concerning the illness of two brothers, material known by both to have been "dear." The presentation confirmed the proto-*yamparru*'s ritual competence and repositioned a small measure of men's material into the domain of women's ceremony, a transmission that both acknowledged the ritual abilities of a sibling and carried larger cross-gender resonances—resonances that serve as the focus of chapter 5.

In 1974, roughly at the age of forty, Judy became a widow. This change in marital status resituated her in one of the quarters for single women (*jilimi*) of West Camp, populated by older women from her residential kin group, and intensified her ritual activity. The decision not to remarry was one reason (but by no means the only one) she was able to expand her ritual engagement. After years of marriage to a man who drank heavily and thus demanded much care, Judy was well aware that a second formal liaison might carry various nonritual responsibilities that could impede ceremonial involvement. However, this should not be taken to mean that widowhood is the means by which women attain or constitute their status as ritual leaders. There is substantial evidence of women amplifying their ritual authority through marriage, but only when such union is made with a man who is himself a *yamparru*.

When Judy determined that none of her potential preferred spouses would in any way amplify her desire to orchestrate ritual, and that the principal liability of her first husband—alcohol abuse—was common to this new crop of preferred spouses, she forswore all attempts at remarriage and devoted herself to ritual business. She told me she was aware of the risks of a bad marriage. Unstable familial environments of any kind can (in fact must) negatively affect one's efforts in ritual; witness the *kumanjayi* Nangala who was denied a role in ceremony because of the troubled son of her deceased daughter. Judy knew that if her future husband took to drink, as her first husband (and their sons) had, no measure of ritual knowledge would counter the obligations of nurturance she would have to undertake. Knowing that weakness in one's family circumstance weakens one's capacity as a ritual leader, she chose to avoid such risks. Judy lingered on the specific pool of potential husbands and not remarriage per se when discussing her prolonged widowhood and ritual activities. All of this argues against any attempt to attribute ritual leadership directly to marital circumstance. In Judy's case, widowhood did not diminish her ritual status; in fact it helped. And though she was repeatedly pressured by her kin to marry again, these pressures in no way restricted their assistance of her ritual development. Marital and ritual pursuits were never seen as oppositionally constituted.

From the time her eldest son completed his *kurdiji* cycle, it took Judy about a decade to attain the status of *yamparru.* This status was never formally bestowed upon her, but was transmitted unceremonially (in all senses of the word) by her classificatory father's sister. The older *yamparru,* with whom Judy had a *marlpa* tie and from whom so much had been acquired, had passed away a few years before, so it fell to other senior performers to express confidence and support in order for Judy to orchestrate events involving ceremonies implicating businesspeople outside the residential kin group. Judy noted that it was this intergroup sanction and her ability to round up and include ritually active women beyond the residential kin group that marked her, at last, as a leader. Early performances were restricted to the presentation of ritual knowledge already known in the other groups, but this was quickly followed by "exchange" events.

This touches on a qualitative difference found in ritual performance. When a ritual (or part thereof) is presented before another group and that group has not seen the material before, that interaction constitutes an exchange, and as such is treated with a larger measure of caution and oversight than usual. Negotiation of the new material's value, and the compensatory action it demands, must be resolved. Indeed, such negotiations often bracket such events. In some exchange ceremonies, ritual knowledge is reciprocally presented. A sand design that was previously unknown to one group is shown in order to compensate another group for the rendition of an unknown song linked to an important itinerary. In other circumstances a group's presentation of new Dreaming material prompts payment of a nonritual nature: money, blankets, cloth. Exchanges, seen as collaborative acts between and among performers and viewers, commonly combine currencies of a ritual and nonritual nature. To reject that collaborative quotient or to offer inadequate compensation is to challenge the authority of those who present it. For this reason, exchange rituals are scrupulously overseen by *yamparru.* Indeed, in the context of exchange *yamparru* lead the songs and dances presented.

The death of Judy's husband coincided with the exigencies of the Land Rights Movement. In the same year Judy was widowed, the Warlpiri—with the help of lawyers, anthropologists, and linguists—initiated their substantially successful attempt to reclaim land through which the Dreamings of the Warlpiri traveled. The intercultural negotiations surrounding this reclamation of a tract of vacant Crown land implicated all Warlpiri ritual owners and managers, since claims could be made only by displays of ritual knowledge and proof of genealogical allegiance, the combination of which served as a stimulant for public ceremonial display. The links between ritual and land, always mutually constituted by the Warlpiri, were now acknowledged by governmental authorities as well. And in light of the often arbitrary dispersal policies of the white authorities during sedentarization, legal claims for the lands required kin from different settlements who shared country (and thus claim) to come together to testify and perform.

Because she manifested both a knowledge of ritual and the desire to display it, and because those displays were appreciated by Warlpiri throughout the settlement, Judy acquired a prominent position in the flourishing ritual discussions that the change in governmental policy precipitated. She was regularly called upon by various governmental and nongovernmental agencies and panels to discuss issues of land rights and identify ritual sites with which she was familiar. Some of these visits brought her to patrilineally acquired lands she had not seen since forced sedentarization. To this day she recalls one such trip, to Puyurru, a site along the itinerary of the Water Dreaming inherited from her father, as a moment of deep joy—one compounded when she and her kin received that land back in 1978. The non-Aboriginal imperatives that instigated such visits also allowed for the augmentation of intersettlement ritual discussion and ceremonial performance of a nonlegal nature. Not surprisingly, Judy's memories of these trips in the late 1970s and early 1980s often precipitate recollections of earlier travels she undertook as a child, prior to sedentarization. Her memories of presettlement travels, in which her kin met up with other groups, evoke a ritual life that implicated men and women during broad migratory activity. Such recollections are noted here because they run counter to the observations of Meggitt, who characterized intergroup ritual gatherings prior to settlement as being restricted to men (1962, 1966). Judy recalled that though before settlement men undertook the majority of such ceremonial travels (most of these associated with initiation expeditions), there were also frequent trips of ritual consequence in which both men and women participated.

From the 1970s on, testimonies of a ritual nature by both Aboriginal men and women were employed to establish kin "ownership" in the courts of the Northern Territory. These efforts, coupled with newly permitted and provided travel (a number of non-Aboriginal researchers emerged willing and able to drive long-sedentarized Aborigines back to homes and countries from which they had been banned), not only enlarged the arena and significance of ritual but enlarged, too, the role women played in it. Consultation with knowledgeable senior members of the settlement of both genders was essential to legitimate land claims. And among women and men, it fell to the *yamparru,* current and former, as controllers of ceremony, if not the Dreamings they celebrated, to broker the intercultural legal exchanges and the resources that emerged from them. Judy and other *yamparru* of her generation reflect on those land claims as a major moment in the history of the settlement's ritual activity, granting as it did ownership that the Warlpiri had always declared and the government only now grudgingly acknowledged. All the Warlpiri, whether directly implicated in negotiations or not, were cognizant of the seriousness of the intercultural discussions, but *yamparru* felt the pressure of the exchange more than others.

As correlative opportunities for administratively sponsored "self-determination" grew, ritual leaders such as Judy found they could—and were in fact obligated to—extend their *yamparru*-ship far beyond ritual. Judy sat on committees dealing with matters of land rights, health, women's issues, and child welfare. She also became co-president of the Women's Museum, a title that gave her control over an invaluable commodity: a four-wheel-drive Toyota Land Cruiser.

Though the primary use of the truck was daily domestic activity—wood collection, hunting, general transport—it served ritual functions as well. Runs for ochre (a material essential for both men's and women's ceremonies) and trips to other settlements for ceremonial activity represented a significant portion of the mileage clocked on the (soon broken) odometer. While on the surface, negotiations regarding the movements of the truck were undertaken in seemingly collaborative fashion, control of the vehicle represented an intense, indeed incessant competition that pitted camp against camp, men against women, and women within camps against each other. At the time, no women at the settlement were able to drive themselves, and the men who did possess the needed skill often were deemed unreliable chauffeurs, their propensity for alcohol resulting frequently in "drink runs" that threatened both the vehicle and its occupants. (Settlement laws at Yuendumu, which is "dry," allow authorities to confiscate any unsanctioned car found to be used for the transport of alcohol. The sanctions, in the form of permits, were generally restricted to the non-Aboriginal population of the settlement.) When Judy spoke of coordinating the use of the vehicle she often lingered on the stresses of resolving conflicting demands. Though no direct connection was made, the language and sentiment closely resembled those raised when describing the reconciliation of competing interests in matters of the repertoire of ceremonial performance. Efforts of accommodation are part and parcel of *yamparru*-ship, whether the commodity in question is vehicular or of a religious nature.

Trucks helped greatly to revitalize the settlement's ritual life. This is not to argue that external policy or governmental largesse in itself transformed indigenous ceremonial activity. Nor do I wish to suggest that the four-wheel-drives be seen as vehicles of spiritual expansion unless the other form of spirit—that is, alcohol—is also calculated into the assessment of effects that attended increased access to transportation. Indeed, Judy isolates among her many tasks as a *yamparru* the search for businessmen out on "drink runs," so as to promote the sobriety needed for the proper enactment of ceremonial life. That the Toyota Land Cruiser may be seen simultaneously as the vehicle of ceremonial renewal and ceremonial assault is but one of the many ironies of the intercultural nexus.

Judy was relatively successful in employing the Toyota for purposes that benefited the settlement in general, and her camp in particular. Inevitably that success, when localized within her residential kin group, led to intergroup fights, with the Toyota (and its successor vehicles) the focus of almost weekly conflict. The ethos of sharing on which so much Warlpiri exchange is based was difficult to reconcile with the competing demands the rare item triggered. In negotiating these multiple requests, Judy suffered the stresses of judicial compromise.

Stress, as I have said, is a primary part of the *yamparru*'s job. That is true whether leaders are rounding up kin to collect and redistribute firewood (with or without the Toyota) or precipitating collective action for the redistribution of ritual knowledge. The authority of *yamparru*-ship is essayed in all gestures and all acts, which is what makes it—and business in general—"hard work."

When Judy and other ritual participants invoke the phrase "hard work," which they do regularly, they mean to suggest that leadership requires strength of spirit and the related quality of social stamina, neither of which can be maintained indefinitely. By the same token, "hard work" establishes the value of the activity pursued and is transformed into prestige for the individual undertaking it. More often than not, "hard work" involves the resolution of conflicts—though by using that phrase I make no allusion to the various conflict resolution rituals. Rather, I refer to the workaday struggles to suppress the frustrations of those denied the limited resources granted to others.

Competing for the preservation of harmony no doubt accounts for the often ambivalent nature of *yamparru* rivalry. I said earlier that Judy was co-president of the organization that controlled the truck. The other titular leader, Lucy Napaljarri, a *yamparru* of Southeast Camp, regularly skirmished with Judy. To observe the two women engage in negotiations about using the truck to travel to big events was to witness a mix of feigned collaboration and hidden resentment, of ritual assistance constituted in ways promoting personal and residential authority at the expense of intergroup cohesion. The words *rebuffed* and *anger* appear frequently in my notebooks to describe occasions when the two *yamparru* came together.

Usually it was Judy who had the upper hand in ritual activity, since her group's domination of ceremonial life compelled Lucy and her kin to rely on them during "big" events. But just as often, Lucy was denied a voice in secular decisions as well. Indeed, the introductory account of the circumstances leading to the subject of this book—my mundane search for suitable housing—was merely one of many disputes between two women vying for personal and residential recognition. Many of their run-ins involved the nuances of ritual and its proper enactment. Lucy and Judy, for instance, were forever undermining—via third parties, to be sure—the virtuosity of the other's *yawulyu* performances, a triangulated censure supported and even encouraged by the kin living in their camps.

As close cross-cousins, Judy and Lucy were tethered to each other in ceremonial performance. In particular, Judy inherited *kurdungurlu* rights for the Red Kangaroo Dreaming for which Lucy was *kirda* by inheritance. Lucy inherited *kurdungurlu* rights over the Fire Dreaming for which Judy was *kirda*. Had the two leaders been on better terms, they would have extended their reciprocal associations to other ritual material each owned, a reciprocity confusingly identified by a secondary application of the term *kurdungurlu*. However, little such expanded sense of mutual *kurdungurlu* obligation in the ritual sphere found expression. The competition between the two, a mirror of the competition of their respective residential kin groups, made such collaboration impossible, and indeed, their unwillingness to assist each other much beyond the strict rules of kinship points to the importance of residency in modifying such rules;

kurdungurlu-ship between individuals of the pan-ceremonial kind is most commonly constituted within a residential kin group informed by the bonds of kinship.

Though obligated to share in ritual activity, each displayed a silent antagonism, a passive resistance to the other's actions. When Judy performed in a *Jardiwanpa* as *kirda,* a role that called for Lucy's *kurdungurlu* assistance, the resentful cross-cousin—who had garnered managerial rights over the ceremony through marriage—often overlooked her reciprocal responsibilities, avoiding the *Jardiwanpa* altogether. This weakened the ceremony and the status of its *kirda* overseer. (Withdrawal from ritual obligation generally indicates conflict but not the attitude of the individual who withdraws. In some circumstances, individuals will avoid the ceremonial arena to diminish rather than exacerbate tensions, even if by doing so the ceremony is impaired.) Judy was equally capable of expressing her disdain for the ritual endeavors of her cross-cousin rival.

In the ten years I conducted fieldwork at Yuendumu, one of the most divisive moments in its ritual life came during a large-scale intersettlement *yawulyu* exchange. The event, which transpired at the Yuendumu Sports Weekend in 1984, brought together Aboriginal groups from numerous neighboring settlements, including Lajamanu, Kintore, Willowra, Papunya, Mt. Liebig, Warrabri, and Mt. Allan. It was the specific *yawulyu* exchanges between Yuendumu's Warlpiri women and their Anmatyerre counterparts from Mt. Allan, the settlement that was the locus of the dispute. The chief instigator of the event was Lucy Napaljarri, whose mother's mother and father's mother were both Anmatyerre and whose other kin were Warlpiri. As such, Lucy's ritual associations straddled both groups. Protocol generally calls for preceremonial discussion among ritual performers of two groups exchanging material, if only to confirm that an exchange is indeed planned. But on this occasion no such talks were held. Lucy believed her ties to the Warlpiri at Yuendumu and the Anmatyerre of Mt. Allan made such discussion unnecessary. This turned out to be a mistake.

The first day of the four-day event was given over to exchange discussions that did not involve the Mt. Allan performers, and so little tension was apparent. The mood changed, however, on day two. At the end of that afternoon, the Mt. Allan women initiated a *yawulyu* that was to serve as part of the ritual currency to be exchanged, one evoking the Honey Ant and Bell Bush Dreaming segments. Accompanied by Lucy, the visiting group augmented dance and song with two ground paintings, a medium acknowledged to be of great value throughout the Central Australian Desert but uncommon in the Warlpiri women's repertoire. Rather than join or praise the actions of their Mt. Allan visitors, Judy and her West Camp mob kept their distance from the Anmatyerre performance, a nonconfrontational rejection noted by all in attendance.

On the third day of the intersettlement events, the women from Yuendumu and the visiting settlements all gathered in separate but contiguous groups to continue their *yawulyu* activities. Lucy, clearly agitated by the West Camp snub to her visiting kin, announced that she and her group should be paid for the two ground paintings and performance of the previous day. Use of the first person plural indicated her association with the Anmatyerre and was a challenge to those who had physically (and spiritually) turned their backs on the earlier events. This request was roundly ignored by Judy and her kin from West Camp and represented yet another affront to Lucy's standing as a ritual leader. Nevertheless, Lucy and the Mt. Allan mob performed the next installments of their Dreaming segments, since obligations to advance the cycle superseded whatever irritations were provoked by the behavior of the West Camp hosts and their leader in particular.

Halfway through the Mt. Allan performance, Judy and her mob moved from their spot on the ceremonial grounds of the Women's Museum to one that offered a direct view of the Anmatyerre actions. Although arrival during a performance is discouraged, in itself it is not a gross violation of ceremonial protocol. However, the subsequent departure of the West Camp group during the ceremony represented a direct abandonment of ritual etiquette.

The other groups present, including Yuendumu Warlpiri from other camps, were agitated by this gesture of rebuke. After the day's events were finished, women from other Yuendumu camps approached Judy and informed her that the Mt. Allan women would be shown the ritual paraphernalia of the Women's Museum. This served multiple purposes. It granted the Anmatyerre women a compensatory measure of ceremonial acknowledgment for their *yawulyu*. Additionally, because it was Judy who was to give that tour, it served as a warning that her actions, and those of her kin, had been unacceptable. Proper behavior was now called for. Unable to reject the request—despite her title as co-president, the museum belonged to all businesswomen—Judy restricted her tour to an unhelpful minimum, pointing out Dreaming designs on various objects but providing none of the ritual knowledge associated with the designs.

This behavior was seen as yet another negation of the legitimacy of the exchange that preceded the tour.

Matters deteriorated still further on the final day of the events. When the Mt. Allan mob completed the Honey Ant and Bell Bush *yawulyu* cycles, their West Camp counterparts failed to show up on the ceremonial ground. Absence at this juncture, when material and intellectual property normally is exchanged, was seen by all as an act of unalloyed contempt, though it must be noted that very little of this dispute expressed itself verbally. The confrontation was more of attitudes and gestures than of articulated dissatisfaction.

What was Judy's rationale for such undiplomatic actions? Much later, when tempers calmed, she explained that she and her kin were only responding to the unilateral (and thus even more impolitic) decision by the Mt. Allan mob and "their" Yuendumu *yamparru,* Lucy, to undertake an exchange. The absence of preceremonial discussion was counter to the modus operandi of ritual transaction, she emphasized. By leaving early and avoiding further negotiation with her rival and her rival's Anmatyerre kin, Judy evaded a ritual exchange that was improperly constituted from the start. That dispute pitted kin and Aboriginal groups, individuals and settlements against each other, though again such distinctions were never expressly stated. It was, to be sure, an extreme case of a *yamparru*'s control by noninvolvement, and of rivalry run amok. More subtle expressions of micro- and macromanagement, however, find their way into ritual life with greater frequency. Indeed, such control is considered part of the *yamparru*'s job.

Oversight of ritual performance (its fidelity, its order, its appropriateness), the rivalry such supervision triggers in leaders of overlapping authority, protection and nourishment of the *Jukurrpa,* the risks of sorcery, the stresses of travel, changes in health or spousal status—all are cited as reasons that leadership is never retained for life.

At the peak of her *yamparru*-ship, Judy supervised exchanges of *yawulyu* ceremonies at other settlements several times a year. Even though the travels rarely lasted more than a fortnight—to minimize the risks of becoming *yirrarru,* or homesick—Judy felt constant pressure while she was away. In one particularly demanding period, involving ritual exchange of *yilpinji, yawulyu, Kankarlu,* and *Kajirri* material, Judy traveled between Yuendumu and Docker River (a distance of some 1,600 kilometers, about 1,000 miles) three times in three months. Because the travel was tiring, she explained, it could have the long-term effect of weakening her essence (*pirlirrpa*). This in turn could increase the dangers of sorcery, which is effective only on individuals with debilitated essence. Though Judy generally considered herself strong enough to counter malevolent *yarda* singing, she knew, too, that the stresses of leadership were taking their toll. The orchestration of ritual activity and the concomitant diplomacy that required her to extend her sense of nurturance and obligation to a large network of kin lasted roughly a decade.

The *yamparru*-ship of Judy Nampijinpa Granites ended in 1985, soon after she decided to remarry. The decision to suspend her ritual authority was Judy's and Judy's alone. When a leader acts properly, as Judy did most of the time, pressure is never exerted to extend or to shorten tenure. This does not mean that decision is received uncritically. Judy's kin did indeed express frustration about her decision among themselves, but never to Judy directly.

Though a change in marital status coincided with a change in her role as a leader, it would be wrong to predicate leadership on spousal disencumbrance, as noted previously. Widows make up roughly half the female *yamparru* population, but their authority is no greater than that of their married counterparts, women with whom they regularly organize events. Indeed, Judy relinquished her authority to a married sister.

It was not the marriage per se that necessitated Judy's renunciation of her role, but the obligations to the particular man whom she married and to her new husband's close kin. Because the new spouse resided with his first wife outside the settlement and had offspring who required much attention, Judy was precluded from continuing her *yamparru* activities. She refocused her energies away from the broad-based, residential matters of West Camp and onto the more intimate needs of her new husband, his children, and her five sons from her first marriage. Such shifts in attention are typical of *yamparru* relinquishing their leadership role. This does not mean, however, that they suspend all ritual responsibility. Active participation in ceremony can still take place, and the analysis of significant nocturnal dreams—a task required of all senior businesspeople regardless of their links to leadership—is still obligatory. Suspension of leadership is usually progressive and informal.

Although *yamparru* women try to instill in their female children interest in ritual, their authority is passed on to other *kirda* with whom they share Dreamings, usually a younger sister. Such siblings must demonstrate desire and competence to carry on the complex orchestration of ritual their older siblings no longer oversee. These new leaders must possess a relationship of friendship and support to allow for the gradual effacement of the former leader and the subtle expansion of her replacement's authority. In Judy's case, that heir was her close younger sister, Dolly Nampijinpa Daniels, an aspiring *yamparru* who held rights to many of the same Dreamings as Judy and shared ownership acquired by both patrilineal and personal connection. Although an accomplished ritual participant, Dolly never organized events without her older sister's approval before the remarriage. Within a few months of Judy's changed status, however, Dolly was rounding up her kin for big *yawulyu* performances, extending her kin obligations throughout West Camp and beyond. In short, she began to act the part of the *yamparru*. How was she received? Both in the West Camp and outside, Dolly had little difficulty taking over the tasks previously maintained by Judy. Her skillful body paintings, her faithful replication of song and dance required to invoke Dreamings (hers and those owned by others), her temperament, and her position within West Camp were all seen as worthy expressions of a *yamparru*.

The intimacy she and her sister maintained enabled her to extend her authority to spheres of influence of both ritual and secular nature. Soon after she started leading rituals, Dolly expanded her involvement in various politico-economic organizations at the settlement. The titles and authority she acquired—co-president of the newly constituted Women's Center, board member of the Warlukurlangu Artists Aboriginal Association and Tanami [Satellite] Network—mirrored many of the earlier roles her sister had undertaken. For example, the control Judy had over the truck, under the aegis of the Women's Museum, was reconstituted by Dolly, whose *yamparru*-ship gave her control over a newer vehicle owned collectively by the Women's Center. In short, the baton of ritual authority and its secular obligations had been passed from one sister to another, thus sustaining the bonds of residential kinship.

When Judy had reconciled the time-consuming circumstances of her new marriage, a process that took nearly two years, she was able to renew her involvement in Yuendumu ritual. However, she never attempted to regain the status she had renounced. She restricted herself to a participatory role, invoking her former authority only when it benefited Dolly in contexts of intercamp contention. When she and Dolly did disagree, a circumstance I witnessed only once, Judy withdrew from ceremonial action entirely to avoid displaying that conflict. Such struggle between the two sisters was rare, however, and Judy regularly expressed support for the actions of her younger sibling. Judy did say that had she wanted to, she could have reclaimed her more visible role in ritual, and with it the title of *yamparru,* but that her sister's competence and strength made such reclamation unnecessary. Absent any long-term survey of multigenerational ritual authority, Judy's confident assessment is impossible to prove or disprove.

The lengthy narrative of Judy's authority, at the most basic level, forces rethinking of those analyses attempting to minimize the role of ritual leadership and the vital part that women play in it. Also resonating through Judy's reflections on becoming a *yamparru* is a fact worthy of repetition: that ceremonial engagement is by no means bordered and separated from the rest of settlement life. Judy's capacities as a ritual leader found expression plurally in other arenas of social engagement beyond the ceremonial grounds. In those arenas, as in the religious one with which she was principally identified, the force of residential allegiance was a constant and palpable presence.

Furthermore, this brief account of Judy's ritual career elucidates that the falsity of the theoretically constructed boundary does more than wrongly suggest the sacred kept at arm's length from the secular. The polyvalence of gender support—the very real ties of men to women—is also reflected in Judy's ritual career. Her prominence was not one constituted by or among women alone, but was instead regularly assisted and recognized by men, too. Her prominence, it must be added, was susceptible to the judgments (positive or negative) of her male and female kin. Judy's leadership coincided with her status as a widow, but it must be stressed once again that this spousal circumstance was not a structural component of the authority she achieved. She shared her *yamparru*-ship with married women of her residential kin group and ultimately bestowed her personal authority on a younger married sister—facts that suggest the locus of authority cannot be linked to the "independence" of a female ritual leader.

Did it help Judy that she emerged from a strong residential kin group? Most definitely. But such allegiance in itself did not enable her to claim the role of *yamparru.* Long-term ritual education, a head for song and dance, skill in the presentation of both, familial stability, the encouragement and pedagogic assistance of close female kin, friendship, the diplomatic talents required to temper "greed" (her own and that of others)—all of these were components that led to her ultimate performative control of ceremony. Judy not only "knew a lot"—a common refrain among admiring kin—but she knew, too, how to use that knowledge. This capacity was not restricted to Aboriginal contexts. As intercultural engagements increased—land reform, "self-determination," and, later, a flourishing international market for acrylic canvases (see Myers 1994a, 1994b, 1995)—leaders such as Judy, especially female leaders, were propelled into European contexts of intense ritual exchange.

The list of qualities required of a *yamparru* is a long one. The rewards that accompany that recognition are not numerous. Certainly the ritual objects Judy acquired for performance were no measure or source of that prestige, for like so many items of value in the Warlpiri universe—intellectual property, money, food—these were quickly redistributed among her kin, and in particular among those kin with whom she had *marlpa* ties. Indeed, whatever personal satisfactions Judy may have acquired often tended to be subsumed under a discourse that emphasized the stress and "hard work" of her efforts. The language of leadership, a language filled as much with burden as with joy, is not unique to Judy. All leaders feel the collective pressure that attends ceremonial orchestration, a pressure sensed most strongly in the obligations to residential kin. For it is there, in the end, where leadership truly resides, constituted by the aggregate force of the relatives' kin with whom and for whom Judy performed. That residential force was felt in all spheres of settlement life, secular and religious.

However egalitarian the goals of ritual performance may be, their enactment is very clearly hierarchic in nature, and that hierarchy functions on a personal level within the residential kin group and at a broader level in the manner by which intergroup ritual politics is conducted. Hence the importance of giving full measure to the language of victory, with its lexicon of *jijami* and "winning." To neglect this spirit in Warlpiri ritual is to deny one of its energizing components.

Ritual competition does exist within groups and among them, implicating their women as much as their men. From the employment of these pairings, however, it should not be presumed that competition is rife between genders—it is not.

Still, does the struggle to win weaken the harmony sought in the exercise of ceremony? Not in the least, for it is through that very competition that the cohesion of the residential kin group—a fundamental locus of Warlpiri identity that links men and women—is maintained. To be deemed winners a group must be collectively judged to have supported and enacted *Jukurrpa* obligations extending kinship beyond the group. That is one of the paradoxes of Warlpiri ritual life.

Ritual was a defining element of Judy's life; that much her testimony makes clear. What must be added, however, is an appreciation of Judy's role in the life of ritual. The concept of nurturance is often invoked when discussing the responsibilities that attend ceremonial engagement. But what is the nature of that nurturance? The next chapter presents one of the more potent expressions of care and oversight and is yet another exploration of how ritual is reshaped and transformed by ritual leaders in order, paradoxically, to preserve its unchanging nature. Reinventing the immutable, through the medium of dreams, is the focus of chapter 4.

4. HOW DREAMS ARE MADE

Innovation, Integration, and Affirmation in Ritual

Though the literature of Central Desert cosmology is peppered with brief references to the integration (or reintegration) of nocturnal dreams into the Dreaming narratives performed during Warlpiri ritual, little exists describing the process and function of that integration or the nature of the attendant pressures. Mutability of ritual expression is generally accepted by analysts of Aboriginal culture, but the forces effecting the expression of cosmological changes rarely find point-by-point explication.

Catherine Berndt notes that the roots of some of the love-ritual songs of women (*tjarada*) have their origins in nocturnal dreams (1950). Munn makes a related observation, identifying the phenomenon of "new" (*jalangu-warnu*) ritual designs revealed during sleep—designs, she notes, that can subsequently find their way into ceremonial activity (1964: 91–92; 1973:37, 146). Other assessments of ritual innovation rooted in dreams surface in the works of Ronald Berndt (1951:71–84), Tonkinson (1970:277–91; 1974:85–86; 1978), Myers (1986a:51, 53, 67), Poirier (1990:263–76), and Glowczewski (1991). None of the authors provides an extended assessment of how nocturnal narratives, songs, and designs (coalesced into "dreams" in a Western sense) enter the ritual sphere, nor of the negotiations surrounding that integration.

The employment of the term *Dreaming*, always troublesome because of the Western baggage it carries, is particularly problematic in connection with this specific aspect of Warlpiri cosmology. A dream specifically identified as a nocturnal episode of a spiritual nature can be intricately linked to the Dreaming. The question is, how? In the opening pages of the first chapter, I noted that in the Warlpiri language both nocturnal dreams and the cosmology of the Dreaming can be invoked by the single term *Jukurrpa,* and that only context provides definitional nuance. This chapter is devoted to exactly that context—to an exploration of dreams and their links to the Dreaming. I will attempt to show how the nocturnal sense of the word can be folded into the religious one—and to what end. The chapter focuses on the production and distribution of Dreamings by the female *yamparru* of Yuendumu. As with all aspects of ritual production, this one is a complex, multistep process that is at times collaborative and at times competitive, a dynamic relying on negotiation and review. In the end, how and why dreams are made reconfirm the functional (though by no means functionalist) importance of residential kinship in the ritual life of the settlement.

For the Warlpiri, dreams (and here I am referring to the visitations of Ancestral Beings attendant to nocturnal sleep) serve a complex set of functions. Among other things, they are part unwritten ritual rules, part records of the mythology, and part vehicles of cross-gender transmission of knowledge that would be more contested if presented in nondormant domains.[1] Dreams, furthermore, enable the Warlpiri to dissipate tensions in the personal and residential dynamics of the settlement by providing a kind of protocurrency of knowledge that allows for circulation, and as such necessitates social exchange. Bearing as they do the potential expression of religious Law, dreams tend to be embraced with a mixture of tentativeness and pride. Ritual power, danger, revelation, guidance, admonition, premonition, and warning can all be found in dreams, and for that reason, dreams must be handled with care. Dreams engender plural functions that often have an ill-defined but consequential impact. They have a role in settlement life every bit as polyvalent as the rituals to which they are so often, and so intimately, allied.

When the Warlpiri sleep, their "spirits" (*pirlirrpa*) leave their body, specifically from the fat surrounding the kidney, via the umbilicus, and wander in the Ancestral Present. These dreamt wanderings retrace the paths of the Ancestral Beings, and in doing so reaffirm and strengthen the *Jukurrpa,* and with it the social coherence of the settlement. So important is the knowledge imparted during this nocturnal process—dreams of ceremonial relevance almost never surface during the day—that the position of one's body, in relation to both the land and one's kin, must be configured in specific ways. How one sleeps at night and wakes in the morning enhances the well-being of the Dreaming by facilitating the fluent movement of the *pirlirrpa* that constitutes it.

To encourage the proper departure, travel, and return of this spirit necessitates sleeping on one's side and in close proximity to the kin with whom one has a *kirda-kurdungurlu* relationship. Sleeping on one's back or stomach, the Warlpiri explain, encumbers the free departure and return of the spirit. An incorrect posture may allow the spirit to lodge itself unhealthfully in the stomach or back, causing physical pain to the dreamer. The nurturance of the *pirlirrpa* also requires one to wake slowly and deliberately. Sudden rupture of sleep can produce dangerous effects by denying the time needed for the spirit to return to the kidney fat whence it came. If such displacement lingers, the individual risks illness that may lead to death.[2]

Shared ownership of nocturnal material deemed "of the Dreaming" can be claimed on the basis of proximity to a dreamer, one reason sleeping arrangements tend to bring together *kirda* and *kurdungurlu.* Husbands sleep with wives, mothers with their daughters, sisters with sisters. Even if preferential kinship pairings are not maintained, ownership of Dreaming material emerging at night will be identified with all who sleep close to the individual who has a visitation. Such acquisition through dreams or proximity to a dreamer can have long-term effects. Initially, the ownership extends only to the Dreaming segment determined to be part of the nocturnal visitation. But there is evidence that descendants of the dreamer and the proximate sleepers may subsequently enlarge their rights to include not only the Dreaming segment but the whole of the itinerary associated with it.

How are such modifications of ownership rights possible? As the women explain it, the dreams of proximate sleepers interact at night. Ancestral Beings crisscross and engage with one another as they travel their itineraries. This engagement sustains (or in some cases establishes altogether new) ritual relationships of the sleepers who lie down close to each other. This, the more ritually attentive women say, explains why one must always sleep in close proximity to those with whom ritual relationships already exist. They say closeness makes the monitoring and reenactment of "new" dreams easier if traditionally sanctioned ties are already in place.

Once awake, dreamers recount almost immediately to those with whom they sleep the substance of the dream, which can include any combination of narrative, song, dance, and design.[3] Understanding the relevance of dreams and their relationship to the Dreaming requires being present at this early stage. This is because much of the most important discussion assessing the potential cosmological value of a dream usually emerges in the moments after a nocturnal dream's initial declaration, in a process of assessment and interpretation generally overseen by the senior kin who are present. The nature of this discussion and negotiation warrants explication.

When businesspeople negotiate or discuss the meaning of a dream, they do not argue its spiritual significance or dispute its narrative content. One rarely observes knowledgeable individuals "correcting" a dream—suggesting, say, the placement of stripes elsewhere, or changing the text of an ancestral song. The "facts" as they are told by a dreamer, once the dream is deemed "of the Dreaming," are never questioned. Such legitimacy can emerge by active verbalized approval or silent acceptance. Nocturnal dreams not taken seriously at this early stage will inevitably fail to gain the support of powerful close kin. Only some of those dreams that are legitimated as *Jukurrpa* will result in wide diffusion. The dream in this early form may bear little or no obvious association to a particular Dreaming narrative or associated site. In fact, much of the early discussion focuses on establishing the relationship of the dreamt material to ritual repertoire and to the rights of the dreamer who had the dream. Meaning and relationship are rarely instantly clear. A series of collaborative discussions among relatives (generally those who slept in close proximity to dreamers) is the norm. Attempts are made (usually) to establish the geospecific site associated with the ritual content of the dream. Once the new material is situated in the existing *Jukurrpa,* the appropriate *kirda* and *kurdungurlu* (generally the dreamer and/or residential relatives) are brought into the discussion.

There are, to be sure, many kinds of dreams dreamt by the Warlpiri; only some manifest spiritual power (*pirlirrpa*) requiring the discussions mentioned above.[4] Furthermore, within the realm of the ritually significant, the *Jukurrpa* finds expression in different ways, and with varied effect. Many spiritually imbued dreams serve to reaffirm ceremonial knowledge already known, and as such may not require intense negotiation.

In order for dreams to become Dreamings, they cannot run counter to existing ritual repertoire as performed, nor can their ritual integration challenge the Ancestral Beings, the Beings' travels, or their actions. The majority of the dreams announced in the mornings are dismissed as "rubbish" or *warungka* (silly), often on the basis of such incompatibility, and consequently ignored.[5] For dreams to be taken seriously—and by that is meant for them to enter the arena of ritual exchange—they must be legitimated, if not exactly sanctioned, by the collective voice of the settlement's ritual community, though often that voice demonstrates its approval in silence. Only then can these dreams find their way into the ceremonies of the residential kin group, of the settlement, and beyond the confines of Yuendumu.

What I failed to see at first but which now proves glaringly clear is that dreams tended to implicate Warlpiri within the network of extended kin—the residential kin groups that serve as a locus of social and ritual life. Wherever a dream emerged, initial confirmation of ritual propriety, which in turn legitimated the potential integration of dreamt material into ceremony, generally depended on the approval of the business leaders of the dreamer's kin group, especially those with whom the dreamer shared *kirda-kurdungurlu* rights.

While the Warlpiri claim that dreams containing ceremonial content can be dreamt by anyone, including the uninitiated, in my decade-long research at Yuendumu I have never registered cosmologically significant dreams emerging from the sleep of the young. When material of a potentially significant nature does emerge from the sleep of the uninitiated, it is often deemed by older kin to constitute a nightmare (*Jukurrpa maju*) that exists outside the realm of *Jukurrpa*.[6] Among the initiated, there is little correlation between ritual authority and the significance attributed to one's ritually charged dreams. Yuendumu has no shamanic presence through which the *Jukurrpa* is channeled. Nor are the Ancestral Beings seen as selecting with special motive particular Warlpiri upon whom distinctive *Jukurrpa* are bestowed. And while it is true that *yamparru* may dream more than most, their dreams carry no greater value because of their ritual status. Neither does the status of the dream increase because of the frequency of the nocturnal visitations. Prestige is arbitrated and sustained in the ritual life stimulated by the dreams, not by the dreams themselves. In short, it is not dreaming per se that grants power; rather, it is the ability to integrate the dream's spiritual content into ritual that is a mark of a business leader.

The Warlpiri recognize among the dreams they deem to be allied to the Dreaming four basic distinctions, though these are by no means conceptualized in an exclusive or compartmentalized fashion. There are, for starters, those dreams that can be called premonitional visitations. This first category associates the dreamer's *pirlirrpa* with the telling of some actual (and by that I mean nonritual) event that has or will occur to a dreamer or a member of the dreamer's residential kin group. Though the prophetic potency of the dream allies it to the Dreaming, the content is in no way ceremonially novel. No ritual songs—a crucial marker of ceremonial significance—will appear in such dreams.

By way of example, a premonitional dream may have a dreamer wake up in the middle of the night and wail because she has seen her child in jail or in a car accident. Such a dream prompts serious response the following day, with dreamers, once awake, making every effort to discover if it has happened, and to protect those invoked if it has not.

The second category of ceremonially significant dream takes the form of an admonition. These dreams caution the dreamer and related kin about behavior incompatible with the Law that sustains the *Jukurrpa.* For example, if an individual dreams of a Rainbow Snake Dreaming (*Warnayarra Jukurrpa*), it is generally interpreted as an indication of some past or imminent transgression by one of the dreamer's kin against the dreamer. But to sanction that interpretation in ritually consequential ways, the kin associated (by *kirda-* or *kurdungurlu*-ship) with the dreamt Dreaming must declare its legitimacy. If that happens, then the dreamer will generally undergo a curing ritual (*nyurnu-kurlangu*). As with the first category of dreams, admonitional visitations do not include ritual songs, though these dreams may precipitate ritual singing to ward off the dangers invoked.

Take the case of the Rainbow Snake just mentioned. I was present when a *yamparru* dreamt of this *Warnayarra* while she was sick. One of her close daughters, a *kurdungurlu* for the *Warnayarra Jukurrpa,* made the connection between the *yamparru*'s illness and some sexual transgression vaguely perceived. The *yamparru* suspected immediately that the source of the dream was one of her sons-in-law—a *kirda* for the *Warnayarra Jukurrpa*—who had been disrespectful to her in the past. This suspicion was confirmed after discussion with other female kin associated with the *Warnayarra Jukurrpa,* all of whom agreed that the son-in-law in question must have had the ill woman "sung." Given the interactive prohibitions between women and their sons-in-law (whether in dreams or while awake), the woman could not respond to her illness or its suspected source directly. To counteract the sorcery, a *kirda* for the Snake Dreaming—a woman who had both *kuyuwurruru* and *marlpa* connections to the *yamparru* (the *kirda* was a classificatory daughter's daughter and friend)—decided that a curing ritual evoking the Dreaming that both she and the suspected son-in-law owned should be undertaken for the sick woman. When the woman had another admonitional dream, the curing ritual was hastily performed by the daughter's daughter. While singing the segment of the Snake Dreaming relating to matters of health, the *kirda* for the Dreaming applied the Snake design upon the ill woman's torso, belly, and upper thighs. The ill woman revived within a few days. No action was taken against the son-in-law because of the speedy recovery. But had the recovery not occurred, it is possible that counteractive sorcery might have been initiated.

Admonitional visitations commonly involve deceased relatives, invocations to the living (the dreamers and/or their kin) of some breach (or potential breach) in postmortem Law.[7] One dream thus interpreted in my presence by various senior women came when a woman "saw" a recently deceased sister in an encounter that directly violated kin-based taboo restrictions that attend mourning. Once awake, the dreamer, in consultation with her residential kin, recalled that a few days before, one of the deceased's sisters-in-law had entered the abandoned camp of the dead woman, transgressing the same taboo that was violated in the dream. The dreamer took this coincidence—coincidence in the sense not of chance but of reiterative action—as a warning from the spirit of her dead sister, whose passage into the realm of the Ancestral Beings would be jeopardized if such encounters continued. The target of the dream's warning was both the woman who had entered the camp and the dreamer, who interpreted the dream as a call for greater vigilance over the territorial domain of the dead sibling.

In another case, a woman dreamt of a deceased husband. Waking in a state of great agitation, she (and her siblings) immediately began to wail (*warrpakarni*) in the ritualized fashion that attends the actual death of a relative. The woman told her dream to senior kin (her husband's mother's brothers and her husband's brothers) and urged them to help interpret its implications. They, in consultation with other businesspeople of the settlement, determined that the dream of the dead husband was an indication that it was time to perform the last postfunerary ("finish-time") ceremonies terminating the taboo on widowhood (see Dussart 1989a, 1992a).

The content of nocturnal dreams of the premonitional or admonitional type is distinguishable in part by the absence of unknown or forgotten elements of the *Jukurrpa*—elements that, once retrieved, can reshape the performance of ritual. In contrast, dreams of the third and fourth categories—which I identify with some hesitation as "conceptional" and "innovative"—do contain new material: narratives unknown, dance steps configured in novel ways, designs never before seen, song texts previously unheard. Songs are especially potent markers of potential ritual significance.

Without a song text, dreamt material cannot be connected to a specific Dreaming or associated site—such is the necessity of "singing the country." Which is not to say that song texts guarantee site-specificity; the extended example of Topsy's dream, which begins in the next section, will show the opposite can be true. Nevertheless, song texts are what most instantly alert a dreamer and the dreamer's kin to a visitation of performative significance. Within nocturnal dreams of the third and forth category, there can be an absence of narrative, graphical design, or dance. Songs, however, are essential. As Wild notes, "The conclusion that the Walbiri myths are secondary elaboration of song texts seems inescapable: there may be songs without myths but not myths without songs, and whereas songs are an essential part of the ritual performance, myths are not" (1975:65).

Designs and narrative innovations that emerge without song texts do not find their way into ritual.[8] The intensity of dream discussion increases significantly when song texts emerge, foreshadowing as they do the potential of ritual performance. Whereas premonitional and admonitional dreams may confirm the power of the *Jukurrpa* by invoking the Law, material of the third and fourth categories can actually become part of the Law. The first two categories of dreams may stimulate ritual activity, whereas the latter ones, and in particular the final, "innovative" category, have the potential to "reenter" and even reshape it.

The third category of spiritually significant nocturnal activity, and one that carries a specific Warlpiri term, is the *kurruwalpa. Kurruwalpa* dreams are those dreams that identify the conception spirit of a soon-to-be-born or newborn child (Munn 1973:89–90; Glowczewski 1988:98). This is generally done through song. Though a woman carrying a child may know where she was impregnated—an important factor in the maintenance of connections between the land and people—there are times when such knowledge is difficult to obtain. In such cases, it is often a *kurruwalpa* dream that confirms the locus of conception. The information need not come from the pregnant woman herself. In fact, usually it is a close relative who dreams the song texts that help establish the site of impregnation. The father's mother, mother's mother, mother's father, father, and husband of the pregnant woman are generally the ones who have dreams that allow them to witness the locus of conception.

The dreams of the fourth category—the most powerful one, which I reluctantly call "innovative"—are generally described as *Jukurrpa-warnu* and *jalangu-warnu*. These are the nocturnal dreams that have the effect of altering Warlpiri ritual life. Such innovation can take many forms. There can be a change by way of new ownership of ritual knowledge (and concomitant rights of performance), a shift that can move across kin groups and settlements and even between the genders (the last transmission will be addressed more substantively in chapter 5). Change can also come by the reconfiguration of myth.

The nature of a dream's new or reconfigured condition is called into question because of the perceptual distinctions surrounding the innovation. The dreamers themselves, when pushed for a specific term, may call what they dream "new." But further amplification reveals that they consider the material to be retrieved or reremembered—reclaimed from the Dreaming after an unspecified time of neglect or amnesia.

Jalangu-warnu, which in its clumsy direct translation means "today belong," does not indicate that material did not belong *before*. Such dissociation would be incompatible with Warlpiri temporal sensibility in matters cosmological. The relationship between the preexisting Dreaming and the dreamer may be new. The associations (to the dreamer and later to the ceremony and the settlement)—not the ritual content—are what characterizes the innovation. And while the Warlpiri acknowledge that this configuration of the material may be new, the material itself cannot be. The "new" dreams are considered "of the Dreaming" and thus part of an immutable *Jukurrpa*. Myers provides the following explanation of paradoxical circumstance of past and present with regard to the dreams of Central Desert Aborigines: "Historical change can be integrated, but . . . it is assimilated to the preexisting forms: The foundation had always been there, but people had not known it before" (1986a:53). The content, forgotten via temporary amnesia that may be a by-product of some taboo or transgression, is thus retrieved.

This fourth category is made up of dream material emerging in nocturnal dreams that is reconfigured and redeployed in ritual. The effect of such retrieval is the reinvigoration of ceremonial activity and the residential kin competition that sustains it.

TOPSY'S DREAM

In the second year of my fieldwork, I entered the first of many notes on what I ultimately labeled "Topsy's dream" (Dussart 1992a). Subsequent reflection, however, led me to conclude the title was wrong-headed, for it obscured the process by which Topsy's ritually significant dream was retrieved, promoted, and reintegrated into Yuendumu's ritual life. It was never really Topsy's dream, at least not hers alone. It belonged as much to her siblings, and in particular to the aforementioned *yamparru* Dolly. Topsy's dream served her close kin as much as it did her. Though an early beneficiary in the ritual negotiations precipitated by the dream, Topsy never made decisions regarding its integration or use in the *Jukurrpa*. She was, or rather her dream became, a vehicle for the ongoing ritual exchange that constitutes the ritual politics of the settlement.

A dream like Topsy's was not uncommon, but access to the circumstances by which it was integrated into the ritual repertoire was. From those observations it became possible to characterize the pattern by which nocturnal dreams are folded into ceremony. The integration of a dream into the Dreaming—that crucial but little-understood shift from lowercase nighttime status to an atemporal mythological realm of ritual relevance that is considered by many businesspeople to be of capital importance—generally observes a multistep trajectory. The broad procedural moments are as follows:

1. *Visitation:* when the "new" dream is first dreamt
2. *Interpretation and recognition:* intimate discussion among the dreamer and older kin sleeping nearby to determine the dream's content and potential ritual relevance
3. *Revisitation:* subsequent dreams by the dreamer or related kin that further support and define the potential ceremonial relevance of the material (serial visitation is generally a prerequisite of a dream's ultimate performance as a Dreaming segment; single dreams almost never find expression in ritual)
4. *Reaffirmation:* a process of broader discussion (within and, at times, beyond the residential kin group with *kirda* and *kurdungurlu* for the Dreaming determined to have been invoked in the dream) that necessitates the involvement of other male and female businesspeople who may not have been present when the dream(s) were originally dreamt or discussed

5. *Ritual integration, part A—"small" performance:* a training session among residential kin that elevates the dream to the status of Dreaming segment, (usually) with a home and associated site
6. *Association/consolidation:* the process by which a particular kin group lays proprietary claim to the Dreaming segment retrieved through nocturnal visitation
7. *Ritual integration, part B—"big" performance:* performance of the dream before businesspeople outside the residential kin group (such presentations may begin at Yuendumu and then extend beyond the settlement, though that route is not obligatory)

It is at this last stage of ritual integration or "big" performance that the full power of the dream as a Dreaming segment (as well as its *kirda* and *kurdungurlu*) is made manifest, a process that reinvigorates the ritual prominence of the kin group performing it, as well as the viability of ceremonial activity in general.

So much for the schema. The actual ethnography is less clear-cut. The basic facts surrounding Topsy's dream are as follows. Topsy, a Warlpiri woman in her mid-fifties, displayed only limited interest in the ritual life of the settlement. Frequently absent from ceremonies in which kinship associations necessitated her participation, she offered a dramatic counterpoint to many of her close kin, active business leaders in Yuendumu's ceremonial life. Her husband, part Bunaba and part Warlpiri, had overcome his limited kin network to establish himself as a well-respected *yamparru.*[9] Topsy's close sisters, both *yamparru,* often earned the title of "big winners" in ceremonial gatherings. Topsy's kin group, the ritually dominant residents of the West Camp, was known for the scope and depth of its ritual knowledge. Because of Topsy's neglectfulness in ritual matters, her abuse of alcohol, and her rumored infidelities, relations between her and her residential kin were often strained. Despite periodic attempts to rein in this behavior, Topsy often succumbed to what relatives called "drinking trips."

During one such expedition to Alice Springs, her husband decided to visit his relatives at Fitzroy Crossing (Western Australia). As he was driving north, the vehicle in which he was traveling hit an embankment. The accident left him paralyzed below the waist, and his injuries were life-threatening. Worse than the accident itself was his distant hospitalization, removed from residential kin so important to the promotion of healing. When news of the misfortune reached Yuendumu, Topsy was still in Alice Springs and thus unaware of the need to perform wailing rituals, a display of grief intended to comfort the dead and the gravely ill.

Topsy's sisters and her husband's close mothers and mothers-in-law all displayed the ritualized grief, but the effectiveness was diminished by the absence of the sick person's spouse, namely, Topsy. The health of one's kin, as is the case with the health of Ancestral Beings, requires constant attention and vigilance; neglect of any kind can have adverse effects that extend to close kin and the settlement at large.

Topsy returned three days later, and upon learning of the accident, she immediately expressed grief in the appropriate manner: by wailing and by shedding her own blood.[10] Certain close relatives who were sanctioned to express their anger—siblings and spouse's siblings—directly chastised Topsy. Other members of the settlement who lacked these formal kinship ties were forced to suppress their resentment. A brother of the injured man announced his anger throughout the settlement by menacingly bearing weapons—spear throwers, spears, and boomerangs—generally reserved for declarations of conflict, anger, and grief.

The anger, whether expressed or not, was directed at Topsy's neglect both of her spouse and of ritual. To fail to attend to a waterhole can result in the source becoming undrinkable. To fail to attend to one's spouse endangers his health. The notion of "looking after"—expressed in the Warlpiri verb *jinamardarni*—applies as vigorously to people as it does to ritual, land, Ancestral Beings, and indeed the whole of the Warlpiri universe. Myers, more than any researcher working in the Central Australian Desert, has mined this notion of "relatedness" and "responsibility" (1986a).

The "responsibility," or the absence thereof, was known throughout the settlement. One month earlier Topsy had failed to attend an important conflict resolution ceremony known as *Jardiwanpa,* a ritual that would have addressed long-standing accusations of marital infidelity (as well as her neglect of her siblings). This dereliction was not invoked overtly as the cause of the accident, but Topsy's general liabilities to her kin group were mentioned repeatedly in the days following the injury. Her relatives recalled often her absence from the *Jardiwanpa* in which two Ancestral Emus ritually singe their pubic hair to atone for sexual transgression.

Faced with the injury of her husband, Topsy's first impulse was to travel to the hospital. This was thwarted by relatives, who angrily denounced any departure from Yuendumu as a violation of her spousal obligations.

In order to help her husband, relatives argued, she had to follow the prescribed proper actions of a wife whose husband is ill. This meant staying close to relatives who were strong. Without the support and surveillance of close kin, her own weak state might be exacerbated. She was counseled to stay in the settlement or risk punitive action, including sorcery by unnamed individuals who could "sing her to death" (*yarda yurnparni*).

Fearful of the wrath of her relatives, Topsy began to accept the responsibilities attendant on proper behavior of a good wife. Though her obligations required she stay at Yuendumu, she sent numerous audiotapes to her husband offering consolation and reassuring him that she "wailed" in an appropriate fashion. This in itself was enough to alert her husband of the redemptive efforts—efforts necessary to give him strength. She enlisted me to serve as technical director for these recordings; it was in this capacity that I spent a great deal of time with Topsy, and it was in this context that I was not only present but ultimately implicated in the cycle of nocturnal visitations that ended up in the ritual performance of a Dreaming.

Topsy's first nocturnal visitation of spiritual significance came two weeks after the accident. In the wake of the injury, Topsy had been on her best behavior, acting as a ritually responsible member of her residential kin group, manifesting the correct mourning behavior, sleeping in the proper configurations vis-à-vis her relatives, avoiding alcohol. On the night of her first dream, she was sleeping with her sisters, Dolly and Lucky.

The dream placed Topsy between two pieces of corrugated iron, a material commonly used to make "humpies," the poorly rigged shelters common to camp life. Sandwiched between these metal sheets, Topsy observed two young, fat Ancestral Beings, women in the guise of Emus. By their body shape, their fair hair, their shiny skin, and their demeanor, it was clear to Topsy that these two females were *Mungamunga,* Ancestral Beings specifically sanctioned to transmit crucial ritual information from the Ancestral Realm to the dreamer. The *Mungamunga,* whose visitation marked an important transmission, danced and showed off their body design on women's dancing boards (*yukurrukurru*). Other elements emerged in the dream. Two ritual poles known as *mangaya* (and subsequently identified by the Warlpiri in conversation as *nullah nullah* and *kurturu*) were planted in the ground. The female *Mungamunga* imitated the movements of Emus looking for special Emu food (which one as yet unspecified). They then approached the poles, sat down, spread their legs, and singed their pubic hair. As a marker of performative significance, the

Mungamunga sang three songs. During the songs, they uttered repeatedly the word *Wilititi* (the personal name of an Ancestral Emu), confirming that an Emu Dreaming (there are many Emu Dreamings, each with a different itinerary) had been performed. The dream was one that invoked punishment in the aftermath of transgression, that much was clear. What was not apparent was the function of these transgressive evocations of Ancestral Beings, and the ceremonies to which they were associated. (The singeing segment in the Emu Dreaming, with its social function of punishment for transgression, can be ritually evoked in many ceremonies, including *yawulyu, kurdiji,* and *Kajirri.* Actual burning, however, takes place only in conflict resolution ceremonies such as *Jardiwanpa.*)

At this point Topsy woke and began singing the songs given to her by the *Mungamunga.* This in turn woke Lucky, who asked her sister what she was singing. Topsy said that the *Mungamunga* had "given" her a *yawulyu* ceremony.[11] Lucky did not dispute this declaration. The following morning, full-scale analysis of the visitation began in earnest with her close sisters Lucky and Dolly.

The appearance of the Dream-bearing *Mungamunga* is a rare event. That Topsy further viewed these Dream-bearers reenact an Emu Dreaming for which she and her sisters were *kirda* gave almost instant legitimacy and importance to the visitation. But the real focus of excitement was on the three songs, none of which had been heard before by the sisters.

The queries from Lucky and Dolly were direct. What had Topsy seen (*nyangu*)? What had she heard (*purda-nyangu*)? From the stress attached to the verbs, it was clear the two sisters' interrogation was targeted at establishing the possible performative significance of the dream.

Further discussion ensued, though at no point did anyone question the specifics of Topsy's dream. The content was taken as is by all present, the noninvasive embrace of such dreams being the norm. In that morning's discussion, the narrative content of Topsy's dream was related to the Emu Dreaming itinerary reenacted in the *Jardiwanpa* ceremonies. No mention was made of Topsy's earlier contrary declaration that it was part of a *yawulyu* ceremony. Lucky, in particular, advocated the interpretation that linked the dream to *Jardiwanpa.* There was no need to justify the statement, for all who were present knew that the narrative content of Topsy's dream mirrored the one in the *Jardiwanpa* ceremony: a story of two male Ancestral Emus, brothers, who fight because of intense spousal and fraternal misbehavior. (The younger brother spears his married senior sibling and elopes with the widow, and both transgressors supplement their crimes by eating the killed relative. To atone for their triple transgression, the runaways undergo a cleansing ritual, after which the younger brother flies north to a place that is both sky and sea.)

However, other ceremonial resonances were clearly also present in Topsy's dream. The *Mungamunga* were generally associated not with *Jardiwanpa* but with *yawulyu,* which is what prompted Topsy's initial nocturnal assessment. Also, there was the matter of the transsexualized nature of Topsy's dream. The male emus were female in the dream. The gender switch of the emus alerted Topsy and her relatives to the importance of the dream but did not provide analytical value. Such changes are quite common in dreams and are a feature of the cross-gender transmission of ritual material, to be discussed in greater detail in chapter 5. Nevertheless, a choice had to be made between stressing the narrative components of one dream (*Jardiwanpa*) or the gender and function of Ancestral Beings who transmitted that narrative (*yawulyu*).

Evocation of two ceremonies did not present a conflict but did necessitate close analysis to establish how exactly the "new" *jalangu-warnu* material should be integrated into Yuendumu's ritual life. The message of Topsy's dream clearly established connections to the *Jardiwanpa,* whereas the messengers (the *Mungamunga*) implied association with the *yawulyu* ceremonies. Such polyvalence is a constituent component of how the Dreaming is made and remade. The term "the Law" suggests some inflexible codified guideline by which the Aboriginal world is sustained, and while the Warlpiri encourage this view of changelessness, they also recognize that no Dreaming exists without nuanced observation dependent on the capabilities of businesspeople who perpetuate its enactment. All of this should partly explain why further analysis involving close relatives of Topsy's would be needed to assess the ritual value of the dream.

Dolly had Topsy sing the three song texts that came during sleep, and retrace the body designs the Ancestral Beings had made. Topsy obliged by drawing with her middle and index finger, on Dolly's chest, the ritual design she had seen during sleep. The methods she used and the designs she drew were deemed ritually appropriate. She began by tracing three parallel lines along the length of the biceps and over each shoulder, down to the breast. These stripes marked the lower legs of the Ancestral Emu. At a spot in the middle of the sternum, Topsy then drew a circle indicating the *mangaya,* the pole in front of which the *Mungamunga* (indicated as a semicircle above the circle) singed their pubic hair. After this, she sang the three songs.[12] The new song texts, along with the new body design, signaled a potential for performative innovation, which in turn would require integration of a new Dreaming segment into the ritual repertoire (re)constituting Warlpiri cosmology.

This activity, and my presence during the discussion, sparked the interest of other female members of the residential kin group who had not slept with Topsy. They gathered to listen to Dolly's rendition of Topsy's dream. As sisters, Topsy, Dolly, and Lucky shared *kirda* rights they had all inherited through their patrilineal descent groups. These rights included the particular Emu Dreaming that Topsy dreamt. As such, Dolly had a proprietary claim further supported by her proximity to Topsy when the dream was dreamt.

Further confirmation of the importance of the Emu Dreaming came from other female members of the residential kin group. It was decided that the anthropologist present should record the three song texts, and I obliged happily. It was not Topsy who sang her own songs but Dolly, which shifted attention from one sister to the other and began to generate interest (and by implication value) outside the kin group. Concomitantly, Topsy's earlier transgressions were overshadowed by the ritual importance emerging from her dream. After the three songs were recorded, the tape was replayed to Topsy. Dolly's rendition received her sister's approval as being *junga,* that is, "correct."

Thus registered, the singing took on yet more importance. It was now clear some "new" material had been obtained and preserved in a form that could be used by Topsy and her kin.[13]

At no point in any of these discussions was the narrative content of the dream compared to the stressful circumstances that preceded it. The Western psychoanalytic logic of cause and effect, rooted in Freudian and post-Freudian supposition, was nowhere present. In fact, the association of the new material to a ritual devoted to conflict resolution or some other activity was not a factor openly (or even covertly) discussed. Topsy and her more powerful relatives were concerned with more abstract (again, to Western eyes) obligations to the Dreaming. They wanted to situate properly the *Mungamunga* message into the repertoire that made manifest the Law. Never was there any talk of processing undesirable material into desirable circumstances.

In fact, throughout the discussions of the dream, there was never any mention of the dream to the sick husband, despite Topsy's regular communication via audiotape. Connections between Topsy's transgression and a dream in which transgressive spirits atone for sexual misbehavior were never made. This was not because they were too obvious, but because no connection was conceived. I asked Topsy and various ritual leaders about this repeatedly, and all dismissed even the most causal connection. "The dream is from the Dreaming," they declared. The *Mungamunga* brought the Emu segment with its cleansing ritual to Topsy not as a specific response to her infractions. She was chosen neither by way of example nor as a rebuke.

What the *Mungamunga* did do—and here it is the anthropologist, not the Warlpiri, providing an assessment—was shift attention away from personal tribulations to matters inhabiting a ritual domain of collective importance. Topsy's dream became a form of ritual currency of as yet undetermined value, to be used by leaders as yet unidentified. How and where that currency would be employed was also open to speculation. Resolution of all these questions would require extensive negotiation that would ultimately extend the nocturnal dream far beyond Topsy's circle of close sisters.

Dolly started to promote the dream outside West Camp in the days that followed. She spoke with other *kirda* and *kurdungurlu* for the particular Emu Dreaming, some of whom belonged to her residential kin group, some not. *Yamparru,* male and female, told in great detail of the visitation, confirmed that the insertion of a new segment into the itinerary of the particular Emu Dreaming was proper. Serious consideration was given to the visitation despite Topsy's ritual neglect, for, as the ritual leaders all explained, she had inherited rights to that Dreaming from her father in patrilineal fashion (as outlined in the first chapter). As *kirda,* she was in a perfect position to serve as a vehicle for cosmological innovation. The gender switch of the Emus via the intermediary of the *Mungamunga* was never questioned.[14]

Dolly never asked whether the segment should be performed, nor did she say outright she expected to obtain the rights to ritual reenactment, but that was understood by all to be a motive behind her movements through the settlement. She had no idea at the outset if or when the songs could be sung ceremonially, or in what ritual such performance might occur. The residential kin group's campaign, spearheaded by Dolly, lasted five or six days. By the end of the first week, the details of Topsy's dream were known by all the owners and managers, men and women, of the particular Emu Dreaming. The urgency and importance of the dream gained clarification when Dolly was approached one week after the dream by the most influential male manager of the Emu Dreaming. He asked, with uncharacteristic adamancy, when "you women" would perform the "new" dream. The question had plural significances. For starters, since the inquiry was made by the most respected *kurdungurlu* of the Dreaming itinerary, it not only acknowledged but legitimated the importance of Topsy's dream. It also clarified how fluently knowledge of "innovative" dreams moves between genders and kin groups. The specific formulation of the question—the use of the "you women"—indicated that he assumed that the ritual integration would take place in a *yawulyu,* thus suspending his personal obligations to perform.

Dolly provided no specific answer to the man, nor to the anthropologist who questioned her silence. What was clear from the exchange was a sense of pressure Dolly did not appreciate. She could recognize the necessity of such reaffirmation in the abstract, but the direct confirmation by the manager also irritated her in ways I have seen repeatedly. One needs confirmation to assert control, but by possessing that control one sometimes resents the confirmation, the new obligation, the organizational responsibility.

The following night Topsy had her second dream. In it, the *Mungamunga* returned to dance around the *mangaya,* only their visitation bore additional details not seen in the first dream. One of the two *Mungamunga* was tall and blond, and the other was short, with no hair color noted. In some visitations, Ancestral Beings, and in particular the *Mungamunga,* take on the appearance of actual or close relatives of the dreamer. This did not happen during Topsy's second dream. The *Mungamunga* did transform themselves into Emus, but that was the full extent of the transmogrification. The dream offered further confirmation of the importance of the first dream, which now clearly represented the core of the Dreaming segment in formation, but offered little in the way of amplification. No new designs or songs appeared during the second dream.

The first and second dreams became the focus of intense discussion among the sisters. It was obvious to the ritual authorities present, Dolly in particular, that while there were components of the conflict resolution ceremony known as *Jardiwanpa,* the presence of the *Mungamunga* suggested that the modified *Jardiwanpa* narrative, the new songs, and the new body design should be included in a *yawulyu* ceremony. However, in this ceremony, while it would mimic in dance the purification activities found in *Jardiwanpa* (that is, the singeing of pubic hair), there would be no actual cleansing. It was on the morning after the night of the second dream that Dolly and her sisters determined that a "new" *yawulyu* should be performed. The word *new,* the lone English term used in talks conducted in Warlpiri, only heightened the foreign, novel quotient of the dreams Topsy had dreamt.

One month after the accident Topsy had her third dream. This one not only confirmed the first two but added new details. The *Mungamunga* provided Topsy yet another song (the fourth) and told her that this particular song had to be sung while the purification ritual was being danced.

The next morning, Topsy, now actively involved in the ritual activities of her kin group, immediately sang the song to Dolly, who recorded it with even greater urgency than she had the first three songs.

By this point, the residential kin group had pulled itself out of the mourning state precipitated by the accident, even though Topsy's husband was still gravely injured. The discussions surrounding the novel dreams very clearly relieved the stress prompted by the accident, and diminished the bitterness of the relatives who had so publicly excoriated Topsy earlier. Further proof of Topsy's reintegration into ritual life came when her dream migrated beyond her sleeping quarters to another sister—an old, erstwhile ritual leader with *kirda* rights to the Emu Dreaming. The older sister, a Nampijinpa whose subsequent death prevents specific identification, dreamt the next installment of Topsy's dream.

Much of the fourth dream replicated the content of the previous three. The *Mungamunga* came and sang the same songs Topsy had heard. But additional material was provided. The two Emus, who in all of Topsy's dreams had been looking for special Emu food, in the fourth dream found and ate some of that food, though again, which kind was never specified. Also added to the ritual material was further detail regarding the appearance of one of the Emus, who resembled Dolly. The inclusion of Dolly in the nocturnal dream was deemed appropriate given her relationship to the Dreaming and her role in its promotion. Details common to the *Jardiwanpa* narrative but absent from Topsy's three dreams also emerged in the dream of the old Nampijinpa. She could see Dolly flying through the sky and entering an unnamed place thousands of kilometers north of Yuendumu in a location above Darwin that is both the sky and the sea.

More discussion ensued, only now it was taking place among a much larger network of residential kin. All agreed that Topsy's three dreams and the dream of her sister necessitated performance.

At this point, Topsy received the qualified approval of her relatives to visit her injured husband. Topsy left the camp the day after the fourth dream emerged. It would be wrong to assume that nocturnal transfer was the motive force behind her relatives' approval of Topsy's departure. They agreed to the trip not because of the dreams' relocation, but rather because of Topsy's proper behavior, including her avoidance of transgressive acts such as drinking. In other words, the ritual material she dreamt was not the focal point of her relatives' willingness to let her go.

That afternoon, Dolly began in earnest the preparations for ritual reenactment. To that end, she convinced the older ritual leader who had dreamt the fourth dream to help her gather various *kirda* and *kurdungurlu* from among their residential kin group. When these women, nine in number, were assembled in a shady spot of West Camp, Dolly oversaw the performance of a "small" *yawulyu*. The diminutive term marks the residential exclusivity of the event. "Small" *yawulyu* often serve as practice sessions in which ritual songs and designs are acquired without the supplemental obligations of dance. The specificity of "small" *yawulyu* performances to a particular camp offers a context in which a great deal of ritual knowledge is exchanged, some of which may not even be directly associated with the event undertaken. Generally, a minimum of two or three such sessions is needed to train the kin who will ultimately combine song, dance, and painting in a "big" performance. "Small" ceremonies, with their intimate relationships of the participants, tend to consolidate the cohesion of a camp, though this is not to say that the sessions are free of tension.

Dolly dominated the afternoon's proceedings, in part because of her singular handle on replication of the body design, songs, and narrative needed to be taught and understood. Since she alone had a close association with the dreamer who dreamt the body design—Topsy being absent from the event—and had been the one who most vigorously promoted its reenactment, Dolly was the undisputed leader of the training session, at least at the outset. During the gathering, she sang the four songs slowly. As she did, certain women present, who possessed a *kurdungurlu* relationship to the material, removed their shirts and brassieres and had their torsos painted by Dolly.

Dolly focused her painting of the design on managers because she felt comfortable controlling the *kirda* responsibilities that would arise in larger ceremonial contexts. The other *kirda* present, who had joint responsibilities for whatever might be performed, shared this comfort and so endorsed her position—a position of leadership that diminished the stresses they might otherwise feel.

Willingness to be painted was a forceful indication of the residential commitment to the ritual innovation. In this particular ceremony, five of the nine women accepted application of the natural pigments Dolly brought to the shady spot. Among those painted was an individual outside the pool of *kirda* and *kurdungurlu* (a *wurruru,* that is, a woman from the other patricouple within Dolly's patrimoiety) whose corporeal acceptance of the designs implicitly reinforced the significance of the Dreaming. To request the application of a body design from a member of an opposing patricouple expressed belief in the events replicated and in the authority of the business leaders providing the songs, narrative, and design.

There were other indications of the validity and importance of the Emu Dreaming now starting to find its way into the ceremonial life of the settlement. Many of those who had gathered were owners and managers of the Emu Dreaming segment by both patrilineal and classificatory association. In this sense, the event satisfied traditional inheritance-based patterns of ritual acquisition and the patterns that emerged from residential habitation.

As Dolly painted and sang, all the women focused attention on her renditions. The songs cannot be transcribed in print because of ritual restriction. The body design, however, absent vocal accompaniment, may be reproduced without offense.[15] The same design appeared on the chests of all five women.

Dolly painted her relatives with confidence and without interruption, which is not to say that the moment was free from stress. The act of painting a body design should, if properly and beautifully executed, prompt the participants to offer praise. *Marrka* is the term used by both women and men to endorse the virtues of a painter's work.

As Dolly applied the pigment, she sang, over and over, the songs her absent sister had heard. She also retold a version of the narrative combining elements of Topsy's three dreams and the fourth from the old Nampijinpa: The Ancestral Emus foraged for food, and they found food—though again, what type was never made clear, at least not yet. After the food was found, the Emus performed the cleansing ceremony in which they singed their pubic hair. This repetition of the songs and narrative took on a distinctly didactic tone, with Dolly stopping now and then to

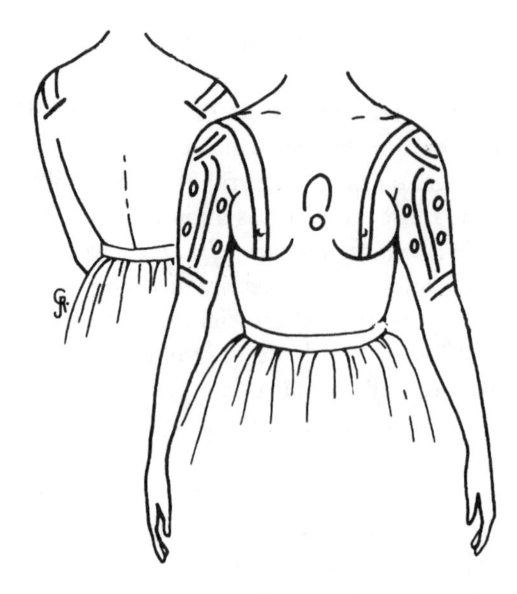

Figure 4. Body design established during first "small" *yawulyu*

correct the repetitions of the other singers. Not all of the songs and narrative had direct connection to the modified design she composed, which contained iconic components that referenced other segments of the Emu Dreaming not directly acknowledged.

Even the most cursory comparison of this "small" *yawulyu* body design and the one previously presented by Topsy evinces similarity and variation. The second design included the circle and semicircle located above the solar plexus, the same iconic representations of the Ancestral Emus (the *Mungamunga*) and the cleansing pole (*mangaya*) that Topsy had seen in her first dream. Other elements of Dolly's design were different. The three parallel stripes that appeared on the biceps, shoulder, and breast were reduced to two and included a single scapular crossbar that ended the movement representing the lower legs of the Emus. When I asked about these differences, Dolly matter-of-factly responded that the modification of the stripes was not different at all, a paradox often encountered in the aesthetic system of the Warlpiri.[16] Additional crossbars, paired, appeared at the bottom and top of the arm stripes, which also represented the Emus' lower legs. Around each of the arm stripes Dolly drew four circles. These circles, she explained, represented the Ancestral Emu eggs lying in the ground—the eggs were *kurruwalpa* conception spirits. Dolly said no more about this sudden inclusion of conception spirits—spirits that had never before been mentioned in this cycle of nocturnal dreams. Nor did any of the women present ask her about these new elements. It is possible to hypothesize that the connection is the graphical similarities of this design with a design commonly painted during *Jardiwanpa* ceremonies.[17] An alternative explanation is that evocation of the conception spirits is a less narrative-specific confirmation of the fertility of the Ancestral Emus central to the Dreaming. But both these explanations inhabit the realm of the speculative, since neither Dolly nor any of the other participants chose to offer any further clarification. A good portion of the narrative implied by the design existed outside the song and narrative actually presented.

From the very beginning, when Topsy first told Dolly of her dream, no one had challenged either the interpretations or the ritual significance Dolly had claimed. The contents of the dreams, and their relationships to the dreamer and her kin, were all deemed legitimate. And that legitimacy, although never authorized in any formal way (that is, through ceremony), was endorsed by the acceptance of those who were told of its appearance. This support continued through the entire performance of the initial "small" *yawulyu.* The first hint of the truly competitive nature of ritual life came after the event was complete, when a *yamparru* present but silent throughout the event expressed serious doubts about the veracity of both the songs and the designs.

Once the painting and singing had ended, Maggie Napanangka, a classificatory daughter to Dolly, stood up and angrily denounced her mother's activities. She said Dolly had not sung the songs correctly, and that the design painted on the bodies of the five women was "wrong." She had never seen the design before, and such ignorance was incompatible, she argued, with her status as a principal *kurdungurlu* for the Emu Dreaming Dolly had just evoked in the "small" *yawulyu.* Dolly countered this attack by reiterating that the nocturnal visitation of the *Mungamunga* had brought her sisters, Topsy and the old Nampijinpa, forgotten designs and songs. Though Dolly never directly disputed Maggie's attack, she said that the stories in the dreams had been forgotten. In this way, she was asking Maggie to suspend her doubts. The *Mungamunga,* in their role as intermediary purveyors of forgotten myth, could legitimate both Dolly's performance and Maggie's ignorance. Dolly then sang the most potent song in the cycle, and by way of confirming her ritual authority, all the other women present, Maggie excepted, joined in. At that point, Maggie fled the shady spot in West Camp, shouting that her kin group had failed to follow the Law and that they were treating the *Jukurrpa* and its reenactment as a kind of "game" (*manyuku*). Dolly responded with equal vehemence that the *Mungamunga* had entrusted the ceremonial activity to the dreamers so that forgotten knowledge could be revived through performance.

Angered by Maggie's challenge, Dolly attempted to legitimate further her status as a *yamparru* by asking those still present to dance. This request was rebuffed. The rejection served many functions. It tempered a tension-filled dynamic within the residential kin group and reined in Dolly's ritual domination. Sensing she had pushed too far, Dolly quickly acquiesced; she decided it was better to suspend the dispute, since personalized assault of any kind would most certainly threaten the well-being of the disputants and their relatives. Since the disputants were themselves closely related, the possibility of sickness emerging from such inappropriate behavior would be intensified.

By this point three issues already troubled me. First, it seemed odd that on the day Topsy's dream was finally starting to enter the ceremonial sphere, Topsy herself was not present. I interrogated numerous participants in the "small" *yawulyu* about this, and they all provided the same explanation, puzzled by my confusion. Topsy's direct involvement was not necessary, since ownership of the dreams was shared with the sisters who were overseeing the event, in this case, Dolly. All *kirda* for the Emu Dreaming being reenacted (and that very clearly included Dolly) had rights over the segment regardless of the source of the innovation. Topsy, to be sure, was the "main" dreamer, but that title carried with it no obligation in the performative sphere. Other members of her patrigroup could satisfy the ritual obligations of the material she had dreamt.

The second question concerned the ceremony performed. Why would a narrative so obviously connected to a conflict resolution *Jardiwanpa* find enactment instead in a "small" *yawulyu* ritual intended to imbue those implicated with a sense of well-being?[18] What emerges from participant observation is an awareness that the relationship between Dreaming segments—in this case an episode previously associated with *Jardiwanpa*—and the ceremonies in which such segments find enactment is never static. However, new content cannot be injected into rituals, such as *Jardiwanpa,* that are already highly structured, since such modification might jeopardize the immutability of the *Jukurrpa.*[19] Presumption of cosmic changelessness demands that the "new" must be integrated into ritual in an innovative way. The Warlpiri explained that there would be no point in situating the refashioned, gender-shifted actions of the (now) female Emus into the old *Jardiwanpa* because it would duplicate a cleansing act in a ritual that already had a cleansing act. This "new" material thus required a new ritual context if the potency of the *Jukurrpa* was to be diffused. Which is not to say that the message contained in songs and designs (that is, the act of purification in the aftermath of transgression) must be employed in specific ceremonies that necessitate such a message being invoked. The "new" material, as ritual currency, can be spent in any ceremony as long as it does not overtly challenge preexisting rituals and as long as the spender (that is, the *yamparru* controlling the performance of the innovative material) has the support of other businesspeople present. In short, the integration of reclaimed narratives, songs, and designs in ritual generally has less to do with the declared function of ritual than it does with the extraceremonial politics surrounding ritual events. To reiterate: It was not the message contained in the ritual or its specific function vis-à-vis the *Jukurrpa* but the employment of the ritual currency at a specific juncture of residential and settlement dynamics that would determine ceremonial selection.

The third problem was the absence of a site to which the new segment would be anchored. In model explanations of the *Jukurrpa,* the Ancestral Beings travel along itineraries with segments that are associated with geospecific locations. But in this "new" segment, no such site was declared. In their discussions of the various dreams, none of the individuals implicated in the reclamation of the forgotten material ever mentioned a ritual location. When I asked about the viability of a free-floating segment dissociated from the terrain that makes up the *Jukurrpa,* they all said that what mattered was the legitimacy of the material's message and the proprietary relationship of that material to the dreamers. In other words, the question of sitelessness could be avoided. A partial explanation was provided by noting that certain kinds of Dreaming segments are part of itineraries that are so long and so territorially attenuated that uncovering a site at which to anchor the Dreaming can be elusive. Such was the case of the Emu segment that Topsy's dreams invoked. The itinerary to which it was associated conjoined mythological terrains of various settlements and various peoples, which meant it had the potential to implicate not only Topsy's residential kin group, but many other Warlpiri and other groups beyond Yuendumu as well. It is here that politics, endorsed by the silence of the Ancestral Beings on the matter of site association, comes into play. The selection of a specific site might well have diminished the intersettlement value of performance and the ritual status attendant on that performance. This fact was never stated explicitly, but in their conversations, the

Warlpiri women who were promoting this segment chose to deflect discussion away from the absence of territorial specificity and emphasize instead the narrative value of a cleansing ceremony known throughout the region.

In short, ceremonial and site association, elements of *Jukurrpa* I had previously taken to be essential and obligatory to establish legitimacy, appeared open to the political needs of the individuals and the groups promoting "new" material, a flexibility that forced me to begin to reevaluate the structural givens of ritual. The checklist, it seemed, was modified when the dreams that were dreamt were "new." When such dreams occurred, the associations created were to the dreamers and their kin rather than to sites and ceremonies.

In the wake of the first "small" *yawulyu,* Dolly's nocturnal life helped to strengthen further the controversial claims she had made during the ritual practice. One week after the fight, Dolly herself began to have ceremonially significant dreams: one dream, then another, then a third.

The first of Dolly's dreams corroborated the modified designs she had painted on the bodies of her kin one week before. Specifically, the dreams presented the two *Mungamunga*—again, in the form of female Emus—looking for food, much as they had in earlier installments. Only this time, the specific food, a berry known as *murnturru,* was mentioned in the dream.[20] The *Mungamunga* went on to retrace in Dolly's dream the contested design Dolly herself had painted while she was awake and overseeing the "small" *yawulyu,* all the while singing the four songs dreamt by Topsy and a "new" one she heard in her dream. In the conversations that followed the first of Dolly's dreams, no one questioned the coincidence of a graphic innovation finding subsequent corroboration in a nocturnal visit of the *Mungamunga.*

For the Western observer faced with the coincidental emergence in dreams of information personally beneficial to the dreamer, it is all too easy to hypothesize an outright falsification (or an unconscious legitimation) of the origins of the dream's content. Such logic runs totally counter to the perceptual framework of the Warlpiri. So important and so potent is the *Jukurrpa* (and this includes the elements of the Dreaming that appear during sleep) that changing any part risks the most serious punishment for transgression: death. Anyone who has worked with the Warlpiri on land claims will know that self-interest rarely, if ever, allows even the slightest modification of how the Dreaming is perceived. Conscious manipulations of the Law are not only unacceptable, they are inconceivable. Dolly's status as a *yamparru* in no way bolstered the legitimacy of the visitation (such bolstering was not necessary), but her analysis was supported by her kin.

Her second dream fleshed out other elements of the reintroduced Dreaming by reaffirming components of the narrative previously established, and adding to it specific dance steps that would have ceremonial value if and when the material was performed. The *Mungamunga,* after presenting their now well-known songs dreamt by Topsy, sang another new one and performed additional dances, and then did what they had done in the old Nampijinpa's dream: flew north toward Darwin and disappeared in that place that is both sea and sky. The second dream in effect consolidated Dolly's near-exclusive control over the material. She had claimed the narrative, four songs, and the design from a sister (at that point living outside Yuendumu), obtained more material from another sister—the old Nampijinpa—and was now given dance steps directly from the Ancestral Beings themselves.

The third dream was perhaps the most politically powerful, for it suddenly clarified where and when all the previous installments—not just those of Dolly's dreams, but those of the old Nampijinpa and Topsy as well—would ultimately find their first formal reenactment. The third dream again had the *Mungamunga* doing what *Mungamunga* do: dancing their special Emu dance, singing another song, and foraging for food. This time, however, close observation revealed that one of these Ancestral Beings was Dolly herself and that her performance was attended by residents of Yuendumu and Lajamanu. Thus Dolly had a dream that foretold the dream's ceremonial value and the context, as well as the narrative starting and stopping points. This last of Dolly's dreams traced the travels of the Ancestral Beings from their initial search for Emu food all the way until they entered a place that was both sky and water. It also alerted Dolly and her kin to the urgency of ceremonial reenactment. To dream of a ritual performance necessitates the reenactment of that ritual, and as such, Dolly's third dream reflected the admonitional dimension of the Warlpiri's nocturnal dream life, within the context of innovated dreams.

The sudden identification of Yuendumu and Lajamanu was obvious to all those Dolly informed of the dream. It was known throughout the settlement that Lajamanu residents would shortly be traveling to Yuendumu. Their purpose was to pick up ritual performers with whom they would present a large-scale cycle of initiation ceremonies, known as *Kajirri,* to various non-Warlpiri groups. Jointly undertaken by both Warlpiri men and women from the two settlements invoked in Dolly's dream, the *Kajirri* were to be held at Docker River, a third settlement to the south of the other two (see map 1). The evocation of Lajamanu and Yuendumu people in the dream was a direct indicator of the context in which the new material could be performed. Dolly and those around her knew that the Dreaming segment of the Emu, in its reworked state, might well find insertion within the *Kajirri* cycle. Nothing was definite, since the decision to perform requires careful calculation of both the internal and inter-settlement politics that are the subtext of all ritual activity. However, there was a good chance that Docker River might provide the context in which to satisfy the performative obligations that Dolly's third dream specified.

All this precipitated a great deal of discussion not just among the women who participated in the first "small" *yawulyu,* but among their male relatives as well. Dolly expanded her campaign. Enlisting three of her actual sisters, she spread the news of the third dream and the Dreaming performance necessitated by the ritual invoked in it. The four sisters told their male relatives—actual, close, and classificatory fathers, elder brothers, and brothers' children, as well as uninformed father's sisters and cross-cousins. In her capacity as a hardworking businesswoman, she made sure that all those who possessed either ownership of or a managerial relationship to the Emu Dreaming would be personally alerted to developments and obligations that were an outgrowth of her serialized visitations. By doing so she situated herself in a position of authority within her residential kin group and placed her kin group in a position of authority vis-à-vis the settlement. "We have to keep this Dreaming. We cannot forget it again," Dolly and her sisters emphasized after telling the story of the female Emus' travels. Dolly was very clear and direct in her claims. She and the rest of the businesspeople responsible for the Dreaming were obliged to be vigilant, and the vigilance meant the ritual would have to be performed.

The collective impact of the three dreams validated Dolly's control of the Dreaming material but did not guarantee performance. Further training would be required. To that end, Dolly organized a second *yawulyu,* this time including *kirda* and *kurdungurlu* outside her residential kin group.

The mood was charged. Maggie, the challenger at the previous training session, was one of the first to arrive, an indication that some form of rapprochement between classificatory mother and daughter had been achieved since the first training session. Dolly initiated the session by announcing that she would teach a close daughter of Maggie's, a woman named Long Maggie Nakamarra, how to apply the innovated design. This served as a concession to Maggie by acknowledging that legitimacy of the design (and related songs) should receive the approval of other businesswomen. The intimate relationship between Long Maggie and Maggie, as well as the newly dreamt material Dolly now presented, enabled the earlier conflicts to be suspended. There was no overt recognition of concession on either side. No discussion preceded the inclusion of the second businesswoman in the painting that took place in the second "small" event. Both Dolly's dream life and politicking in the days following the last event (from which she received the support of relatives) necessitated a change in Maggie's disputatious attitude. In both social and ritual senses, Maggie changed her tune; she willingly sang the songs she previously had ignored, and allowed her breasts to be painted with the "forgotten" and now revived design. Thus classificatory parent and child, who were also *kirda* and *kurdungurlu,* were reunited and the ritual strength of their residential kin group was reconfirmed. It was clear to those present that the "new" Dreaming had been legitimated for imminent use in a more formal context. And though it was by no means guaranteed, most of those present at this second training session assumed that this context would be Docker River. By the time Dolly, with the assistance of Long Maggie, finished painting the body design on Maggie's upper torso, Maggie further confirmed the "correctness" she had previously questioned by noting that she could now feel the "life forces" of the Emu permeating her body, a sure sign of proper design promoting proper enactment.

The second session, like the first, lasted almost two hours, during which time Dolly's stress visibly diminished. Potency and legitimacy are additive. The more *yamparru* willing to perform a segment or sing a song, the more correct it is, and thus the more powerful it becomes. All those present sang the songs previously dreamt: the four that came from Topsy's dreams, and the two that came from Dolly's.

Still, conflict did emerge. In much the same fashion as in the first training session, the second witnessed a direct challenge after all ritual activities were complete. This time, a classificatory sister-in-law to Dolly stood up and objected. Like Maggie before her, this woman had a *kurdungurlu* relationship to the segment. Her rebuke was almost identical to that of Maggie's earlier (now unmentioned) complaint, and so was the timing.

Ritual activity is too potent to be interrupted, which is why ritual participants tend to raise their objections either before or after performance. It is generally in pre- and postceremonial activity that struggles take place. Argument swirls around performance, not in it, since the material content is too powerful to risk declaring impropriety simultaneous with presentation.

The reestablished design and songs were "not really from the Dreaming," the sister-in-law declared with the curtness that often attends such disputes. Though she had the proper managerial relationship to the material to raise the objections she did, her criticisms were ignored by Dolly and the rest of the ritual participants. The reason: The woman lacked the ritual authority to make such overt challenges. Whereas in the earlier conflict Dolly had felt compelled to defend herself and the Dreaming, this new assault, lacking as it did the force of ritual respect, failed to warrant a response. Soon after, all the ritual participants replaced their brassieres and T-shirts and thus marked the end of the event.

If the challenges were stressful at the two training sessions, they only increased as the scope and stakes of the formal enactment grew. The Docker River rendezvous was scheduled three weeks after the second training session. Had all gone according to the admonitional imperatives of Dolly's third dream, the Dreaming segment would have been presented formally as part of the "big" ceremonies held at Docker River, where the people of Lajamanu and Yuendumu would gather to perform. But as so often happens in the ritual life of the Central Australian Desert—especially when that ritual life brings together Aboriginal peoples from different settlements and different linguistic groups (Warlpiri, Pintupi, Luritja, Pitjantjatjara, Anmatyerre)—little went as planned. When the *yamparru* from Lajamanu arrived at Yuendumu and began various preceremonial discussions, conflicts between the Warlpiri businesspeople of the two settlements quickly surfaced. At issue was what portion of the *Kajirri* cycle should be performed, and by implication (though that implication was only obliquely expressed) who should control that performance. A divisive, even rancorous, argument broke out. Tempers flared. It had been the intention of ritual leaders from both Lajamanu and Yuendumu to present jointly portions of the *Kajirri* owned collectively by the Warlpiri. This performance would have presented some ritual knowledge unknown to the non-Warlpiri and sanctioned its recirculation in subsequent rituals. In exchange, the Warlpiri would receive similar rights to Dreaming itineraries that crisscrossed lands outside their ritual domain.

In this way, the Docker River rendezvous was intended both to elongate and to intensify knowledge of ritual travels undertaken by the Ancestral Beings of the whole region. When the Warlpiri were unable to reach a compromise over the specifics of the presentation, many of Yuendumu's most powerful *yamparru* decided to forgo the trip. Only a handful of Yuendumu's Warlpiri joined the caravan as it moved south. Eight women and four men chose to be present at the "big" events. Included in the group was Dolly. The trip was from the start perceived to be risky. As has been stated in other contexts, ritual protection emerges when the Warlpiri stay together. That there were only twelve Yuendumu Warlpiri, in the context of ceremonial events in which hundreds of businesspeople (Lajamanu Warlpiri as well as ritual participants from other non-Warlpiri settlements) would perform, threatened the potency of the material presented, and by implication their standing as ritual leaders at Yuendumu. The events would take place far from Warlpiri homes and sites, far away from kin. The same cautionary declarations Topsy had faced when she first expressed interest in seeing her ill husband were now invoked when Dolly and the other eleven expressed their intention to attend. There were other risks Dolly accepted by attending the events. The gross gender imbalance meant the relative success and failures that came with participation would fall squarely on the women, since they represented the majority of the Yuendumu travelers. Dolly's senior position, enhanced (and put in jeopardy) by her decision to go, was further enhanced by a linguistic capacity that made her indispensable to all the Warlpiri women (both from Yuendumu and Lajamanu), namely, her ability to speak Pitjantjatjara, a language understood by most of the non-Warlpiri attending the Docker River events. As Dolly left, it was clear to all that she would represent (or misrepresent) the interests of her residential kin group and indeed all Warlpiri participants when the ceremonies began.

The Docker River delegation from Yuendumu included Dolly, four of her sisters (though not Topsy), a sister-in-law, and two classificatory daughters, including Maggie. As such, Dolly had the necessary owner-manager relationship to present certain (but not all) portions of the "new" Dreaming as it had been constituted at the second "small" *yawulyu*. They were not, however, able to participate as actively as they had hoped in the *Kajirri* cycle that was the inspiration for the gathering.

For three days and nights Dolly and her residential kin group served as the dutiful assistants to the more dominant Lajamanu Warlpiri as they sang, danced, and painted their itineraries to the hundreds who were present. During this time, Dolly muted her ritual knowledge, fearful of both clashing with the Warlpiri of the other settlement and offending those relatives who had chosen to stay behind.

On the last afternoon of the ceremonies Dolly tracked down three Pitjantjatjara women with whom she had exchanged knowledge seven months prior, and offered to paint their bodies with what she called "our group's Emu Dreaming" (*Yankirri Jukurrpa, warlaja-nyani*). The three women, classificatory sisters to Dolly and thus ideal candidates for ongoing ritual exchange, immediately accepted. Dolly painted the women that afternoon, sang all six of the songs flawlessly, and ended the preparation by stating that the dances would be shown that evening, when all the ritual participants would be gathered.

For the actual "big" performance, Dolly was accompanied by her sister Judy, whose ritual life cycle was outlined in the previous chapter. At no point then or subsequently did Dolly or her siblings mention that the material was "new." In fact, none of the nocturnal origins of the Emu segment was discussed.

Whereas Dolly had been nearly silent and protective in the early gatherings, in this performance she displayed the confidence of a *yamparru* well in control of material she knew would not be challenged.

The performance began with two Napanangka sisters (including the once disputatious Maggie) in the role of *kurdungurlu* planting two *nullah nullah* in the ground and singing while the *kirda* performed. The wooden poles (linked by hair strings that serve as part of the *Kajirri* cycle, signifying spiritual potency) marked the locus of the cleansing ceremony undertaken by the transgressive Emus. This cleansing dance was performed by Dolly and her sister Judy, who mimicked with noteworthy precision the dance of the Ancestral Beings. All the Warlpiri sisters sang.

The performance lasted only five minutes. In that time all six songs were sung, the design was displayed to all viewers, and the dance steps Dolly learned in her dream found ceremonial expression before an audience of nearly three hundred Central Desert Aborigines. No spoken narrative was presented, but the songs and the dance provided the ritually significant elements of innovated *Jukurrpa*.

"Ancestral Emus are looking for food" was the message the first sung text conveyed; this was the song Topsy heard in her first dream and which was heard again by the old Nampijinpa.[21] The number of Emus was never specified but was clear to all those watching the event, since Dolly and Judy danced as Ancestral Emus dance. The second and third songs performed had initially emerged respectively during Topsy's and Dolly's first nocturnal dreams. "Ancestral Emus eat Emu food" was the message of the second song presented at Docker River; "Ancestral Emus approaching the *mangaya*" was the message of the third song.[22] The fourth and fifth songs, which employ the word *Wilititi* in sacred syntax that cannot be reproduced in print, announced that the Emus spread their legs and singed their pubic hair to atone for sexual transgression. Both of these songs had initially been dreamt by Topsy. The final song presented was also the final song dreamt by Dolly, and it tracked the travels of the *Mungamunga* as they made their way up north to a place that was both the sky and the sea. And with that, four months of negotiation and competition found expression in a formal, intersettlement context. Because non-Warlpiri with classificatorily suitable connections had participated in the event, legitimate channels of intergroup transmission (in this case between the Warlpiri of Yuendumu and the Pitjantjatjara attending the Docker River event) had been opened.

The Dreaming segment could subsequently be inserted into the ritual performances of the Pitjantjatjara; the painted women could legitimately transmit the knowledge they had acquired at Docker River to their close kin, who in turn could perform while bearing these designs. Subsequent encounters with these Pitjantjatjara women confirmed that the designs were very much part of their ritual life, though the details of that integration were never spelled out.[23]

The involvement of the Pitjantjatjara women also validated Dolly's struggle to establish the veracity of the plurally dreamt Dreaming segment. In short, what the exchange at Docker River showed was that prestige comes not only with the acquisition of someone else's knowledge but through the acceptance by others of one's own.

The full extent of the personal and residential benefits of Dolly's decision to perform at Docker River and other events was not immediately obvious—such benefits rarely are. Ritual "winning" tends to be confirmed and consolidated slowly, compounding over time. The Warlpiri from both Lajamanu and Yuendumu noted that the performance was "entertaining" (*manyu-ku*), but its ritual value vis-à-vis Warlpiri ceremonial life was never addressed. There was no talk at the moment of a "big" victory.

For currency to have value it must be exchanged.[24] That exchange continued to occur. The Yuendumu and Pitjantjatjara women gathered a few months later in a more intimate context, and in this context Dolly provided additional ritual information that she had held back in the more combative context of Docker River. She mentioned for the first time to other non-Warlpiri that this Dreaming segment, with its designs, dances, and songs, had its origins in the dreams of her sister Topsy. They accepted this explanation as legitimate because of Dolly's relationship to Topsy and Topsy's *kirda*-ship over the Dreaming.

In the months ahead a consensus emerged regarding Docker River. There was general agreement among ritual leaders that despite their minority status at the *Kajirri,* the Warlpiri businesswomen of Yuendumu proved to be the most successful performers. Pitjantjatjara and Warlpiri (from both Yuendumu and Lajamanu) all recalled the events of the final night, when the Yuendumu mob attracted the attention of all convened.

A dream initially associated with the narrative evoked in *Jardiwanpa* ceremonies was subsequently taught to various *yamparru* in a "small" *yawulyu* session, preparation for more formal presentation in the *Kajirri* cycle transacted at Docker River. The ceremonial adaptation did not stop there, however. The Emu segment resurfaced in conflict resolution ceremonies (*Jardiwanpa*) and initiation cycles of various kinds, including *Kajirri* and *kurdiji.*

The combination of components (narrative, song, design, dance) were never replicated in the same way in different ceremonies, since the Law prevents such overt modification of what is by definition immutable. In performative terms, the six songs were sung only during the *Kajirri;* however, they also were invoked in the preperformance painting that attended *Jardiwanpa* and *kurdiji* events. As for the story of the two female Emus cleansing themselves in the wake of transgression, it became a variable feature of both ceremonial and nonceremonial narrations. A similar adaptive diffusion accompanied the design that Topsy dreamt and Dolly "modified." It underwent further modifications, but again, these modifications were deemed inconsequential by the overseers of that design.

One element present in all ceremonial contexts in which the Emu segment was invoked (in whatever fashion) was its early and most staunch advocate: Dolly. The Emu segment ultimately became hers in all but name, a kind of property without title, coin not of one realm but of many, a currency that only she and other *kirda* could exchange. And by teaching her knowledge to other Warlpiri and non-Warlpiri, Dolly ensured that the segment would survive her. Still, was it only Dolly's to use as she wished? No. For Dolly to use that currency she needed (and would always need) the sanction of others. When she performed she did so at many levels, individual and social. The spirit of "relatedness"—found in the painting of an acrylic canvas or the distribution of kangaroo meat—is rooted, too, in the labored negotiation of dreams that become Dreaming segments, a move that enables nocturnal visitation to enter the realm of ritual.

It was not the possession of this segment but the ability to use it that manifested Dolly's strength as a businesswoman. That strength came, as it must always come, in her ability to negotiate with the others in her residential kin group, and in their subsequent ability to negotiate with other groups.

CONCLUSION

Topsy's dream, as I have taken pains to show, was not Topsy's alone. Nor was it Dolly's. It was a commodity jointly held, if not jointly controlled. There could never be any explicit territorial or proprietary claims made over a nocturnal dream and its ritual reenactment. The material pieced together from the dreams of West Camp ultimately entered the general cosmology of the Dreaming, circulating in and around the kin group, the settlement, and the region. To this day, the story of the female Emus, their search for food, and the cleansing ceremony that followed is told often in casual, nonceremonial contexts. Circulation means life, be it in blood, in banking, in the ritual objects of its active participants, or in the ritual currency of its business leaders.

That fact seems far more important now than the questions I attempted to pose early on, focusing as I did on issues of "inconsistency" and "mutability," the narrative and psychic utility of nocturnal dreams, and the discrepancies between the template of the Dreaming and the facts fieldwork provided.

Was the Dreaming immutable? It was clear that "new" material was being inserted into Dreamings. Or was that, in fact, clear? For the dreamers, the elements that came to Topsy and her sisters were more accurately reconfigured components of past, preexisting Dreamings and did not challenge the unchanging nature of the *Jukurrpa*. For the Warlpiri such temporal distinctions of "new" and "old, "past" and "present" are of little utility. Dolly and the other *yamparru* of Yuendumu saw in their dreams the material that is the Law and that which is not. That which is happens also to have been, and no doubt will be. The expression of the reality of the Dreaming may be modified because of what is forgotten and retrieved, but the reality of the *Jukurrpa* does not appear to change (see Myers 1986a:53ff.).

Did Topsy's dream serve a personal function? Topsy may or may not have had her transgressive dream because of the social pressures and sense of censure she felt upon learning of her husband's car accident. His injuries, which ultimately proved fatal, confirmed the neglectful nature of his wife. But the transgressive dimension of the dream was quickly subsumed by larger, social concerns. The ritual leaders to whom she was related very quickly forgot, if indeed they ever recognized, the tragic events contemporaneous with the innovative dreams. The dream, in the end, had little to do with Topsy, and she, in the end, had little to do with the ceremonies it precipitated.

My efforts to establish the connection between the narrative content of dreams and ceremonies were also misplaced. To the question of what the connections are between the function of ritual and the narrative content of the dreams they enact, the answer is that there is very little connection. As I hope I have shown, ceremonial selection has not much to do with the stories in the dreams or even the rituals initially associated with those dreams. The choice of what ceremony is used combines unspoken elements of political calculation that must coincide with cosmological sanction. The Dreaming segment that was so laboriously reclaimed, reworked, and reestablished could have been (and indeed was) invoked in any number of ceremonies. What mattered was not in which ceremony it was invoked but how and why it was used as a declaration of ritual competence in an arena of social exchange. Dolly used the material in the *Kajirri* to consolidate her status as a *yamparru* vis-à-vis other leaders of her residential kin group (Maggie, for example), vis-à-vis leaders outside her kin group (all those Yuendumu Warlpiri who had argued against traveling to Docker River), and vis-à-vis the Warlpiri from other settlements (the Lajamanu *yamparru* who outnumbered their Warlpiri counterparts at Docker River events).

The six songs, one design, series of dances, and story were the trump cards Dolly used to achieve her "big" win. But "trump card" is perhaps the wrong metaphor, for one does not make, nurture, negotiate, and fight for a trump card the way Dolly made, nurtured, negotiated, and fought to perform at Docker River. Where the analogy is apt is in the manner with which Dolly could play the knowledge she had acquired. It is important to note another limitation of the ever-present vocabulary of value: Ritual currency cannot be spent down. In fact, the more it is used, the more valuable it becomes. To keep one's ritual knowledge to oneself is to diminish the force of that knowledge. The act of spending, through performance, is the most obvious and most fundamental manner by which a business leader may declare, sustain, and accumulate ritual authority. It should come as no surprise, therefore, that such declarations are rife with struggle and stress.

Until the first performance of the nocturnal material, at the "small" *yawulyu,* Dolly's interpretation of the content had never been challenged. There was no need, since the material was divorced from the ceremonial domain, and it is in ceremony that authority is declared. The ritual context is what gave the dream its currency. It was ritual that provoked the competitive impulses of other *yamparru.* When the nine women first gathered under the shade of the West Camp tree to learn what Dolly knew, Dreaming material that had previously been discussed in a non-contentious fashion and calmly associated with the *Jukurrpa* became disputed, reconfirming the competitive nature of ritual and the currency that allows it to be enacted. In much the way that secret knowledge tends to be legitimated by the ritual act, so is the value of innovated dreams established. And lest it be assumed that the dispute arising from the "new" material was restricted to some marginalized sector of Warlpiri social life, it is important to reiterate that a dream that emerged in the quarter of West Camp inhabited by single women was ultimately enacted in ceremonial events that brought all of Yuendumu's ritual leaders (men and women) together.

That left the problem of the site, or rather the absence of a site. How could a Dreaming find legitimate enactment when it failed to be anchored to a specific territory, home, and country? This question troubled me for a long time, in part because of the contradictory information I had gathered. In the months after the performance at Docker River no specific site was associated with the segment. Three years later, the segment was very definitely anchored by Warlpiri businesswomen to a specific spot of land owned by the Warrumungu, where the Emus invoked in the *Jardiwanpa* ceremonies performed the cleansing ritual. But because the Warlpiri did not know the name of this distant site, they could not establish the kind of site-specificity that attends Dreamings closer to home.

In the case study presented above, it was women's dreams that were integrated into a women's ritual event—at least at first. But the material quickly moved into a ceremonial domain shared by men and women. Much of the responsibility for the dream's integration into the ritual repertoire rested on the efforts of a single female *yamparru*. However, her residential kin, including men, were implicated at important junctures of the process. Lest we forget, it was men who provided support that aided in the confirmation of the dream's relationship to the Dreaming. And without subsequent encouragement by the male relatives who traveled with her, Dolly and her sister might not have presented the "new" Dreaming segment in the *Kajirri* ceremony at Docker River. This support between the genders constitutes a central component of how settlement ritual life works.

Gender-exclusive ritual exchanges among Aboriginal women, and similar transactions among Aboriginal men, have been substantively addressed (principally by anthropologists of the gender under scrutiny). Intergender exchanges of ritual material, however, have been less closely addressed. The movement from dreams to Dreaming, like so many social acts in the settlement, necessitated the joint obligations and commitments of men and women. Topsy's dream only hints at the scope of such cross-gender assistance. A more substantive analysis of this connection, focusing on cross-gender transmission, is the focus of chapter 5.

5.

"ENGENDERING" KNOWLEDGE

The Exchange of Ceremonial Material between (and among) Warlpiri Women and Men

During the last twenty years, the concept of "gender" has effectively supplanted the stodgier "masculine"/"feminine" distinction once used to classify and assay the social engagements of women and men. Whereas in the past researchers of Aboriginal religion cleaved the ceremonial world into sex-bound domains of ritual activity, identifying spaces—psychic as well as physical—inhabited by one group, the other group, or the two in informal conjugation (for example, joint ceremonies in the case of the Warlpiri), the lexical fashion now, quite rightly, challenges the biological construct, and in so doing erodes its presumptive dichotomy. As put to use by the current generation of anthropologists working on matters of ritual and kinship, the nominative form of the word *gender* is as much a grammatical and cultural construct as it is a biological one, a word that bypasses overdetermined distinctions of sexuality.

Perhaps the most subtle ethnolexical definition of the term comes from one of its most sophisticated analysts, Marilyn Strathern. Strathern generates a lengthy assessment of *gender* as an "unqualified noun" serving as a type of category differentiation that extends beyond notions of identity and subsumes the forms *male* and *female*. She writes: "Whether or not the sexing of a person's body or psyche is regarded as innate, the apprehension of difference between 'the sexes' invariably takes a categorical form, and it is this to which gender refers" (1988:ix). Strathern goes on to argue against a language of gender that reflexively promotes contrast, opposition, domination, exclusion, and antagonism. As she notes throughout *The Gender of the Gift*, even in gender-specific rituals (and in actions extending beyond ritual), the interests of men and women are mutually constituted (1988:101).

Based on this appealing notion of complementarity, I would extend the lexical function of the word *gender* by shifting from the nominative to the verbal form. To resurrect a secondary meaning of *gender* as a verb—that is, *to gender*—serves nicely to clarify how Warlpiri men and women often exchange their ritual knowledges. As a transitive verb, *gender* (and the related *engender*) suggests "to give rise to, bring about, produce, engender (a feeling, state, etc.), as well as associative notions of regeneration."[1] These meanings, obscure though they are, are useful enough to be dusted off in order to diminish the male-slash-female distinctions of those midcentury ethnographic discourses that separate the actions of men and women. And by reclaiming for analytic purposes the word *engendering,* we have a term better suited to the social and ritual commerce that gets transacted among groups. I say *among* rather than the more grammatically correct *between,* because the "groups" in question often act less as men versus women than they do as individual actors tethered to a residential kin group. Indeed, at Yuendumu, in the time when I conducted research, there was a flourishing, at times overt, exchange of seemingly gender-bound ritual knowledge, an exchange that spoke, and still speaks, to the cloven nature of Warlpiri ceremonial life. (As for the word *cloven,* I must repeat the observation set down in chapter 1, where I noted the apparently oppositional notions of "adherence" and "loyalty" versus "separation" and "dividing blow" buried in the word. What we have, then, is not one but two terms that point to the connected separateness of Warlpiri ritual. Yuendumu is a cloven world in which men and women engender knowledge—that is to say, conjoin it—and by doing so sustain it.)

There are many contexts wherein knowledge is engendered, but three stand out in ways that warrant close, extended analysis: nocturnal dreams (a focus of the previous chapter), the cross-gender exchange of knowledge in ceremonial contexts, and the collaborative use of iconography in the production of acrylic art. All three of these engagements reveal men and women transacting business in ways that undermine gender-specific notions of spatially separate dominions of ritual action. In fact, these cross-gender exchanges of ritual material point to the allegiances of residency, whereby siblings, spouses, and children of the opposite gender, linked to one another residentially, dilute traditional paths of ownership and responsibility, and do so quite overtly.[2]

CONTEXTS OF RITUAL EXCHANGE: NOCTURNAL DREAMS

As the previous chapter suggested, nocturnal dreams constitute a principal context in which *Jukurrpa* narratives find (re)generation and subsequent exchange. The segments that emerge from such nighttime visitations, and the ceremonies that these nocturnal dreams have the potential to trigger, though usually gender-specific, can produce knowledge that migrates between men and women. When this occurs, the flow generally sustains residential affiliation, with husbands, brothers, and fathers passing on material to their female relatives, and mothers, wives, and sisters proffering knowledge to men to whom they are related and with whom they live (see also Poirier 1996).

While I was at Yuendumu, a Japaljarri had a dream. In that dream he "saw" (*nyangu*) a men-only (*watimipa*) segment of the Fish Dreaming (*Jirri Jukurrpa*) situated at Napperby Creek. In one standard version of the men-only form of the Dreaming, the eponymous Fish Being is male. However, in the Japaljarri's dream, the segment was performed by two Ancestral Women (*Tiyatiya*), a modification of the enactment heralding an engendering event of tremendous consequence. In consultation with other male *kirda* and *kurdungurlu* of that particular segment, the Japaljarri was authorized to communicate the *watimipa* segment, in an altered form, to a close sister. By transmitting the segment to his relatives, he diversified the repertoire of his Dreaming in a fashion that reified the bonds of residential kinship—bonds that would protect the Dreaming and its overseers. In other words, a Japaljarri segment remained a Japaljarri segment but became a Napaljarri segment as well. That transfer was slow and delicate, and rife with ambivalence and fear on the part of both donor and recipient. Though the women desired to acquire new material and had no choice but to embrace the modified Dreaming, there were innumerable unspoken risks accompanying the integration. Specifically, the version communicated to the women featured the Fish Being carrying a *rdumpa,* a curse bag that often figures in the most restricted of men's business. The inclusion of the *rdumpa* made the women wary of the symbolic burdens associated with this object. How, then, did the sisters deploy this bequest? They restricted the diffusion of the knowledge, at least initially, to other female *kirda* and *kurdungurlu* at Yuendumu, so as to tether control of the segment to the settlement, and more specifically to the brother's and their residential kin group.

The transfer of knowledge from the male domain to a female one was no small or simple matter. The Japaljarri first had to consult the *kirda* and *kurdungurlu* at Yuendumu, and then widened his request for authorization to men at other settlements. Only after several weeks of intersettlement discussion was he sanctioned by the men to approach his sister. The men residing at Yuendumu sketched the segment—on cardboard and in the sand—for his sisters, a transmission that transpired over several days. This transaction in turn enabled the women to perform the segment, which they ultimately did—not in a joint context with their male relatives, but in a *yawulyu* event where only women were present. That *yawulyu* ceremony, the culmination of nearly three years of (often pressured) discussion among both men and women implicating women in the Fish Dreaming, was deemed proper by all concerned. As such, it constituted an important expansion of the ritual repertoire, one in no way thought to be less legitimate for its innovative origins. The men encouraged the women to perform the *yawulyu* to maintain the *Jukurrpa,* and though the women were responsive to such entreaties, they proceeded with caution because of the powerful life forces associated with the segment. Indeed, the women I spoke to repeatedly noted how cautious they had to be in reconstituting the Japaljarri's nocturnal dream in a ceremonial context of their own. Only after repeated representation of the segment in "small" *yawulyu* performances at Yuendumu did the women determine that they had the strength and knowledge to visit the actual sacred site implicated by that segment. Once they had traveled south to the creek bed at Napperby associated with the Fish Dreaming segment, they felt "strengthened" (*wirijarrijalu*), a fact confirmed by the health they managed to maintain in the weeks following the visit to what was previously a men-only location. As a final acknowledgment of the propriety of the exchange, the women who received the rights to the Fish Dreaming compensated their male relatives with payments of blankets and money.

It is important to note that though the narrative dreamt by the Japaljarri was considered jointly shared as a narrative, the performative obligations of the segment as dreamt resided among the women alone. In other words, the knowledge was shared, but the right to display it in a ritual context remained gender-specific, transferred (while still being retained), in its altered state, from men to women.

This transfer in no way diminished the power of the knowledge. On the contrary, the Japaljarri's dream enabled that segment to find broader ceremonial representation, and thus strengthened the position of the expanded company of overseers (managers and owners alike) in the ritual life of the settlement.

Exchange rooted in nocturnal visitation can also move in the opposite direction, whereby women dream material of ceremonial significance for male residential kin. During one such episode, Peggy Nampijinpa dreamt, while pregnant, of two Jangala brothers being pursued by *Warlu,* the mythical Fire Being. As so often happens in the cosmological narratives of the Warlpiri, images of fire tend to be intertwined with images of rain (see also Hale 1967:6; Munn 1973:180; Bell 1983:190). This particular nocturnal visitation was no exception. Peggy saw that the pursued brothers were followed by a large rain cloud (*mangkurdu*) from which white smoke (*yulyurdu*), in lieu of rain, descended. The narrative significance of the dream was further compounded by the geographic location where the visitation took place. Peggy had her dream within a few kilometers of the actual site she "saw" (*nyangu*). In short, the dream and its locus, plus the condition of the dreamer (that is, her pregnancy), combined to trigger lengthy ritual analysis among Peggy and her kin.

After much consultation with male and female relatives, a number of men in her residential kin group—specifically, her brothers and fathers—undertook to reenact the narrative in a ritual context that excluded women. Because of the dream and the resulting performances by men, Peggy Nampijinpa was able to lay claim to a version of the narrative she had dreamt. In addition, it was collectively decided by *kirda* for the Fire Dreaming that she could display a body design that alluded to, but modified, the restricted version of the *Warlu Jukurrpa.*[3]

Whereas many other female *kirda* of the segment of the Fire Dreaming that invokes the Jangala brothers could wear body designs chronicling the narrative, only Peggy's pattern included the vertical hatching below the clavicles. These white marks—representing the white smoke she had seen descending from a rain cloud—constitute an iconic adaptation of the images that came to her at night.

When I asked all concerned why Peggy was granted rights to the design, the responses were the same. The dream alone did not precipitate ownership of the design, even though she was *kirda* for the Fire Dreaming. The iconographic rights were generated by the overlapping of dream, dream site, and pregnancy. The combination personalized her relationship to that segment of the Fire Dreaming, established the conception site of her unborn child, and granted Peggy newfound rights of associated

Figure 5. Peggy Nampijinpa's personal body design for the Fire Dreaming

representation. Because the narrative's ritual employment was restricted to the ceremonies of men, the body design (at least among women) was retained by the dreamer alone.

Not all important nocturnal dreams precipitate ceremonial activity. In one case, a *kumanjayi* Nangala "saw" male incarnations of the *Tiyatiya,* whose ceremonial actions were determined—again by cross-gender consultation in the wake of nocturnal visitation—to be allied with the Emu Dreaming (*Yankirri Jukurrpa*). These actions very clearly took place in a *purlapa* (men's public) event, though no such actual business was being performed by men at the time. The visitation did not modify the actions or narrative but did alter the context of those actions. Nevertheless, though it was determined, in the wake of the dream, that the *Yankirri Jukurrpa* could be performed in public, no such action was taken, at least within the ten subsequent years during which I conducted fieldwork. That is not to say that no reenactment will ever take place, only that such nocturnal dreams do not constitute mandatory ceremonial obligation. Because the segment was already being nurtured in restricted *watimipa* and *karntamipa* contexts—specifically in *parnpa* and *yawulyu* ceremonies—the pressures to perform it in a public *purlapa* event were diminished.

From the accounts described above, and others like it, some general comments can be made regarding the cross-gender dynamic of ritual exchange at Yuendumu in the 1980s and early 1990s. Men were willing—indeed desirous—to broaden certain ritual responsibilities to include female relatives. Women, for their part, reciprocated, though with less overt ceremonial repercussions; that is to say, while their narrative material was acknowledged to move from the dominion of women's business to that of men's, it did not necessarily find ritual reenactment. Significantly, the material transferred from women to men and from men to women rarely found expression in joint ceremonies, but rather in gender-specific rituals to which the other gender was privy. Such recirculation of ritual currency tended to honor the *kirda-kurdungurlu* dynamics that characterized "traditional" ritual connectedness, while pointing to the ever-growing role of women in the reproduction of the Dreaming in public ritual performance.

How does this engendered use of nocturnal dreams fit with earlier ethnographic accounts of the Warlpiri's gender-specific links to the cosmology?

Whereas Munn acknowledged the transfer of ritual material via the intermediary of nocturnal dreams, she noted a number of constituent elements in such exchanges radically at odds with the situation I observed during my fieldwork. For starters, Munn observed no dreams by women that touched matters of men's business (1973:38, 90). Men, for their part, did have dreams that were relevant to women's business. But here, too, there were distinctly different patterns at work. The transfers from men to women were, during Munn's fieldwork, exclusively spousal (as opposed to the broad residential exchange I observed) and bestowed honorary ownership over dreamt material unconnected to the exchange process as it is now undertaken (Munn 1973:37; see also Wild 1975:18). Furthermore, Munn found no reciprocal acts of payment in those instances whereby material such as *yawulyu* designs shuttled between husbands and wives in the wake of nocturnal dreams. Those correlative exchanges that did take place—principally in the form of food exchanges—did not, in her estimation, constitute a formal transaction, since such transfers were already "built in" to the marital relationship (Munn 1973:38–39).

The circumstance has changed considerably during the half century since Munn first conducted her work with the Warlpiri. The reciprocal relationship made manifest in the marital unit is still very much in place, but accommodates—indeed, seems to require—regular, formal acts of engendered payment when nocturnal material moves from men to women and from women to men. Even though payment is not always made, it is nevertheless expected, and can take the form of money, blankets, or other durable goods of value.

One structural component of the transfer that Munn documented does remain very much a constant in the transmission of nocturnal material between men and women, and that is its potential for recirculation and revaluation in the ceremonial arena. Munn noted that men's dreams had a direct effect on the *yawulyu* ceremonies of women. The men could traffic in designs, songs, and narratives on behalf of their spouses. Such cross-gender ritual negotiation has increased in frequency and widened in scope, now moving in both directions.

CONTEXTS OF RITUAL EXCHANGE: CEREMONIAL PERFORMANCE

Although both Munn and Meggitt focused on gender-specific manifestations of ritual knowledge—the so-called masculine and feminine orbits of ritual activity—they did not explicitly deny the covert flow of knowledge between men and women for ultimate enactment in ceremonial contexts (Munn 1973:44, 51; Meggitt 1966:209–10). This exchange of knowledge between genders often begins before the Warlpiri engage in formal ritual activity. Young women, even those as yet uninitiated into their own gender-specific ceremonial activities, will nevertheless take it upon themselves to assist male kin navigating various necessary rites of passage that consecrate ritual ascendancy. This impulse to nurture and protect, educate and monitor, is particularly strong among siblings. Brothers regularly take an interest in their sisters' ritual careers and vice versa. The bond strengthens as siblings advance toward ritual maturity. In its most naive and public manifestation, such cross-gender exchange can be seen in the gentle nudge a teenage girl might give her younger brother when he fails to recognize the importance of a site jointly visited during a hunting and gathering expedition. Neither she nor her relatives (both male and female) will have any qualms about alerting the inattentive young brother of the significance of a rock hole invoked during ceremony. This youthful dynamic among siblings on the cusp of ritual engagement evolves into more formal exchanges that generally require reciprocal payment, though that payment may not always be easy to detect.

During the time I was gathering various versions of the Fire Dreaming

(*Warlu Jukurrpa*), I spoke to a number of men and women who were *kirda* for both the territories and the performative rights over the itinerary. In the course of piecing together the complex and lengthy narrative (some of which is public and some restricted), I learned that in a public version two mythical brothers were born out of a spearwood tree (*winpiri*).[4] One of my most helpful and knowledgeable friends, Molly Nampijinpa, interrupted me during the transcription to ask rhetorically, "*Nyarrparla nyinaja Napangardi?*" which translates roughly as "Where was [their mother] Napangardi in the Dreaming?" Two weeks later, in another conversation about the *Warlu Jukurrpa,* Molly mentioned without elaboration or prompting, "There is no mother," a fact suggesting possible connections to portions of a restricted initiation ceremony performed only among men. Molly said nothing more, and at the time I did not register the significance of the comment. But two days later, the ritual value of her remark was clarified when her older brother, Kumanjayi Jampijinpa, approached me and asked in a matter-of-fact fashion for payment. I was confused, since such requests are generally associated with assistance and we hadn't worked together. I asked why he should be paid, and he said he had been the source of the information Molly had provided about the absence of the mother in the *Warlu Jukurrpa.* He offered no further elaboration of the Dreaming narrative. The request indicated for the first time a social dynamic I later observed played out with great regularity, a flow of ritual material between a brother and a sister that would precipitate triangular payment.

The exchange of ritual knowledge grows as siblings enter the ritual sphere. They regularly assist each other and offer support on visits to sacred sites and in meetings with governmental officials on matters that require ritual discussion, such as the reclamation of vacant Crown land. But the most potent exchanges are those directly concerned with ceremonial performance, a context in which the bonds between men and women—and in particular brothers and sisters, and husbands and wives—are regularly nurtured and strengthened.

Take the case of Sheila Napaljarri. A day before she was to perform a segment of the Vine Dreaming (*Ngalyipi Jukurrpa*) during a *yawulyu* ceremony, Sheila left the confines of the *jilimi* to ask her brother, Paddy Japaljarri, about certain narrative components of the Dreaming. The cross-gender request was made because the women normally in a position to educate Sheila—that is, her father's sisters—had either died or moved away from Yuendumu. As Paddy Japaljarri explained (and Sheila confirmed), seniority had granted him access to the ceremonial representations of the women's business that Sheila wished to perform. He had seen the same *yawulyu* enacted by his father's sisters a generation before. In the absence of actual/close father's sisters and/or elder sisters, elder brothers can pass on knowledge to their sisters about the Dreamings that they share. This conduit of knowledge is not only common but obligatory, according to numerous ritual performers, male and female. As the sole knowledgeable relative, Paddy felt obliged to bestow (*yuuly-pungu*) the details of the design. He did so by drawing out a male shield pattern on a piece of scrap cardboard, omitting those elements beyond the scope of the women's business. This assistance was provided to Sheila in the presence of his wife. The inclusion of Sheila's sister-in-law during this engendered transmission codified the wife's managerial role in the performance of the segment, reinforced the links among the three principals—the two women and the man—and pointed to how residential pressures often trump subsection affiliations and rules of assistance. Although there was no shortage of women who had inherited *kurdungurlu*-ship over the segment in question, none resided in close proximity to either Sheila or her brother. That is why they were bypassed when it came to establishing managerial rights to oversee the knowledge Sheila would perform.

How did Paddy's modified shield design find graphic representation when it entered the repertoire of women? Not as he had drawn it, but in a recomposed form that ultimately was represented on Sheila's body. This alteration of medium—from shield design to body design—reflected how shared (if partial) knowledge commonly finds gender-specific representation.

Significantly, Sheila's body was painted by Japaljarri's wife with the design Japaljarri provided. The communication among the three, while reconstituting the cast of performers, did not disturb the other senior women associated with that Dreaming segment who did not perform. Sheila ultimately became the principal overseer of the segment, teaching it to the other women who had inherited managerial and ownership rights to the Dreaming itinerary but who lacked the accompanying ritual knowledge to nurture it. That single segment helped Sheila, Sheila's brother, and his wife strengthen their ritual status. From then on, each time this particular Dreaming segment was reenacted in *yawulyu* performances, Sheila served as *kirda,* and her sister-in-law served as primary *kurdungurlu.*

The transmission of ritual knowledge between Paddy Japaljarri and his wife, Bessie Nakamarra, did not exist solely through the mediated presence of his sister. During my fieldwork, I observed the couple exchange specific knowledge about the Dreamings that they inherited both as managers and as owners. Beyond that, however, they also conversed regularly, and with intensity, about other Dreamings to which they were privy. For example, when I observed Paddy give the specifics of a *Jardiwanpa* for which he is *kurdungurlu,* Bessie, as a *kirda,* had no qualms interjecting various correctives and amplifications she felt her husband had neglected to mention. He accepted this intervention and was even grateful for it. The same spousal attentiveness also made itself apparent when Bessie discussed her Dreamings in the presence of Paddy.

The spousal exchange also finds modified replication when a spouse dies. If a woman loses her husband, the affinal ties between the widow and her husband's brothers will often substitute for the dynamics lost through death. That is to say, the widow and her brothers-in-law will exchange ritual knowledge and promote the nurturance of the Dreamings that they oversee. (Likewise, the death of a woman will recalibrate the cross-gender exchanges between a widower and his dead wife's sisters.)

Indeed, some of the ritual currency the Warlpiri deemed most valuable (*wiri*) and which I observed being passed from men to women implicated widows and the brothers of their deceased husbands. Well into my first stay at Yuendumu, I was privy to one exchange between Judy and a brother-in-law. For some time, I had observed Judy showing concern about the neglect of her segment of the Creeper Dreaming, the site at which she had been conceived. The site—long unsung by women and (according to Judy) less than adequately sustained by male residents—required performative reinvigoration.

Judy considered the circumstances dire. Those women who held *kirda* and *kurdungurlu* rights to the Dreaming segment either had died or no longer lived at Yuendumu. She worried that further neglect would result in the land "becoming sick" (*maju-jarri*), a condition that would jeopardize both fauna and flora. To rectify the situation, Judy called upon her brother-in-law to provide graphic details of the site so that she could maintain its well-being through ritual activity. He obliged her in much the way Paddy had helped in the example cited above, that is to say, by showing his sister-in-law a modified shield design that could be used in women's business. Whereas Paddy had used a scrap of cardboard, Japangardi relied on a more traditional method and medium, drawing the design in the sand with his finger. At no point in the exchange did she ask

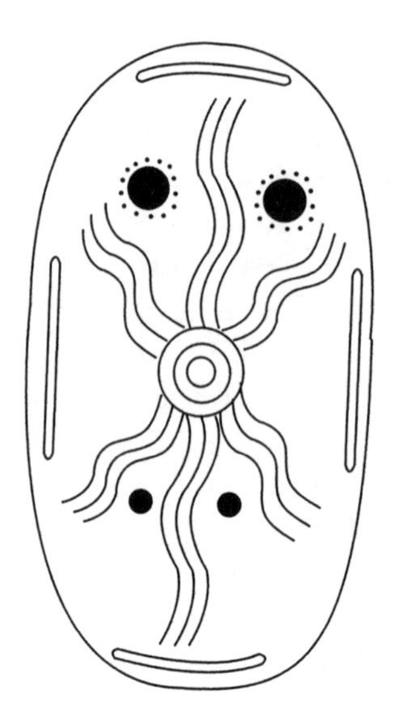

Figure 6. Design of the Creeper Dreaming on baby carrier

questions of her male relative. She did not have to. She knew she was entitled (indeed required) to reproduce the reclassified sand drawing of a shield design in a variety of ways. She did so first by applying the pattern to a *parraja,* or baby carrier, and then by requesting that a sister copy the design onto her body. Even though Judy lacked the collaborators required to perform the Dreaming in a "big" *yawulyu* (that is, with narrative and song accompanied by dance), she was able to undertake "small" events, singing the associated songs and overseeing the reproduction of the newly engendered design.

As I noted, though the Japangardi referred to the pattern as part of a *yawulyu,* it was clear to both Judy and her brother-in-law that the pattern had iconic origins in a shield design, that is, in men's business. How much that men-only (*watimipa*) design was modified for women's business was never stated, at least in my presence, but it was clear that the instruction transmitted rights and responsibilities whereby the material was legitimately repositioned in the province of women. To repeat, Judy could—indeed had to—undertake modified representation of the *wiri* men's pattern in various ritual fora overseen by women. She confirmed the immense significance of this cross-gender exchange and instruction two paydays later by giving the Japangardi a third of her widow's pension (a sum of $A 60) for the help he had provided.

Judy told me that without the assistance of the Japangardi, the Creeper

Dreaming segment would not have been taken care of. The lines he drew in the sand allowed the segment to reenter the repertoire of women, where it has grown (and continues to grow) in ritual significance.

But not without conflict. A few months after Judy had begun wearing her new design, a senior ritual leader—one of her mother's brothers—questioned the accuracy of the design, one for which he was *kurdungurlu.* "That Japangardi got it wrong," he declared. The error, it became clear, was one of propriety rather than accuracy. The *kurdungurlu* was concerned that the reclassified design retained too many of the *watimipa* components of the original shield pattern. A few days later he provided a modified alternative that Judy accepted unquestioningly, in part because the suggestion came from a ritual leader with substantial experience shifting ritual material from one gender-specific domain to the other. Judy never replicated the original version again. The modification appeared as follows:

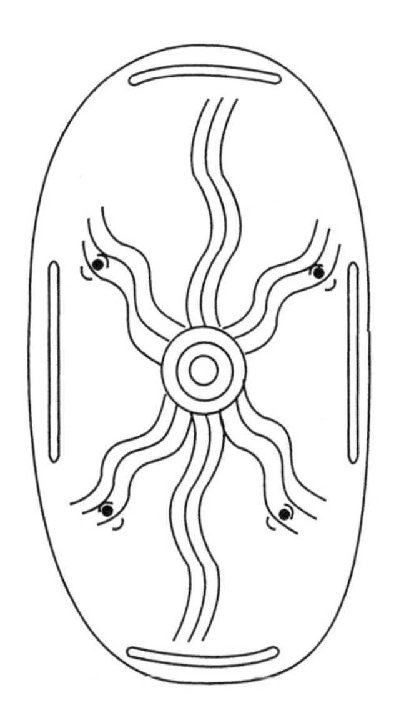

Figure 7. Modified design of the Creeper Dreaming on baby carrier

The question remains why the man offered up a shield design rather than reassure Judy that the nurturance would be taken care of by men. Judy never accused the Japangardi overtly of neglecting the segment. Still, it was obvious to all the relatives privy to the exchange that male ties to the site were at the time nearly as fragile (that is, in need of nurturance) as the women's, and that this particular brother was a manager over a segment that lacked a living male owner at Yuendumu. They thus lacked the prerequisite configuration to perform (and so sustain) the Dreaming.

Cross-gender exchange of knowledge also finds expression in kin-based noncollateral contexts, through the offspring links that accompany remarriage. Although men are more likely to remarry than women, it is important to note that widows who find new husbands often expand their ritual knowledge more broadly than men. The reason for this is quite simple: Second and third marriages by women frequently create bonds to new homes and associated Dreamings, whereas widowers often remarry within the kin group of the former spouse and thus only minimally expand the repertoire of their ritual knowledge (Dussart 1992b).

The enlargement of cross-gender ceremonial knowledge through remarriage does not presume a concomitant expansion of performative rights. As I showed in chapter 3, remarriage can mark the relinquishment of ritual leadership while preserving access to knowledge that will be deployed by others. In the case of Judy, ritual leadership ceased with remarriage; nevertheless, the flow of ceremonial knowledge between Judy and her new husband continued. In other words, a woman (or man, for that matter) may, via marriage, learn a great deal about the Dreamings of a spouse—knowledge that in no way presumes engagement (let alone control) of associated ceremonies.

Remarriage in general will bring greater ritual benefits to the offspring of the widow than it will to the children of the widower, because the lines of ownership are broadened more for women's kin. It is typical in such contexts for the new husband to teach the children from his spouse's previous marriage his Dreamings. A new wife will act similarly with her spouse's children, though her stepchildren's potential for expanding their ritual knowledge is minimized because of the managerial relationship between the stepchildren and the spouse.

Perhaps the most vivid example of the benefits that emerge from remarrying "right"—that is to say, in a manner that sustains the patricouple and land connections established by the first marriage—can be seen in the second marriage of two widowed Warlpiri, a Nungarrayi and a Jangala.

The remarried Nungarrayi lived with her new husband in another settlement. At gatherings for ceremonial activities, one of the Nungarrayi's daughters, a Nampijinpa who was an active ritual leader, would receive ritual knowledge from her new father (who had other female offspring from other marriages). This substantiation of the father-daughter dynamic yielded tremendous ceremonial consequences. Because the Jangala was *kirda* over significant segments of the Wattle Dreaming (*Watiya-warnu Jukurrpa*) located south of Yuendumu and his daughters (through remarriage) possessed *kirda* rights over segments of the Wattle Dreaming to the north of Yuendumu, the marital union, via the knowledge transfer (and accompanying control) it legitimated, strengthened all the women when it came to the expression of the *Jukurrpa* in ceremonial contexts. (As for the man's possible expansion of ritual authority, no data were available.)

According to the women, each time the Jangala saw his younger female relatives he would give them various elements of the ritual knowledge he owned: stories, designs, and songs related to his segments of the Wattle Dreaming. Some of this ritual currency was incorporated into the women's performances of their Dreaming, though the modification in no way diminished the primacy of the segments of the Wattle Dreaming the women owned through their actual father. I was present at one particularly poignant exchange in the long-term process of engendering nurturance. At an initiation event at Mt. Allan, the relatives all gathered to perform a series of men-only and associated joint ceremonies. The women, for their part, painted the Wattle Dreaming on their bodies and danced for several nights. The following morning, the Jangala approached his new wife, her daughter, and her daughter's three sisters bearing a cloth bundle. He joined them in the shade of a humpy and placed the bundle in the middle of the group. When he unwrapped the bundle, the women were all taken aback, insofar as the Warlpiri express such an emotion. The cloth contained four dark green stones (*pirli*), Dreaming stones clearly associated with a domain almost entirely off-limits to women. He immediately confirmed what was suspected by the women, noting that the smooth fist-sized stones were "*tarruku*."[5] The term *tarruku* in this context was being used to indicate power, potency, and danger, a "dear" knowledge generally beyond the reach of women, but now rendered "halfway" by the engendering gesture. (See chapter 2.)

After he said what all the women suspected, he noted that the Dreaming stones were a potent manifestation of the Ancestral Wattle Trees. He asked them to touch the stones, and after some hesitation (given the power the stones possessed) the women did so. Once this tactile connection had been made, the Jangala promptly closed up the bundle, and the "exchange" came to an end. The whole interaction lasted fewer than ten minutes, but it was clear to all present that the display would create a long-term benefit (and obligation) for the women present. Once the stones were bundled back up, the Jangala's wife (a *kurdungurlu* for the Wattle Dreaming) reiterated to the younger women the value of what they had seen, while making clear to all present that she herself had seen the stones before.

A few days after the end of the initiation events, the Jangala's wife pestered her daughter to give a ritual gift (*jarnarrpa*) to the Jangala for showing the women the stones; the next week he received two large woolen blankets, an extremely valuable item among desert residents.

Even though the narratives and songs and designs of the Wattle Dreaming were in no way modified by the sight of the four green stones, the ceremonial status of the women who were *kirda* over that Dreaming improved significantly after the viewing.[6] This was made clear in the weeks and months ahead, when the women performed the Wattle Dreaming in women-only contexts. During the instructional portion of the ceremonies, the four daughters were able to take control of various aspects of the ritual by virtue of their direct contact with the Ancestral Wattle Trees. The engendered viewing—the cross-gender presentation of men's material—granted them the right to discuss the existence of stones with other women associated with the Wattle Dreaming who had never seen the green stones and did not know they existed. Additionally, the Jangala's display extended the women's performative rights to include the southern segments, though no accompanying land rights came with their broadened ceremonial oversight. Furthermore, over time, these four women started to take a pedagogic role in the dissemination of the Wattle Dreaming, a role that they were confident would ultimately allow them to sanction performance by women who had never seen the stones. The diffusionary transmission of knowledge—from men to close female kin to women of less intimate association—plays itself out regularly in the ritual life of the settlement. Once women attain the role of *kirda* for ceremonial enactment, they can sanction knowledgeable kin to perform that ceremony in their absence.

In the main, ritual assistance that brings men and women together transpires outside actual ceremonial performance. However, there are cases—rare, to be sure—in which a man will enter, at his relatives' behest, into the actual ritual and offer assistance. I was privy to one such intervention, a cross-gender exception that shed light on the perceptual frameworks of the Warlpiri with regard to gender separation. The intervention by a male *yamparru*, a *kumanjayi* Jungarrayi, was triggered by preceremonial negotiations surrounding efforts to reenact a segment of the Flying Ant Dreaming (*Pamapardu Jukurrpa*). The *yamparrupatu,* though initially confident the segment could be properly overseen by a *kumanjayi* Nangala, had to rethink their decision when it became clear that she possessed knowledge of the designs and songs but could not reproduce the associated dance. Incorrect dancing, the women decided, could threaten the entire *yawulyu* event. To alleviate the pressure on the woman, they turned to the *kurdungurlu* for the Flying Ant Dreaming, but she, too, lacked the knowledge (to say nothing of the performative rights) associated with the Flying Ant segment under scrutiny. Clearly, some external assistance was required. That assistance came, in the end, from the Nangala's husband, a *kumanjayi* Jungarrayi who held managerial rights to a stretch of the Flying Ant Dreaming that included the segment in question.

The *yawulyu* ceremonies took place as planned on the lawn of the Women's Museum. From the outset, the Jungarrayi posted himself inside the museum grounds, atypically close to the locus of the women's business. Two segments were performed before it was time to dance the *Pamapardu.* When it came time for the Nangala's segment, two female *kirda* for associated segments of the Flying Ant Dreaming called over to the Jungarrayi, requesting assistance about how to proceed. Rather than call back details of the dance the women wished to perform, he danced the segment himself. The women took on the function of *kurdungurlu,* offering guidance to the dancers about the steps they should take and the songs they should sing. This atypical intervention lasted no more than three minutes but was enough to provide the necessary nurturance. The performance was deemed proper, and in fact initiated the long-term integration of that segment into the performative repertoire of the dancers who were already *kirda* for related segments. These women told me that even more material might have flowed into the women's business from this particular Jungarrayi if he and his wife had not died prematurely. Their death placed a taboo on that particular segment.

The decision to bring in the Jungarrayi, one reached by consensus among the ritual leaders overseeing the *yawulyu,* did not require lengthy discussion. Nor did it prompt much comment during or after the event. It was deemed perfectly okay to call in the man, even if such requests are uncommon. Furthermore, the intervention was perceived in spousal terms insofar as the women who were *kirda* of the related segments decided to direct payment (of blankets and money) to the Nangala's helpful husband as well as to the female *kurdungurlu*. There was no stress attending the engendering exchange, no suggestion that what took place had been in any way improper.

That is not to say such stresses are absent from ceremonial life. Quite the contrary. The communication of ritual knowledge between men and women is dangerous enough that mismanagement can indeed threaten the spiritual health of the whole settlement.

Because the act of engendering ritual knowledge transfers often requires participants to make use of men-only material that is meant to inhabit a space outside the domain of women, a collective vigilance must always be maintained when that material is reconstituted for wider use. There are rare circumstances when the clearly defined barriers separating men from women are considered to have been transgressed. When that happens, the repercussions can reshape the geography and repertoire of ritual life for years to come.

I was present at the settlement when one such violation of taboo took place. This transgression speaks to the response by both men and women with regard to the nurturance of ritual. The matter concerns a breach of secrecy that occurred early in my fieldwork, in October 1983.

Men and women had started discussing the annual circumcision event: which boys had to be "caught" (*rdarri-mardanu*) and placed in seclusion, which ritual leaders would oversee the staging of the *kurdiji*. The men-only material was, late one night, made unacceptably public by a man who, inebriated in the wake of an alcohol run to Alice Springs, started to perform various details of Warlpiri ritual life. His early displays were harmless; a generic imitation of the stylistic differences between the dances of women and men. But then his drink-induced performance trespassed the boundaries of acceptable or "proper" behavior. He stumbled over to the *jilimi* where his mother-in-law resided, and called out her name. His close kin quickly intervened to remove him from proximity to his mother-in-law and thus defuse this mildly unacceptable gesture. Insomnia got the better of him, and a few hours later he exacerbated his earlier misbehavior with more egregious violations of social and ceremonial taboo. He began to sing, in a loud voice, various song verses from the men-only portion of the ceremony associated with circumcision, songs that were highly *juju*, that is, wholly beyond the purlieu of the uninitiated. His singing woke the whole of West Camp. The locus of this misbehavior added to the gravity of the breach. Not only were there women and uninitiated youth camping within earshot of the man, there were also numerous male *yamparru* cognizant of just how inappropriate the singing was in so public a context. Several older men immediately tried to stop him, but without success. After several hours, the man finally fell asleep.

The next morning the transgression was the major topic of discussion among ritually active men and women of the settlement. Though the specifics of conversations, which took place in gender-specific settings, differed in explicitness, both the men's groups and the women's groups spoke of the incident as though anticipating death and preparing for a long period of mourning. By the end of the day, it was clear to all concerned that the Law had been transgressed and that a "death" of sorts had occurred. The victim was the circumcision ceremony, which the older men collectively decided could not take place in the vicinity of Yuendumu. The Warlpiri youths to be "caught" in the settlement would have to undergo initiation at another location where no violation of the Law had taken place. That year, Yuendumu's young males were taken to Mt. Allan for the *kurdiji* ceremonies. The ban lasted two years. During that time, the violator of the Law was not punished. (At least, he was not punished in ways that were known to the senior women of the camp. In the past, such violation would have resulted in the death of the transgressor, according to some of my male informants.)

At the end of the second year of the ban, a large group of senior Yuendumu men, desiring to reclaim control of the ceremonial arena, campaigned to complete the second set of circumcision events back at their own settlement. How to restore the health of the setting generated considerable discussion. Because there was no precedent for this kind of transgression by the Warlpiri at Yuendumu, the senior men had to invoke nonlocal precedent in figuring out an appropriate ceremonial response. One man offered details of the ritual reaction by some Pitjantjatjara faced with a similar dilemma, and it was decided that such intervention could serve as a model for the Warlpiri response. To that end, the men left the settlement for two purposes: first, they punished the man who violated the taboo, and second, over a period of several days and nights, they performed a purification ceremony, a response consistent with the follow-up to death and mourning. The men then returned from their "business" trip and announced what they had done. They next performed another set of purification ceremonies, this one intended to be viewed by both men and women. This new set incorporated modified elements of the transgressive material that caused all the problems in the first place. In other words, a group of senior men attempted, after a two-year hiatus, to "engender" men-only songs that had been made public into a broader dominion, one that was open to women as well.

The men hoped that this expanded ceremonial context would be seen to nourish the *Jukurrpa* and thus appease other male ritual leaders troubled by the drunken display. Unfortunately, no consensus among the senior men emerged from this intervention; the efficacy of the "reopening" ritual was considered inadequate. However, the sanctioned cross-gender display precipitated by the unsanctioned one had long-term metaceremonial impact that may have led, a year later, to the lifting of the ban. Using the songs and narratives provided by the men during the purification ceremony, women who were *kirda* over the Dreaming itineraries associated with the songs that men sang began to paint associated designs on acrylic canvases. It came as no surprise, and triggered little consternation, when the following year's set of circumcision ceremonies was once again performed at Yuendumu. In fact, the reestablishment of the circumcision ceremonies prompted a settlement-wide sense of relief.

ACRYLIC PAINTING: A METACEREMONIAL CONTEXT FOR THE ENGENDERING OF KNOWLEDGE

What is often called "acrylic indigenous art"—a seemingly paradoxical term reflecting the larger societal oxymorons of sedentarization (playing up to, as it does, the notion of the "modern primitive")—has yielded innumerable insights into the contestations (economic, formalist, epistemological, and so on) among the producers, purveyors, and purchasers of a synthetic and nonindigenous art form that the Warlpiri, among others, have been producing commercially in the Central Australian Desert since the late 1970s. Indeed, because of the very nature of the medium, acrylic offers a lasting record of the engendering process—a process often less tangibly and impermanently constituted in the "closed" contexts of cross-gender ritual activity. And whereas the art critic, the aesthete, and the ethnographer—to say nothing of the curator, collector, art advisor, and dealer—have proffered assessments of the "dot" painting phenomenon, deploying their own techniques and languages, methods and motives, such insights stand beyond the focus of the current discussion, which is restricted to the intracultural dynamics of this declaratively intercultural medium.[7] In short, what concerns me here is the specific evolution of internal gender relationships as played out during the history of acrylic art production. The question I wish to pose is this: What can acrylics teach us about how men and women have negotiated their social identity as Warlpiri and as members of residential kin groups with the Warlpiri universe? How do acrylic paintings manifest, as I believe they do, the engendering process characterized in the discussions above?

While the iconic repertoire placed on the canvases by Warlpiri women and men is of limited performative significance, it nonetheless incorporates material of tremendous ritual value. To be properly produced, the designs—"open" (*warraja*) versions of the Dreaming (or, more accurately, segments thereof) directed to a non-Warlpiri audience—must avoid the use of restricted material. There is no such thing as a "private" or "secret" acrylic; the designs applied are purposely modified (as are the stories that accompany them) to obviate the dissemination of knowledge prohibited to the uninitiated. Failure to withhold such restricted designs and narratives—and by that I mean those elements of the cosmological patrimony that the Warlpiri identify as *wiri*—can only result in problems. Fear of sorcery—the threat of "being sung" into blindness (or even death) for transgressive representation—is an ever-present risk when artists undertake the unsanctioned production of *Jukurrpa* designs. For that reason, a canvas that borrows from the visual vocabulary of Warlpiri ritual iconography must systematically hide as much, if not more, than it reveals. What does get revealed, furthermore, must be shown schematically, protectively, reductively. As I have written elsewhere, the acrylic canvas is, more often than not, part Morse code and part Kabbalah: a coded key to a Dreaming that must remain less than wholly readable to uninitiated viewers (Dussart 1999).

All of this, then, should go a long way to explain why painting the *Jukurrpa* is a stressful undertaking. Many religiously knowledgeable Warlpiri do not involve themselves in such adaptive expressions of traditional cosmology because of the forces that permeate the designs. Those painters who do create acrylics are quick to point out that the tension accompanying such activity often requires mitigation by the same social networks in place during the performance of ritual; that is, kinship, residential affiliation, and travels to foreign places to accompany exhibitions.

For all these reasons—and others that implicate the markets that the artwork reaches—acrylic is a gesture of translation, a shift of iconic representation from the initiated to the uninformed. This translation and distribution demand a great deal of internal negotiation to guarantee that the ritual currency undergoing (ex)change—from the restricted sphere to a public one, and (for the purpose of this analysis) from the male domain to the female—retains its properness and related potency. This is not to imply that male equals private or that female equals public, a matter of some complexity first addressed in the terminological overview provided in chapter 2. In point of fact, the phenomenon of acrylics allows us to observe—indeed, highlights with a boldness reduplicative of the medium—the manner by which the Warlpiri use intercultural exchange to reconfigure various intracultural social relations, relations that defy any single dichotomous cleavage, be it defined by gender, market, or structural function. For the postsedentary phenomenon of "dot" paintings constitutes a kind of metaceremonial act: the replication of the visual component of ritual repertoire in a form that underscores the social exchanges found in more traditional media. Indeed, acrylic brings to the fore many recurrent phenomena of contemporary settlement life. These phenomena include:

1. *The collaborative ethos surrounding all matters implicating ritual.* Despite the single names that often appear on the canvas—a nod to the Western conception of the artist, which is as alien to the Warlpiri as the synthetic paints they now use—approval and execution of ritual designs generally follow traditional (if residentially modified) lines of kinship, whereby the owners and managers associated with the designs must "sign off" on the artist's work. In other words, acrylic confirms, in a different, intercultural key, its ritual precursor. It underlines, in the adaptation of the Warlpiri vocabulary of visual design, the patrimoietal organization predicated on a collaboration cleaving *kirda* of the graphically represented Dreaming segments from the *kurdungurlu*. There is much collective consultation and assessment before the first dot or line is applied on a design that has not been previously authorized.
2. *The compensatory negotiations that attend the distribution of ritual material.* Whether the iconography appears on the body of a male ritual leader or a piece of store-bought canvas, and whether the design moves from the domain of men to that of women (or in the opposite direction) or stays within the repertoire of a single gender, payment must be made. In the case of acrylic art, a rare source of hard currency, the money received from a sale is distributed in much

the way other resources get recirculated. Though an art advisor in the settlement might designate a single painter as the payee, it is understood that when funds are received they must go toward satisfying the obligations of kinship and residential affiliation, as well as the territorial and ceremonial links associated with the painted design.

3. *The revivified legitimacy of seniority in matters of ritual and meta-ritual activity.* In a settlement environment where some of the traditional gerontologically constituted economic and political positions have been weakened, the phenomenon of acrylic production has reinvigorated a knowledge system that privileges seniority (Myers 1986a, 1994a). Older ritual leaders have been able to reclaim a small measure of their traditionally constituted social status by creating or monitoring the reproduction of modified ritual designs in the newfound medium.
4. *The engendering of ritual.* As with ceremonial material that is negotiated after dreams and during ceremonial performance, the paintings of the *Jukurrpa* allow for the flow of knowledge between (and among) men and women. Acrylics serve as a kind of visual currency, a spiritual inheritance that is both separate and shared among women and men. Indeed, Berndt's famous two-sex model of Aboriginal consciousness—that of digging sticks and spears—can be profitably modified by the inclusion of a third tool: the paintbrush, an implement wielded by both women and men in ways that further complicate our understanding of their "divided" ritual world (Berndt 1974).

The introduction of acrylic art to Yuendumu, a process that began on a large scale during my second year of fieldwork, in 1984, can be traced in practical terms to the desire on the part of some thirty women—all ritually initiated—to raise money to purchase a new Toyota Land Cruiser. At my suggestion, these women decided to generate funds by painting their respective Dreamings on canvas for sale to nonindigenous visitors and collectors. Within months, the remunerative value of such public replications of the *Jukurrpa* became clear, and some dozen men (also ritually active) joined the undertaking, independently producing public versions of their (that is, male) designs. Because women possessed more designs already inhabiting the public sphere—the patterns applied to their exposed torsos were particularly adaptable—they were less hampered. As a measure of the art project's success, the women purchased their Toyota by the end of the year, and the men, too, quickly began bolstering the fragile economy of the settlement through the sale of acrylic art.

Though the paintings were never seen as formal extensions of ritual activity, their production was perceived, from the outset, as potent enough to necessitate the replication of the proprietary and managerial configurations traditionally put into action when designs were produced for ceremonial purposes. In other words, the intercultural adaptation ratcheted up the negotiation of ritual material in a nonritual context. The obligatory collaborations seen during, say, a *yawulyu* ceremony, whereby a Napangardi with *kurdungurlu* responsibilities would monitor the displays of a Nangala possessing *kirda* rights, were similarly played out when a public version of the Water Dreaming was painted on a piece of canvas for sale to a local art advisor.

During the actual painting by an owner-artist, the managers monitored how the main symbols were configured, how the design was filled in, and how the story accompanying the execution was told. For instance, early renderings of a segment of the Skink Dreaming (*Warrarna Jukurrpa*) were rife with impropriety, visual and verbal. As a result, inappropriate oral references to the actions of a mythical relative, a Blue Tongue Lizard (*Lungkarda*), had to be expunged, and unauthorized use of certain icons near an arc representing the Mythical Skinks had to be modified to make the acrylic proper (Dussart 1999). Similar conflicts arose over a Bush Tomato Dreaming and the visual representation of a ceremony of initiation performed by women. The duties of deletion typically fell to the manager, a kin-based rigor maintained by both men and women.

In the early years of the "dot" phenomenon, men tended to paint with men, and women with women. Few if any examples of "engendered" canvases—say, an acrylic representation of a joint event implicating men and women—were painted collaboratively during the formative years of the acrylic movement. Furthermore, the production of canvases, whether by initiated men or women, tended to be produced in a context of avoidance. That is to say, the uninitiated—as well as the initiated of the opposite gender—were informally discouraged from approaching the artists and their overseers during the production of a canvas. Even with these precautionary efforts, gender tensions ran high. Because the available repertoire of public patterns was limited, artists were forced to consider adapting versions of designs that sometimes implicated *kirda* and *kurdungurlu* not involved in actual production. This often devolved into touchy discussions of the redistribution of money generated by the sale. Additionally, the tension between men and women quickly intensified when women began painting ritual sequences taken from the iconography of joint ceremonies without proper consultation with the men associated with the traditional performance. The men who felt slighted warned that unauthorized use of the shared designs, which they considered sacrilegiously represented, could make the women artists *parnpa,* that is, blind. After these accusations were leveled, the women in question discussed the matter among themselves and decided to paint over the problematic designs to avoid the stigma of transgression. However, this form of response was subsequently tempered; women soon after began to modify rather than obliterate shared restricted designs. To render a representation suitable for nonindigenous viewing, the women would, for example, change a circle into a semicircle, thus diluting or otherwise emending totemic significance. Alternatively, a crucial line could be deleted to allow a painting to be shown (Dick Kimber, personal communication, 1984).

Within a year, the women increased their collective independence with regard to men. Though the women never intentionally circumvented the boundaries of restriction, they did allow a few canvases containing nonpublic motifs to find their way to a nonindigenous audience. If, after the completion of a canvas, a design was deemed improper (such determinations were regularly reached by a *kurdungurlu,* a *kirda,* and even the artist herself), the work was either effaced or sold discreetly to a knowledgeable outsider, a practice that was adopted by men soon after. The logic legitimating the latter action held that inadvertent delineations of restricted material on canvas could be sold without liability if the work ended up in the possession of an individual familiar with and respectful of Warlpiri spiritual traditions. The practice was abandoned by 1986. After that, very few representations of restricted designs found synthetic representation.

When material not specifically owned by the painters was found to have been painted, the money generated would inevitably have to be redistributed in much the same way resources were allocated during the exchange and use of ritual material. Artists became increasingly proprietary of "their" designs, and disputes were quite common.

The exclusionary protocols of the early months evolved slowly into gender-specific collaborations that mirrored the exchanges of traditional material. That is to say, the force of residentiality began to insinuate itself into the making of paintings. Men who possessed managerial rights derived from nontraditional residential circumstance started providing assistance to their male residential kin. Women, similarly, pursued their patterns of assistance, helping those female relatives with whom they lived.

During the early months of the acrylic movement, joint painting by men and women was a rarity. Before such overt collaboration began, however, painters did negotiate ritual knowledge from their gender-specific domains for use, in modified forms, on the canvases of residential relatives of the opposite sex.

In December 1984 a Japanangka gave a *Jukurrpa* sketch to two of his sisters for use in the production of acrylic art. His sketch evoked a funeral ceremony that constituted a significant segment of the *Wardapi Jukurrpa,* or Goanna Dreaming, that tracked through Yinaparlku, a sacred site also known as Mt. Theo, located to the north of Yuendumu. Although the narrative associated with the iconography was already part of the women's cosmological patrimony—both women were conceived at Mt. Theo, a traditional connection further reinforced by the *kirda* rights to the land that they inherited from their father—the sisters were not familiar with the graphic representation, a clear indication of the material's restricted male status. For that reason, the women approached the prospect of public representation with a strong measure of caution, one compounded by the fact that most funeral events inhabit a decidedly nonpublic sphere. Faced with the obligation to render as "open" material variously characterized as "closed," *tarruku,* and "dear," the women began to produce a series of boards based on the Japanangka's sketch. As was common in the formative period of acrylic production, the women worked in relative isolation while they struggled to compose a proper visual translation, fearing that restricted components of the original might be inadvertently revealed.

Their first two efforts to finesse the problem of restriction deployed a tactic of camouflage. They hid the ceremonially "dear" design in the sketch in a thicket of icons that possessed limited spiritual significance. After two such improper attempts, a disagreement between the two artists erupted openly. The cause of the dispute very clearly focused on the propriety of the engendered works. One of the artists felt the boards were too revelatory. Specifically, she felt that the version of the Dreaming presented in the Japanangka's sketch had been rendered too fully, that certain details—for example, the illness that killed the Mythical Being, the method of burial, and the mourning procedures bracketing interment—

had no business finding expression in a nonindigenous environment. "It's a 'dear' one," she said, adding, with no small measure of agitation, "It's men's business." After some private discussion, the two painters eventually decided not to release the boards publicly. In the end, they sold the contested works to a non-Warlpiri, but one who possessed the ritual knowledge of an initiand—an anthropologist privy to, and respectful of, the ceremonial activities depicted. The women then painted a third version based on the sketch, but this time they began from a premise of omission. They removed the iconic representations that cued the cause of the Mythical Being's death and all references to burial, but retained the symbols of mourning and the geospatial markers identifying the locus of the schematized Dreaming. This pattern of graphic intervention is quite common when restricted material must be translated for a nonindigenous market. Location tends to be preserved, while the narrative that transects the site is dramatically altered or excised outright.

It is important to note that in rendering a once-restricted event public, the women did not believe they had diluted the importance of the Dreaming segment, even in this simplified, edited form. Quite the contrary. Increasing the audience (albeit in a metaceremonial medium) broadened the network of nurturance, situating their residential kin group's patrimony front and center in the spiritual and economic life of the settlement. The engendering process exemplified in the male-to-female migration of material—the move from sketch to board—underscores the domains through which ritual knowledge now often seems to travel: the shift from "inside"—the restricted space the Warlpiri sometimes identify as *kanunju*—to "outside," that is, the public space known as *kankarlu*.[8] And while gender is implicated in that movement (usefully conceptualized, too, as an act of translation, vulgarization, or paradigmatic shift), it is not the only motive force, or indeed even the primary one, behind the alteration. On the most superficial level, the rebuke by one sister of the other—that it was clearly "men's business"—might seem to suggest gender-bound exclusion. That was not the function of the admonition, however. Implicit in the phrase was that the design was part of "our men's" business, that is to say, part of a restricted patrimony owned by all three principals in the undertaking: the Japanangka and the two Napanangkas. The execution, embellishment, and ultimate deletion were undertaken to strengthen, preserve, and protect a ceremonial inheritance shared by the women, their brother, and relatives associated with the

Goanna Dreaming. At the same time, the adaptation was one of many efforts to expand the repertoire of "public" designs to satisfy the growing market for Aboriginal art.

By 1985, the residential kin template of assistance was further strengthened by the active participation of men and women on each other's canvases. This collaboration took two general forms. Either relatives would help the principal artist(s) by filling in the backgrounds, a typically tedious process of "dotting" few artists wished to complete, or an artist would sanction relatives to paint his or her design, and then share the proceeds, a workshop system that brought men and women together in a manner that sustained gender separation. By that I mean that in some instances a woman would paint one of her designs and have her husband "fill in." Male and female artists rarely collaborated as equals in the conceptualization of a story and the canvas it spawned, but the dynamic of residency enabled spouses and in-laws to assist in the completion of designs putatively designated "men's" or "women's."

In other words, the ever-changing composition of ritual life was observable, in a microcosm, in the negotiations leading to the composition of acrylic art. The production and consequential resource reallocation played out—at an accelerated pace—along lines of kinship and residency. The ritual material of women and men migrated back and forth among the ritual leaders, who were also, not surprisingly, the leaders of the art movement, a process of collaboration that distinguished itself from ceremonial transactions as traditionally constituted. In short, acrylic canvases expressed cross-gender connectedness both in product and in process.

Soon after, around 1986, husbands and wives began to allow themselves to paint contiguously. And though assistance might be offered, spouses did not tend to collaborate simultaneously, nor did they share Dreamings on a single canvas. At this juncture, few canvases were produced that bore the names of women and men. By 1988, however, demonstrably collaborative production began to find its way into the commercial market, with spouses conceptualizing and executing canvases as partners. This declarative engendering never overwhelmed the more common gender-specific procedures inherent in both ceremonial and metaceremonial undertakings, but it was frequent enough to point to the awareness—indeed, a thorough familiarity—that men had of women's designs, and women had of men's.

What we see in the production of acrylics, then, is a process of engen-

Figure 8. Photograph of *Janmarda Jukurrpa* (Bush Onion Dreaming, 342/87) at Wakurlpu (Courtesy of Jeannie Nungarrayi Egan, Tom Jangala Rice, and Warlukurlangu Artists Aboriginal Association, Inc., of Yuendumu)

dering, with three distinct phases spanning less than a decade. Phase one constituted gender-separate production in isolation. Phase two evinced separate but contiguous production. Phase three marked a process of joint production in which women and men worked together. The impacts of phases one through three have been multiple. We see the conflation and simplification of an expanded visual repertoire in a medium of metaceremonial value, and the engendering of production leading ultimately to the degendering of content.

How could the iconographic vocabulary seen in Warlpiri acrylics have stimulated both simplification and expansion? The answer requires us to unpack at least three components of a painting: the relationship of the acrylic to the medium of origin (for example, traditional forms of body painting, ground painting, and patterning of ritual objects), the fidelity of the canvas to the traditional design (independent of the medium of origin), and an overview of the changing repertoire of public acrylic design and its connection to the restricted *Jukurrpa* representations.

Whereas the repertoire of acceptable segments has increased as the movement gained popularity, the methods of iconic representation have been modified to avoid the violation of restrictions. Dreaming segments previously banned from nonindigenous use appeared in modified form. This modification, coupled with the nonindigenous nature of the medium, rendered the works proper.

Consider Warlpiri women and their use of traditional body designs when painting a canvas. Early on in the acrylic movement, nearly all the designs women painted for sale were exacting adaptations of the ceremonial designs applied to their torsos—designs generally associated with unrestricted iconography.[9] Over the last decade, however, women have all but abandoned any overt references to traditional corporeal surface, choosing instead to reproduce an iconography that has little direct connection to any single medium. This "infidelity" (or innovation) has broadened the repertoire and given new meaning to the notion of disembodying art (Dussart 1997). Additionally, the more recent canvases, while expanding the topographic and narrative representation of the *Jukurrpa,* withhold crucial information (or designs) that might provide access to the most profoundly "inside" *kanunju* readings of the Dreaming. Take, for example, three iterations of the Initiated Woman Dreaming (*Karnta Jukurrpa*) segment linked to Minamina, a sacred site to the west of Yuendumu. When it was first represented on canvas, in 1984, the Dreaming replicated a public body design that made visual reference only to a generic group of older women performing a "big" women's ceremony, or *yawulyu.* A year later, the relationship to the traditional medium (that is, body design) was no longer apparent, and the iconography was more complex. Specifically, a broad U-shaped symbol appeared at the bottom of the canvas, with a series of short parallel lines filling the concavity. That cluster revealed a newly "opened" graphic, though its narrative value remained closed until two years after that. In 1987, the women began to reveal that the broad U and internal hatch marks chronicled the fact that the Initiated Women in the Dreaming were sleeping. This conditional observation might seem inconsequential to the uninitiated, but to the Warlpiri familiar with this Dreaming, any reference to sleeping in the context of *Karnta Jukurrpa* indicates a ritual activity jointly undertaken by women and men. This connection was publicly declared when the women painted the same *Jukurrpa* with not one but two new iconographic clusters of cosmological significance. Considered separately, the added meander and grouping of some half dozen semicircles would have yielded little in the way of narrative significance. Together, however, they cued a public account of a *kurdiji,* an initiation event implicating women and men. What does not find representation in public in the 1987 version is the changing nature of that cross-gender engagement, a piece of the *Jukurrpa* known only to initiated men and women and ceremonially performed by men alone. Although an outsider may view this movement as one predicated on a trajectory toward "openness," there are other indigenous psychic imperatives also at work when acrylic canvases are painted. Because painting offers a metaceremonial method of nurturance, artists often select their subject by its relationship to the spiritual landscape it implicates. A rock hole that hasn't been sung and requires attention or a Dreaming track in need of evocation can gain some small measure of sustenance through the decidedly non-Warlpiri medium of brightly colored acrylic paint. Even art intended for the "public" will serve an unexpressed internal function. Often an artist will paint a series of canvases in the order that tracks the itinerary of a Dreaming he or she owns, and reflect on the benefits such serial representation provides, whether or not ceremonial activity is taking place simultaneously. As a measure of the connections drawn between the ritual and the representational, it is worth noting that artists in the early years of the movement regularly expressed consternation when the linear path they wanted to paint was at odds with the desires of the marketplace.

The long-term effect of the flourishing art movement was that the variety of segments increased (for both men and women) while the diversity of the originating media—that is to say, body paintings, sand designs, ground designs—constricted. What now gets painted may have connections to the patterning of traditional ground and body paintings, but they are connections that have been blurred. The engendering process has led to the cross-fertilization of Warlpiri iconography in ways that have precipitated a degendering of its style and content. It is now possible (if not common) for a Warlpiri ritual leader to be unable to identify the gender of the artist of a particular work, a form of iconic homogenization difficult to imagine within the repertoire of traditional designs.

CANVAS: THE SIZE/GENDER QUESTION

There has been some discussion of the correlation of canvas size to the gender of the artist. In the early days of Yuendumu production—that is to say, in 1984 and 1985—men's canvases tended to be larger than those painted by women. The reason has its origins not in the will of the artists but in the actions of Yuendumu's first art advisor, a non-Aboriginal man who resided in the settlement in 1985. The advisor, viewing examples of acrylic art produced during the previous decade by Aboriginal men residing in Papunya, a settlement due south of Yuendumu, determined that their large-scale paintings represented the dimensional characteristics of the gender-specific medium of ground painting. Based on this presumption, he distributed canvases at Yuendumu sized according to gender. And because women tended to adapt body designs to acrylic, the art advisor provided them with canvases dimensionally suited to their art. He never clarified this reasoning to the women, but did so to the men. The gender-based distinction was quickly corrected by the advisor's replacement, a woman who arrived at Yuendumu in 1986 and sensed that the size criterion caused no small measure of distress to the female artists. The female artists argued that because they were every bit as knowledgeable about the *Jukurrpa* as their male counterparts, and because the adaptations of the original media (that is, ground versus body painting) were for all intents and purposes conflated—engendered—there was no reason to maintain the difference. The Warlpiri women, and men, for that matter, situated their interests not in matters of gender, but in more personal and kin-based loci. As soon as the artists learned of the correlation between canvas size and the prices the art generated, economic consideration overwhelmed the nonindigenous discourses touching on issues of traditional media.[10]

Indeed, the economic repercussions of acrylic art were so pronounced that they offer further insight into the paths by which knowledge and the modest economic rewards associated with the distribution of that knowledge move through the settlement. Although acrylics were initially the bailiwick of older male and female ritual leaders, production has broadened, in the wake of monetary dividend, to include younger relatives of those early older painters, relatives who frequently lack the requisite knowledge and confidence demanded when painting a public version of a Dreaming. To mitigate this fear, senior ritual leaders often oversee, correct, and approve the acrylic representations of the Dreamings generated by their young relatives. When payments make their way back to the settlement, the overseers receive shares in ways that replicate the patterns of obligation associated with ceremonial exchange. Typically, young painters feel obliged (or are made to feel obliged) to redistribute some of the money from a sale (up to a third) to a senior relative (or relatives) who sanctions or in less formal ways promulgates production. Payment rights might be established through a classic *kirda* connection to the

Dreaming represented by the artist, or may be legitimated through residential affiliation. In cases where a senior ritual leader connected to the conception of the public representation refuses immediate payment from a junior executor, the debt remains and is considered due at a future date, in a form determined by the elder—a mode of obligation that correlates nicely with the compensatory transactions surrounding the exchange of ritual material as it is indigenously negotiated. This dynamic, like so many others, holds true as much for women as it does for men, and it is unaffected by moves between genders—an example of the ways in which the patterns of acrylic activity, like the patterns themselves, have come together. Payment issues, like the issues of canvas size and canvas repertoire, have less and less to do with the gender of the artist. The process of engendering has degendered the iconography, the medium, and the transactions that they precipitate. The sex-specific elaborations Munn observed within the "graphic code" shared by women and men find only limited iconographic expression in the acrylics produced at Yuendumu, subsumed as they are under the overarching pressures that attend residential affiliation (Munn 1973:112). The Dreaming canvases, however generically "Warlpiri" they have become (with men and women planning, producing, and narrating work in ways that very clearly overlap), manifest a network of connectedness that reaffirms (in the nature of the collaborations and the benefits derived from those collaborations) a model privileging the expressions of social identity of individuals and individuals' residential camps over those of settlements or "Aboriginals."

The canvas has, in short, provided a field for much more than the exchange of ritual material between men and women. It documents the associated struggles, desires, aspirations, connections, and collaborations of the artists and their kin. What was once a segregated undertaking now accommodates, indeed encourages, the interaction of women and men, and in so doing documents in a stable medium the more transient engenderings that emerge in the wake of nocturnal visitations of the *Jukurrpa* and in the ceremonial exchanges such dreams often provoke.

CONCLUSION: ENGENDERING RITUAL

The increase in cross-gender exchange is a response to residentiality, a realignment of ritual activity that comes in the wake of forced sedentarization. But to characterize the change in solely quantitative terms—of increase, expansion, and so on—belies a radical revision of the configuration of ceremonial responsibility. The observations of midcentury anthropologists, documenting, as Munn did, "the relatively low ritual status and power of women," represent a picture wholly at odds with the circumstances of today, where the status and power of women at Yuendumu not only are not low, but are irrefutably crucial to the reproduction of the *Jukurrpa* and the correlative psychic health that accompanies that act of reproduction.[11]

This change brings to mind one of Strathern's many trenchant meditations on matters of gender, specifically on the nature of sociality that matters of gender differentiate, and its relationship to domination. I will quote her remarks at length because their nuanced oscillations point to certain qualities that make Warlpiri ritual so distinct.

"In the end," Strathern observes, "men's and women's domains are not socially distinct. Rather, each may act in a same-sex or cross-sex way, in contexts that are always conceptually transient. Time, duration, and sequence are as important to form as they are to the gift." Strathern goes on to offer up an example, taken from New Guinea, of a gender-specific scope of action distinguishing women from men. Men of the Highlands, she notes, "enjoy both a collective life and the relations of domestic kinship, whereas women appear confined to the latter." Strathern, with predictable subversiveness, quickly undermines this generalization in elegant contradistinction to the presumptive dualism. "We must get the mathematics right," Strathern ends up cautioning, and indeed she is right. Binary formulations, whether attached to Highlanders or the Warlpiri, generally result in something worse than gross miscalculation. The nature of those variables we label "man" and "woman" undergo such constant change that any attempt to construct an equation based on such X's and Y's (or should it be XX's and XY's?) would be predicated on untenable formulas.

At Yuendumu, where the collective and domestic are constantly converging under the strain of external, nonindigenous dominance, Strathern's comments take on even greater weight. Is it any wonder that in a ritual life where Warlpiri men no longer assert ritual dominance over women, the content and form, structure and expression of the cosmology should display concomitant transformation? Overt exchange of ritual material between women and men—whatever the medium—is the material expression of social transformation. "Engendering" is a reflection of changes in process, product, and producers. Strathern's insights on notions of transience play themselves out each time women and men come together to exchange (or not exchange) ritual material. Engendering is simultaneously the cause and the effect of ritual.

I have tried in this chapter to document just how the transfers of material between men and women have tended to loosen the restrictions associated with ritual representation. Yet even when engendering requires material to retain its indigenousness, revision of the restricted repertoire has a profound, and generally salutary, effect. The exchange of material, regardless of its "open" or "closed" status (to use Aboriginal English's handy pair of antonyms), invigorates the Dreaming, and that, in turn, invigorates the Dreamers, which in turn, invigorates the Dreaming.

Engendering highlights just how responsive the Warlpiri and the *Jukurrpa* are to each other and how responsive both have been to the external pressures long suffered. Indeed, a large measure of the cross-gender exchange of ritual and the reconfiguration of its (broadened) public enactment can be treated as the material response to the ubiquitous pressures of acculturation.[12] For as the final chapter shall show, cross-gender exchange goes hand in hand with cross-cultural exchange. Both moves require the de- or reclassification of ritual material. Both force the abandonment of whatever static notions of the Dreaming some have managed to retain. Indeed, the public promulgation, defense, and maintenance of the *Jukurrpa* recapitulates so many of the issues raised in previous chapters that it serves nicely as a closing chapter to the study of Warlpiri ritual as seen through the bifocals of kinship and gender.

6.

FROM *PURLAPA* TO *YAWULYU WARRAJANYANI*

Public Ritual and the Projection of Social Identity

While there has been much anthropological inquiry into the constitution and function of "secret" ceremonies among Central Desert Aboriginal groups, significantly less attention has been paid to the indigenous significance of "open" ritual, those ceremonies unencumbered by restriction. Indeed, there has often seemed to be a taint of illegitimacy associated with rituals accessible to the uninitiated, as if their very enactment somehow delegitimated or diluted the value of the information on display. Justification for this perspective is easy enough to come by; the Warlpiri themselves equate the word *warraja* with the English words *open, free,* and *cheap,* a synonymity that might, at first glance, confirm the limited value of ritual material or the events in which such material gets circulated. And yet, as I have taken pains to point out in chapter 2, the last of these words—the seemingly pejorative term *cheap*—refers more to the accessibility of a Dreaming than to the quality of its cosmological potency or social significance. Access may be "cheap" insofar as it is free of the costly burdens of initiation, but the material content that finds ceremonial expression in no way lacks value. As such, public men's ceremonies (which are known as *purlapa*) and their equivalent performances in the repertoire of women's ritual (*yawulyu warrajanyani*) are both characterized as *wiri,* which is the word the Warlpiri use to acknowledge a profusion of spiritual power.

Far from being considered illegitimate, tarnished, or in any other way less than genuine, the public event constitutes a valued arena in which the Warlpiri derive ever-growing material reward and cross-cultural legitimacy.

In fact, public ritual clarifies the valences of Warlpiri social identity in ways that "closed" events often cannot. The public execution of ritual is frequently accompanied by similarly open articulations of methods and (putative) motive in ways restricted ritual is not. It is in reference to open rituals that the Warlpiri are apt to dilate on the protection, nurturance, and connections generated by ceremony in general. Indeed, the word *jinamardarni,* which, as noted earlier, means "to look after," "to protect," "to hold," "to keep," carries a very explicit tenor of faultfinding if uttered in a restricted context. But the very same term used during "open" ceremonies retains a different connotation; it is used with the positive intent to confirm the connection of performers and viewers. With reference to *purlapa,* the word celebrates a collaboration of place and people.[1] My point: Explication is encouraged in some ritual contexts and avoided in others. Public ceremony, among its many functions, serves to declare the potency of the Dreaming in ways restricted ceremonies cannot. I leave to others reflections, both figurative and literal, created by the bond between indigenous performer and the non-Aboriginal audience.[2] For the purposes of this study, it is the internal moves and motivations of the Warlpiri in a domain that externalizes ritual that I wish to address. Public ritual does much more than proclaim the richness of *Jukurrpa* beyond the settlement. It also serves to recirculate ritual knowledge, and in the process sustains if not revivifies social networks, which in turn stimulate correlative reconfigurations of prestige and economic circumstance. In this sense, public performance simultaneously functions as a mirror and projector of Warlpiri culture. The forces of gender, kinship, and residency are all brought into high relief when the neglected history of Yuendumu's public ceremonial life is laid out for inspection.

Viewed schematically, three distinct, if overlapping, stages of public ritual activity can be isolated from the half-century chronology of the settlement. Stage one in this timeline, which stretches from the late 1940s to the mid-1970s, is one of almost entirely indigenous consequence, limited to the *purlapa* of men. In stage two—marked, if not exactly precipitated, by the Aboriginal Land Rights (Northern Territory) Act of 1976—public ritual was externalized to include an intercultural audience. Expansion can be seen, too, in the representation of public enactment, which began to include Warlpiri women performing "open" ceremonies parallel to those of male kin. With this broadening of constituencies among performers and viewers alike came an expanded set of motives, many of which subsumed earlier priorities to external legal demand prompted by governmental land rights legislation. Deployed for the *kardiya* (loosely translated as "light-skinned people," that is, non-Aborigines), public events, by the end of the second stage, were overseen in large measure by women. *Purlapa* in effect yielded to *yawulyu warrajanyani.*[3] As the legal actions diminished in frequency, another cross-cultural phenomenon, the acrylic art movement, seemed to take over as a catalyst for public ceremonial activity. The third stage in the history of public ritual at Yuendumu, which began in the early 1980s and continues to this day, has been fueled by the international demand for so-called dot paintings. The newfound demand for public ceremony linked to art exhibitions has meant the periodic export of public ritual beyond the settlement gates and, by implication, beyond the homes and countries of the Warlpiri's Ancestral Beings. During this final period, Yuendumu's businesswomen have served as the primary advocates of the *Jukurrpa* as it is ceremonially presented to the world at large, but there advocacy is focused on matters that transcend the circumstance of sex.

To be sure, the changes in public ritual performance have tended to play themselves out more ambiguously than the above historical trisection might suggest.[4] Nevertheless, the fact remains that the baton of public representation has passed from men to women with little or no analysis of why that switch has occurred.

STAGE ONE: CONJOINING "LOOSENESS" AND "SOLIDARITY"

The two principal researchers working with the Warlpiri in the 1950s, Munn and Meggitt, dedicated little more than a few lines to public ceremonies per se. Nevertheless, their brief observations provide a useful basis upon which to confront *purlapa* and public ritual in general.[5] Meggitt downplayed the significance of men's unrestricted events, likening *purlapa* to "medieval European mystery plays that edified and expressed group solidarity as well as providing entertainment" (1962:244). Munn, for her part, noted on the basis of the two rituals she observed that "*bulaba* [*purlapa*] do not have any specific aims beyond general entertainment and the dramatization of *djugurba [Jukurrpa]*." She added that the execution of public designs was loosely organized in ways that denied the strict endogamous structures present in secret events, and that they did little beyond "yield feelings of general well-being"(Munn 1973:53).

Putting aside the theatrical language Munn and Meggitt share, there is a component in each researcher's description worth retaining. Meggitt's identification of "group solidarity" as a rationale for enactment and Munn's recognition of "looseness" were both substantiated by the older ritual leaders I queried on the subject of *warraja* events in the days just prior to and following sedentarization.[6] These same informants, male and female alike, while not dismissing the "entertaining" nature of the *purlapa,* were quick to note the competitive and stressful circumstances that attended theirs, particularly in the wake of forced settlement, when various Central Desert groups were summarily corralled. Still, as I say, "looseness" and "group solidarity" are concepts worth preserving in any discussion of public ritual at Yuendumu. In fact, the consolidation of those two phrases goes a long way in capturing the spirit of "open" events. Then and now, it is the looseness of public ritual that seems to accommodate the expression of group solidarity.

What was the nature of the loose group solidarity affirmed by public ritual? It depends how and to whom the question is posed. A member of a residential camp lacking in ritual authority might invoke general notions of diversion and cohesion that are consonant with the language of entertainment. But the ritual leaders (and their close relatives, male and female) who were directly implicated in the performance of *purlapa* at the time tend to have a very different take on dividends that accrue through the enactment of public ritual. They invoke the prestige such events generate for the residential camp identified with the ritual leaders overseeing performance. Given that "well-being" is a goal of most ritual activity, the phrase does little to distinguish the specific function of *purlapa,* which has at least one ever-present, if implicit, motive: the declaration of territorial and cosmological authority that is by and large camp-specific. Additionally, public ritual can serve to stimulate subsequent intergroup exchanges of restricted ceremonial currency, used in effect as a training ground for "closed" events. Relatively free of the dangers of trespass or transgression—the threat of sorcery that hovers over the more potent forms of the Dreamings—public ceremony provides a context in which the Warlpiri more freely express the parameters of performance rights and the motivations beyond the selection of a repertoire and the performers who enact it.

Purlapa events, in the early days of settlement, were overseen by senior men who recruited circumcised youth beginning the initiation process to help perform enactments for all who wished to observe. Older ritual leaders recall that these events were more common before the local restrictions that attended sedentarization were set in place. Indeed, work and school schedules imposed on the residents of Yuendumu by white authorities circumscribed all manner of indigenous ritual. *Purlapa* especially suffered. Because it became necessary for the Warlpiri to compress a year's worth of ritual activity into the final weeks of the year, when their overseers retreated to celebrate the nonindigenous ritual of Christmas, the Warlpiri focused on "required" ceremonies, that is, those obligatory events associated with rites of passage. Big, nonessential ceremonies such as *purlapa* diminished in frequency.

That is not to say that the impact of *purlapa* on the collective consciousness of the settlement's ritual leaders diminished. Uni Nampijinpa's reflections are particularly telling, since they constitute a woman's observations about erstwhile events performed by men alone. Like other older *yamparru,* male and female alike, she is quick to identify *purlapa* as "real" business, that is to say, ceremonial activity of great social and cosmological consequence. She recalls that the public events were enacted, when possible, each time a new group entered the settlement. Asked if it mattered whether the newcomers were Warlpiri, she said that it did not, adding, "Whenever a new mob came in, we [would] perform a *purlapa.*" The "we" she used—*nganimpa*—requires clarification. It was used in a way that suggests a decidedly exclusionary quality; the "we" did not connect Uni to other Aboriginal people generically (*yapa*), or even to other Warlpiri. She deployed her "we" to invoke her connection to the West Camp mob (which was then in the process of formation), the residential kin group with whom she had come to identify. She went on to say that her mob had overseen the bulk of the *purlapa* events in the early days and had usually ended up "big winners." This is how the residents of West Camp became "one mob" (*jintajuku*), according to Uni. Her observation underscores an earlier point: that residency is often destiny in matters of Warlpiri ritual. That single word goes a long way in overwhelming the usual expectations that attach themselves to gender-specific performance. Uni's allegiance to the male actors was so presumptive that it is easy to lose sight of its significance. A Warlpiri woman was generating prestige directly, and without qualification, from the ritual acts of men. In short, the benefits of ritual attach themselves not only to the performer, but to the performer's residential kin as well—a form of "engendering" that transcends the cross-gender transfer of ritual currency.

This is not to say that more wide-ranging motives of Aboriginal nurturance were absent from the *purlapa* performed in the opening decades of settlement. However, events stimulating broader expressions of indigenous solidarity were usually generated in contexts of cross-cultural contestation—contexts as far removed from the language of "entertainment" as Uni's proud recollections of triumph. Performances of *purlapa* for nonindigenous audiences (that is, whites) were rare during the early years of sedentarization, but at least one such engagement warrants mention insofar as it foreshadows subsequent cross-cultural protocols. The *purlapa* most regularly invoked by senior Warlpiri—one that came to serve as a template for future public representations triggered by the Land Rights Movement—took place in 1971, after a mining company came to Yuendumu in search of uranium. The company's tests focused on a ritual site near Yampirri-Parnturnu. Although the site was implicated in the Fire Dreaming rituals of both men and women, only men had access rights to Yampirri-Parnturnu itself. As the Warlpiri now explain it, it was the site restriction that precipitated the gender-specific ceremony performed for the miners. However, women actively participated in the prefatory discussions leading up to the *purlapa,* and they remained close at hand when the ritual took place. What made the event anomalous, however, was not the involvement of women (all of whom came from the patrilineal descent groups of the men who performed), but exclusion of the younger males from the enactment or its viewing. The mining *purlapa* was a hybrid event evincing qualities of both "open" and restricted ceremonies. The long-term impact of the event was a clarification of the role business leaders of both genders would play in the cross-cultural negotiations characterizing the second stage of public ritual at Yuendumu.

The mining *purlapa* triggered a series of discussions between the performers and the geologists. Because the mining company ceased prospecting (for reasons that had more to do with profit than any newfound appreciation of the *Jukurrpa*), the Warlpiri presumed their efforts had paid off. I made inquires about the locus of the victory; the big win privileged the performers and their female residential kin. Once again, location and agnation took precedence over gender. The big winners were identified (by themselves and others) as the West Camp mob associated with the Fire Dreaming, a localization of group identity consonant with earlier observations.

Even though the cessation of the geological testing was misattributed to ritual enactment, it established a correlation between performance and territorial politics that would prove increasingly useful as a medium for cross-cultural advocacy. The mining *purlapa* served as a template for the deployments of public ritual prompted by the passage, in 1976, of the Land Rights Act. That single piece of legislation dramatically expanded the function and frequency of public ritual, and in doing so reshaped the makeup and motives of the medium.

STAGE TWO: PUBLIC RITUAL AS POLITICAL ACT

Soon after the passage of the Aboriginal Land Rights (Northern Territory) Act, Warlpiri ritual leaders began to deploy public ritual more regularly as a means of cross-cultural advocacy. Many of the "open" ceremonial manifestations in the decade after the act was passed were a direct response to the legislation, which allowed ritual activity to be used as a tool for legitimating indigenous claims to vacant Crown lands. Because the legislation necessitated proof of traditional land ownership or genealogical connection to the traditional owners of the land under review, the Warlpiri (and other Aboriginal groups) began tendering evidence of affiliation in various forms that included public ritual. *Warraja* events did a nice job conflating genealogical and territorial claims by declaring simultaneous connection both to the lands and to their ancestral owners. Public ceremony provided an aptly intercultural setting in which the nuanced obligations of indigenous Law could meet the black-and-white provisions of governmental legislation.

The two territorial proceedings of greatest consequence for the Warlpiri at Yuendumu were the Claim to Areas of Traditional Land by the Warlpiri and Kartangarurru-Kurintji (1978) and the Claim to Chilla Well Pastoral Lease by the Warlpiri (1985). The first case predates my fieldwork; however, I was able to witness firsthand the effects of the second intervention, and in doing so observe the expanding role of women in the enactment of public ritual.

By the time the Chilla Well claim began, the baton of public representation had very clearly been passed.[7] The move from *purlapa* to *yawulyu warrajanyani* was accompanied by a marked increase in the frequency of public events now undertaken by women. Though exact numbers are hard to come by, it is fair to say that during the 1980s, *purlapa* events occurred at Yuendumu at a rate of roughly one or two a year. Women, by contrast, were performing *yawulyu warrajanyani* at an ever-growing pace, culminating with twelve ceremonies in 1988, a year in which I was able to record only one single *purlapa* enactment.[8]

Many of the women's ceremonies were "practice" sessions for formal court hearings—a means of perfecting, of rendering fluent, dances that would legitimate territorial claim. No fewer than thirteen public *yawulyu* were undertaken in direct response to the demands of the Chilla proceeding, which was thirteen more than the men performed. When I asked a principal male claimant, a *kumanjayi* Jungarrayi, why no correlative *purlapa* were undertaken, he said that the actions of his female relatives were sufficient to demonstrate the claim. The Jungarrayi noted that his relatives had exposed their breasts (*lampanu*) ceremonially, thus legitimating the claims of "his mob." He added, to further underline the strength of his personal connection to the actions of the women's event, that he had played the preperformance role in the negotiations surrounding repertoire, a neat inversion of the gender dynamics present when it was women who aided men prior to the miners' *purlapa*. In each instance, only one gender performed, and yet both planned the events, both monitored them, and both ultimately shared the benefits the events generated.

Single-sex public ritual seems to reflect mutually constituted obligations and concerns. As for the restricted rituals performed for the court (by both men and women), these tended to sidestep details of design or song deemed too dangerous for display in the presence of the uninitiated. A case in point: Amid the welter of evidence presented before the judge, absent was a design associated with the Rat Kangaroo Dreaming (*Mala Jukurrpa*) with an itinerary that crosscut Jila, the epicenter of the disputed area. (The map designation was transliterated as "Chilla Well.") No explanation was provided as to why this design was omitted while other restricted knowledge found representation in various forms (objects, dances, designs, and songs). Relevant to this discussion was the process by which the facts of the design's omission was communicated. Men first approached to show me a representation of the Dreaming segment, warning of its *tarruku* status. Women then separately approached me to confirm that the design had been displayed, noting that it was part of their own restricted repertoire as well. The men and women were linked to one another by the bonds of residentially constituted kinship, and linked to the deleted Dreaming segment by traditional *kirda-kurdungurlu* ties, yet another manifestation of the cohesive separateness of Warlpiri ritual life. The content of the *Mala* design ultimately found material representation in a *yawulyu* event performed by the women owners on behalf of those kin—male and female—linked to the site and segment in question.

An obvious question comes to mind: Why the gender shift? Why did public ritual, once the province of men, slowly become the duty and right primarily of women? The answer touches, to some degree, on one of the more insidious consequences of forced sedentarization: alcohol abuse. One of the by-products of the ever-present risk of inebriation at Yuendumu was the inappropriate (to the point of transgressive) revelation of restricted ritual material. Because men drank more than women and also had access to a wider range of restricted information, it was inevitable that indiscretions, and outright violations, of performative norms befell them more than their female kin. This risk only increased when ritual activity transpired beyond the drink-restricted borders of the settlement. To obviate this problem, women began to take over the public duties of their male relatives. Men considered that they could depend on strong (*wiri*) women in these contexts, and it was this reliability that was invoked to explain the switch of performative responsibilities. And yet the transfer was not seen by the ritual participants, then or now, as an abdication or appropriation. In fact, the change in representation tends barely to be acknowledged, and it is shrugged off when raised by curious ethnographers. One ritual leader explained that he withdrew his commitment to perform *Jukurrpa* publicly because of a brother who was regularly getting drunk and threatening the protocols of performance. The *yamparru* said he had gotten his sisters and daughters (that is, female members of the performers' patrilineal descent group) to step in and perform a parallel Dreaming from the women's repertoire of public events.

This wholesale transfer of performative responsibility, like the smaller migrations of ritual knowledge described in the previous chapter, reflects more than the mutability of Warlpiri ceremonial life and the aforementioned constancy of change; it underscores the gender-specific methods by which residential kin groups retain their strength. Ritually powerful men burdened by the stresses attending restricted events were only too willing to have female kin take over the performative duties of the settlement's public ceremonial life. Neither the erstwhile performer of *purlapa* nor his female replacements conceptualized the cross-gender transfer as one that diminished male authority; it did not enhance the status of the women in relation to their sidelined relative. What was retained, the women and the men stressed, was the place of the residential kin group in the ritual life of the settlement. That, in the end, was what mattered.

Some observers might be tempted to hypothesize that these Warlpiri women were "granted" the right to perform because they were unaware of men's restricted business and thus incapable of the transgression the man risked when performing with his brother. Yet that logic would run counter to fact. Two of the women who took over the ritual duties were themselves powerful *yamparru,* leaders who possessed a great deal of the knowledge that the male relative wished to protect. The risks of indiscretion were just as great for them, and the punishments similarly severe.

The increased deployment of women in public representation of the Dreaming was, in effect, a self-regulating response by ritual leaders of both genders to the social circumstances threatening to undermine the distribution (or, rather, nondistribution) of ritual currency. But this begs a second question: Why didn't the Warlpiri share the burden of public representation by performing joint events that would acknowledge their unexpressed collaboration? The reason is that joint ceremonies, while overtly implicating both men and women, do not avoid the risky use of restricted material in the way that certain gender-specific events can. To perform jointly and openly would not have been possible unless Warlpiri ritual leaders had negotiated how and what to delete to make such enactments proper. And since women already possessed a large body of unrestricted material—itineraries filled with unrestricted Dreaming segments that could be reenacted with little risk of impropriety or indiscretion—it seemed best to pass the reins of public ritual to them.

Yet another question must be asked: Did land claims, and the associated ritual activities that resituated the role of women in public ceremonies, expand women's ritual power? Or did they instead express that power in a new intercultural context with greater regularity? A simple answer is hard to come by. When women in the settlement increased their role in the public representation of ritual, they did so as both members of a residential kin group and as women. Yet when the overlapping motivations for action are weighed, what emerges is a sense that the female performers undertook the obligation to nurture their residential mob and to enhance that mob's prestige in the universe of the settlement and beyond.

That is not to say the expanded role was accepted unquestioningly. With the status came performative expectation, and not just from indigenous sources. A number of female *yamparru* overseeing the *yawulyu warrajanyani* during this period recall how white public servants, local teachers in particular, demanded improper representations of ritual in order to legitimate land ownership. On more than one occasion, the same nonindigenous authorities urged the enactment of multigenerational rituals that required the use of uninitiated women, a situation that ended awkwardly, with expressions of embarrassment (*kurntangka*) coming from novices and *yamparru* alike.

While land rights legislation, alcohol consumption, and the misguided, if well-intentioned, efforts by public servants all had an impact on public ritual, they did little to change the substance of the material performed. The Dreaming narratives themselves managed to retain their indigenous integrity despite various external pressures—pressures that expanded in the mid-1980s, when there was sudden demand for ritual enactment beyond the territories of the Dreaming. It was this exportation of representation that marked the third phase of public ceremony, an intercultural phenomenon that reveals with remarkable clarity many of the intracultural dimensions of Warlpiri ritual.

STAGE THREE: FROM COURT TO CANVAS

In the mid-1980s, a new factor was added to the list of ceremonial stimuli: the international interest in the acrylic canvases painted by various Central Desert Aboriginal groups. The Land Rights Movement, in effect, slowly gave way to a movement of different kind—one that propelled the iconography of the Warlpiri into the maw of the international art market. With the demand for "dot" paintings came related solicitations for ceremonial enactment of the Dreamings depicted on canvas. In fact, the three most important art exhibitions of the 1980s to feature work by Warlpiri painters—an event in Sydney in 1982, another in Darwin in 1985, and an Adelaide exhibit that took place in 1988—were all inaugurated by public ceremonies. While newspaper accounts of these performances typically relied on a rhetoric of pan-Aboriginal "spirituality," there was in the choice of performance and repertoire a hint of the camp-based competition that characterizes so much of Yuendumu's ritual life.[9] More significantly, the three events, while sharing certain superficial qualities, demonstrate in their differences the evolution in tactics used to lay claim (and counterclaim) to a reinvented form of ritual—one that, by virtue of its novelty, has generated a reconstituted form of prestige.

In 1982, a group of ten Warlpiri women traveled to Sydney and performed a *yawulyu warrajanyani* at the Australian Museum in conjunction with a show featuring dancing boards, baby carriers, and other female ritual objects. Though museum officials limited their efforts to the artworks, the Warlpiri saw the show as an opportunity to make manifest the richness of the *Jukurrpa,* and to that end decided to enact a series of Dreamings. The women who ventured to Sydney, all older ritual leaders, were chosen after a settlement-wide negotiation that brought to the surface some of the basic pressures that attend ritual performance. Indeed, the foreign invitation raised many of the same questions a local event taking place at, say, the ritual grounds of the Yuendumu Women's Museum would have prompted. But it also added to those questions new ones relating to the distance of the performance site from home (*ngurra*) and the substantial scale of the ceremonial representation.

The "business" talks preceding the trip centered around what Dreaming should be enacted, what version, and what segment, and also how it should be performed and by whom. Beneath often blandly articulated queries and suggestions were the unspoken but well-known affiliations that each Dreaming, segment, version, and performer had in the constellation of *Jukurrpa* and the authority that came with each.

In the end, the ten women chosen were selected for a variety of reasons. All were considered ritually fluent—that is, praiseworthy as dancers, singers, and painters. In addition, all were deemed capable of travel. (Some women had to be taken off the list of potential performers because they risked *yirrarru,* or homesickness, perceived by all as a health hazard that could spread to other kin group members.) The selection talks ultimately yielded a number of women who were deemed (both by themselves and by their kin) capable of reproducing the Dreamings of all six of the principal residential camps at Yuendumu. This criterion for selection was by no means a given at the start, but the end result of many weeks of bargaining and negotiation.

By settling on a repertoire reenacting versions of the Water, Goanna, and Bush Yam Dreamings, the negotiators agreed they could represent the six principal residential camps of the settlement. Indeed, the rationale, and the roster and repertoire it produced, were all hammered out in a series of training rituals conducted before the trip. In closed and stressful settings marked by exhortations to train (*piljipiljijarrimi*), the ritual leaders weighed what could and could not be transmitted in Sydney, and how and by whom, measuring among themselves the relative risks and rewards attached to each of the segments considered for public viewing. In addition to training events, where only women were present, preparations for the

Sydney ceremonies included lengthy discussions with male relatives over the capacities of individual performers and the risks attendant to the Dreamings being considered. Preparation very clearly elided the interests of women and men, even though the discussions focused on the ceremonial actions to be carried out in a public setting where only women would perform. The display, the women decided (again, after consultation with male relatives), would bestow knowledge on the museumgoers, and that offering of knowledge would in turn stimulate reciprocal responsibility. The use of public ritual as a precipitator of mutual obligation—a logic governing the earlier miners' *purlapa*—found renewed expression at the *yawulyu warrajanyani* in Sydney.

Did this strategy succeed? Partially. While the cross-cultural dividends did not meet expectations, there was a feeling that the performance had been successful (*nyanungu nyayirni pinjaku*) insofar as it declared the vitality of the Dreamings overseen by all six of the settlement camps. The diffusion of ceremonial legitimacy was confirmed in concrete ways by the even distribution of the small sums received during the event. The money was shared based on the Dreamings represented, an act with symbolic significance, if only limited economic impact. The cohesion and settlement-wide goodwill were short-lived, however. To satisfy the interests of all camps, the Sydney dancers were forced to modify the protocols of performance; owners of the Dreamings were allowed to perform without proper managerial oversight. This suspension of the *kurdungurlu* protocol was particularly ill received by those groups who had the representation necessary to undertake rituals in a properly monitored fashion.

What emerged in the wake of the Sydney performance was a conundrum that would permeate much subsequent discourse on matters of public ritual: whether to pursue a policy of inclusion or one guided by principles of ceremonial rigor. Because some of Yuendumu's residential kin groups lacked the necessary complement of managers and owners, the principle of pluralism proved dangerously at odds with traditional protocols that emphasized properness.

The dilemma this choice presented was exacerbated in the wake of the next set of public rituals tethered to an art exhibit. For the Darwin exhibition, eighteen ritual leaders—men and women—traveled north, though again only the women performed. Again, the performative imperative was stimulated by indigenous discourse, not curatorial request. And as happened before in Sydney, the Darwin negotiations established a performance repertoire that effectively relaxed the owner-manager proviso of enactment to accommodate a wide, highly representative cycle of dances. And as happened after Sydney, the return of the performers was met with heated debate over the protocols of ceremony. This time, the settlement's ritual leaders agreed to regulate more vigorously the reciprocal obligations of owner and manager. The net result of this decision was to grant substantial control of subsequent public rituals to those residential camps that included among their ritually active members the requisite configuration of owners and managers. Ritual representation, and the correlative authority it implied, constricted as Dreamings were one by one omitted from the repertoire of representation on the grounds of insufficient management.

By the time the Adelaide performance took place in 1988, a single kin group dominated the public ceremonial activities exported from Yuendumu. The Nangala and Nampijinpa from West Camp were able to push through repertoires favoring their Dreamings. The Water Dreaming from Mikanji and the Fire Dreaming from Ngarna flourished with regular nurturance. The Dreamings owned and managed by residents of the settlement's weaker camps languished. Many of the less powerful groups reacted to this situation by withdrawing from the performance. One senior woman whose residential camp had helped finance her trips to the Sydney and Darwin exhibitions decided not to attend the Adelaide event because, she said, she could not count on the assistance of the West Camp mob to perform her own group's Dreamings. To attend without performing would have diminished her prestige and the prestige of her mob, she explained with a rare display of bitterness.

Those kin groups still able and willing to travel had their Dreamings marginalized by West Camp ritual leaders, who were able to determine repertoire and duration of the dances and songs performed.[10] The irony here is that demands for the preservation of traditional rigor—that is, the maintenance of *kirda-kurdungurlu* oversight—allowed West Camp to rewrite the guidelines of public ritual enactment in ways that obviated traditional guidelines. Unrestricted ceremonies eventually came to be controlled by various close agnates of West Camp members. Not only did the members of the group privilege the Dreamings they owned as *kirda,* but they extended their residentially conceptualized power by promoting the performance of Dreamings they managed as *kurdungurlu* even when there was inadequate or tenuous representation by the owners needed for proper enactment. Embracing a rhetoric of pan-Aboriginal or pan-Warlpiri identity—"we are all one family" was the expression most often used to justify these adaptive performances—West Camp proved capable of both privileging the Dreamings they owned and expanding the performative repertoire of the Dreamings they managed. The group repeatedly modified the protocols of ritual enactment—this after having prevented modification after Darwin—by pressuring weaker residential groups to help perform Dreamings that would enhance the status of the West Camp even though their partners had only limited (for example, subsection) connection to the material presented. The weaker groups usually accepted this argument, earning a small measure of prestige by their association with intercultural reproduction of the Dreaming.[11]

One other seemingly significant difference characterized the 1988 Adelaide event: Men performed. Why the performative involvement after nearly a decade of limited performative engagement? It was, as the men and women explained, reluctant recompense for the efforts of two knowledgeable male anthropologists who worked for the South Australian Museum and who had been crucial in the repatriation of a number of important sacred ceremonial objects. The *purlapa* was undertaken as a reciprocal act with these two anthropologists, who were *ngampurrpa* (needful, desirous) of "seeing" men's business they had never before witnessed. Absent from the explanation was any internal discourse on the relationship between the women's *yawulyu* and the men's *purlapa.*

What was more clearly part of the Warlpiri consciousness was that the pluralism of Sydney had yielded, in less than a decade, to the camp-specific repertoire of Adelaide. Which form of public enactment was more characteristically "Warlpiri"? The question misrepresents the motive forces at work.[12] Broad-based nurturance and residential allegiance were present in some fashion in all three ceremonial negotiations, and the fluidity of these imperatives constitutes a defining characteristic of Warlpiri ritual life, whatever ultimately gets enacted. Furthermore, the either/or construction obscures the actual tenor of the events in much the way gender dichotomy misconstrues the collaborative nature of separately performed rituals. The basic integrity of Warlpiri ritual life was maintained even as these changes were taking place.

During my decade-long survey of ritual, I took notes on the motives proffered for public performance. These included education (for example, the transmission of an open version of the *Jukurrpa* to a *kardiya* audience); remuneration (through the sale of the art and other monetary compensation for performance); negotiation (over matters of land rights, mineral rights, and so on); protestation; association; and "identification."

The last rationale was one pegged more to camp-specific kin group pride than to broader Aboriginal declarations of self. One motive, however, appeared absent from the ritual negotiations of public ritual: gender. Gender seemed beside the point.

When I asked after the Sydney event why no men were involved in the performances, I was corrected. The men might not have performed, but their involvement was never in doubt. After all (the men and women explained), the Dreamings were as much theirs as they were the Dreamings of the women who performed. Yes, Sydney and Darwin witnessed women's ceremonies, while Adelaide was privy to the enactments of both women and men. But that was not what the performers focused on.

For the Warlpiri, the gender shift in the public ceremonial life of the settlement actually hides a more telling component of sedentary existence: the primacy of kin-based residency. To be sure, the Dreaming performances, especially those at art exhibitions, have become the acknowledged domain of senior women. Businesswomen have accepted an ever-expanding role in the extraterritorial protection (and promotion) of Aboriginal identity through its various cosmological media. Their role as gatekeepers has grown to include an ambassadorial component.[13] But to restrict analysis to the performative dimension of the change is to dislocate the nature of Warlpiri connectedness. Both in the settlement and beyond, the performance of public ritual and the negotiations surrounding it are infused with a desire for ceremonial preeminence that situates itself in networks of residential kinship.

The evolution of public ritual from *purlapa* to *yawulyu warrajanyani* has been one of marked shifts in gender responsibility, as well as of changes in the tactics surrounding the selection of repertoire. And yet there is, consonant with that ever-changing nature of function and performative representation, an indigenous constant of competition often unnoticed by the nonindigenous spectators for whom such events are arranged.

CONCLUSION

Toward the end of my fieldwork—a study that had started by focusing on the iconography associated with rituals, but which then ventured (stumbled) into broader issues of gesture, gender, kinship, and word—I took notes on a verb the Warlpiri offer up to characterize a *kurdungurlu*'s single-minded (usually stressful) absorption with matters of ceremonial action: *miirn-nyinami.*[1] This verb has rarely strayed from my thoughts during the many years spent completing this book. Emerging from more than a decade of research, I now still find that Warlpiri expression offers correlative insight into the nature and intensity of the process known as "writing up." That the language of Aboriginal ceremony and Western fieldwork overlap should come as no surprise. The ritual of ethnography is as imbued with nervous-making restrictions and performative expectations as the Fire Dreaming of Ngarna presented during intersettlement events. The audience for a monograph or a conference paper is as quick to judge if a presentation is *junga,* or proper, as a *yamparru* weighing in on the execution of a "small" restricted ceremony by a close kin group member. In short, swift value judgments are in no way limited to the Warlpiri. And to expand the analogy just a bit more: In much the way the Warlpiri have been forced to learn to create ritual enactments for a broader audience, so, too, have anthropologists. Both groups now find themselves obliged to tread carefully, to be aware of how and when to edit what is said and shown. Cavalier revelations of restricted information are as unacceptable in the academic universe as they are in the public performances of *wiri* designs by a Nangala dancing for patrons of a Sydney art gallery.

With this recalibration of temperament and methodology in mind, it is fair, I think, to characterize the preceding work as a decidedly *warraja,* or "open," version of how the Warlpiri approach their ritual life. By choice, I have avoided the language of the ethnographic initiand—the more obscure locutions and conceptual tools so commonly deployed by my French brethren and their American heirs. That decision was made in part to avoid causing offense (or consternation) to the individuals kind enough to allow me access to their world. But there was a more self-serving rationale as well. All too often I have seen the brilliance undermined by a relentless inaccessibility of style. Some of the most important works in the field of anthropological studies, sadly, have been egregiously undervalued because they are as difficult to decode as the indigenous worlds they claim to decipher. This self-imposed stylistic "restriction" will not be seen as a diminishment of the discourse so much as a redefinition of the parameters that frame it. For as I have tried to show, to understand ritual, even as it is publicly expressed, is to understand the profound if entangled forces of gender and kinship, and related notions of power. To understand ritual is to understand the nature of competition and negotiation and the manner in which systems of hierarchy and equality can be simultaneously nourished, a paradox (one of many) at the core of the Warlpiri world.

In the early phases of fieldwork, when the theoretical underpinnings of the project were predictably shaky and the data collected thin, I relied on oppositional constructs to propel my research. I posed the question of social identity in terms that privileged either kinship (that is to say, the network of affinal and cognatic associations) or gender (the status of individuals as either women or men). To be sure, I made an effort to temper this dichotomy with a notional nod to the language of the "individual as social actor" so effectively developed by Myers. But in the end, my analysis was so overly deterministic that there was little semblance between what I hypothesized in the drafts I composed and what I had seen in the field. I shuttled back and forth between data and theory, weighed the false incompatibilities of kinship and gender, and attempted to legitimate different (and seemingly conflicting) strands of feminist theory, all the while trying to situate what I observed in the context of the slim historical record on matters of ritual undertaken by women. When theory and data collided, as inevitably happened, I wavered on how to proceed. A similar indecision arose when I hit upon conflicts within the domains of method and material. Each step, or misstep, created its own problems. Whenever I cut this questionable conceit or that inconsistent narrative many more problems would emerge, hydralike, in the void the cuts created.

I did find some early solace in the scholarly attempts to merge the theoretical models. Particularly noteworthy were the works of Strathern and Weiner, and a volume on kinship and gender edited by Collier and Yanagisako optimistically subtitled *Essays toward a Unified Analysis.* But more often than not, my indecisions found resolution in common sources infrequently cited. Truth be told, I spent as much time squinting over the compact edition of the *OED* and my battered *Petit Robert* as I did turning to Meggitt or Munn, Durkheim or Geertz. It was in my unwieldy and tattered tag-sale Webster's that I discovered that *gender* and *kinship* shared a single lexical ancestry—that both are rooted in *genus.* With that legacy in mind (a legacy that always seemed to sanction a maneuver around the ethnographic debate), it became easier to reunite the concepts after long and strife-filled separation. Those same nonethnographic resources also offered etymological links between "business" (as the Warlpiri regularly characterize their ritual activities) and "the negotiation of social identity." For, as the *Petit Robert* clarified, what is a *negociant* if not a businessman?

Ambiguity was further diminished (or at least comprehended) when I was trying to make sense of the complex relationships between the owners and managers of Dreamings. I settled on the idea of "cleavage" because it seemed to be the notion that most felicitously captured the sense of adhesion that is firm, close, loyal, and unwavering (those descriptors coming from one definition of *cleavage*) while at the same time suggesting division in two parts by a cutting blow. The two uses of the word *cleavage* captured the reciprocal forces present in the reproduction of the Dreaming, with the owner executing the work and the manager making sure it is *junga,* or proper. The two principals (and the principles their actions sustain) are at once bound by loyalty (to each other and to the Dreaming) and divided by the labor that the expression of that loyalty demands. Understanding this relationship brought with it insights into many other cleavages that make up Warlpiri life, the most important of which is the cleavage of women from (and to) men. And that returns us to the theoretical cleavage of gender from (and to) kinship. Whether we choose to designate the links of men and women as an expression of "interdependent independence," as Berndt calls it, or as a bond of another kind, it is important to recognize the links that are ever-present (Berndt 1974:75). Yes, women at Yuendumu have in recent years taken on an increased role in the public expression of ritual. But it is a public expression that relies on support from men and their engagement. When studying so seemingly bifurcated a ritual universe, there is the risk of overstating the function of gender as a criterion for *determining* action. To do so runs the risk of succumbing to a subspecies of illogical reasoning that rhetoricians call the "fallacy of composition." It is dangerous to mistake the part for the whole. The obviousness of this point escaped me more than once while I was trying to reconcile the Warlpiri perspectives as expressed at Yuendumu with those written up at nearby settlements, or when attempting to configure the Warlpiri at Yuendumu circa 1950 with the same group thirty years later. If long-term fieldwork has taught me anything, it is to retain a suspicion of pan-Aboriginal theory. Space and time alter more than the expression of ritual; they change just as quickly the theoretical gambits brought to bear on the subject of study.

That said, there are some constants worth restating. As I have taken pains to point out, Warlpiri ritual is a "business." It is a world characterized by transactions that rely on a very special, if at times intangible, kind of currency whose value is forever in play. As such, the business leaders of Yuendumu, the men and women who handle this currency, are principals in the evocation and negotiation of social identity. Ritual events, in communion with various correlative social and economic activities, sustain (and are sustained by) residentially modified patterns of kinship, and as such constitute a cosmic and social mastic for an Aboriginal settlement whose spiritual and economic condition is forever under external pressure. That said, it should come as no surprise that the business of ritual ends up being hard work, a stressful undertaking that incorporates (the prevalence of economic idiom is inevitable) a great deal of competition and concomitant pressures of nurturance. On the surface those two terms—*competition* and *nurturance*—may seem antonymic, but closer examination has, I hope, shown that for the Warlpiri these demands are not only compatible, but inextricably connected by their mutual regulation. Here, then, is yet another of those intertwined conundra at the root of Warlpiri ritual life. Without nurturance competition is jeopardized. The complementarity of seemingly rival concepts is at the root of much of Aboriginal social engagement. That is not to say I wish to fall prey to the easy paradoxology that the false heirs of Marx are quick to abuse, the kind of linguistic deception that so often inverts or subsumes cause and effect. The concept of chiasmus serves literature better than it does anthropology. And yet the connections—or better yet, cleavages—implicit in tropes of inversion and paradoxes seem to be present in so many aspects of Warlpiri business: in the nature of egalitarian leadership (explored in chapter 3), in the dynamic permanence of the Dreaming (invoked in chapter 4), in the shared separation of engendered knowledge (a focus of chapter 5). When I began my work, I hoped (arrogantly) to write a definitive work. I found I have written a definitional work, one much smaller in scope. As I hope I have shown in the lexical portions of the book, one cannot begin to assess the place of the Dreaming among the Warlpiri until the plurality of meanings attached to *Jukurrpa* and related terms find exact explication. Only after that work is complete is it possible to explore how the expressions of ritual are linked to broader forms of engagement tying the Warlpiri to each other and to their cosmological landscapes.

To be sure, such terminological efforts take us only so far. The five meanings of *Jukurrpa* may, for example, hint at the pervasiveness of the Dreaming, but they do not show us the operating factors that stimulate its enactment. And while Warlpiri as a language provides many of the nuances needed to distinguish different forms of ritual knowledge (a matter explored in chapter 2), it does not grant the nonindigenous scholar correlative terms to characterize the allegiances by which such knowledge is put to use. The residential configuration of the sedentarized mob or camp as it exists at the end of the twentieth century necessitates the tweaking (if not outright abandonment) of classical models and lexicons. Kinship charts take us only so far, and must be correlated with both residency patterns and the genealogies of inheritance before a clear sense emerges of how the Warlpiri enact their ritual universe. It often seems that for each term that enhances our understanding of the Dreaming, there is one that serves to obscure it. Take the genealogical vocabulary tethered to the now-suspect prefix *patri-*: *patrilineal, patrimoiety, patricouple,* and so on. In the wake of the mid-1970s feminist analysis of Aboriginal culture, that whole family of descriptors was jettisoned by many scholars because of the subjugation the prefix presumed. Certainly I did so during much of this book's composition. But then I had a change of heart and returned various forms of *patri-* to the text. The fact is that the inheritance of ritual material among the Warlpiri at Yuendumu often travels a patrilineal path, and it would do a disservice to distort or deny this pattern of transmission. Still, the legacy of the patricouple does not, in the case of the Warlpiri, imply patriarchy. Far from it. Women are as much the beneficiaries of such inheritance flows as men are. Women have managed to establish a position of ritual prominence in the public expression of the Dreaming (a transfer of ritual responsibility taken up in chapter 6). Yet to couch the enhanced role of women in public ritual life as an expression of their triumph over men is to misrepresent the collaborative nature of the *Jukurrpa*. The competition that finds regular expression in the life of the settlement is not one that the Warlpiri see as pitting women against men. To imply that kind of division distorts the situation at Yuendumu in ways that would reflect the sensibilities of the observer more than the values of the observed. Competition, as it plays itself out in Yuendumu, is more often than not an intercamp, intersettlement, or intercultural affair. Social identity is more a product of residential habitation than it is of gender, though it must be pointed out that space is itself the by-product of the multiply constituted forces of kinship and gender. In short, gender-specific dichotomies deny the complexity and ultimate coherence of ritual, and the manner by which the settlement's business leaders support it. That is why I have taken pains to explore the phenomenon of "engendering" at both the material and structural levels (chapters 5 and 6). The transfer of knowledge—in the wake of nocturnal dreams, during ritual, when paintings get painted—suggests a ceremonial world mutually constituted and jointly made manifest.

Linked to the obligations of the ritual performer are the duties of the viewer, who shares the burdens and satisfactions that infuse the business of ritual. As an anthropologist who has had the good fortune to study Warlpiri rituals for more than a decade, that bond of reciprocal obligation is one I feel with unflagging intensity and gratitude.

Jinamardarni.

NOTES

INTRODUCTION

1. See the entries for *gender* and *kin* in *Webster's Third New International Dictionary.*
2. Fred Myers has written extensively about the influence of residence on social identity; see Myers 1986a, 1986b, 1994b, 1995.
3. The term *yamparru* was regularly used by ritual participants while I worked at Yuendumu to refer to business leaders. Male and female users explained that such a person was "strong" enough to understand the Dreaming and could be trusted to orchestrate ceremonies and guide the actors in the reenactment since she or he knew ceremonies, designs, and their meanings. Though more commonly applied to women, the term *yamparru* is sometimes used to refer to male ritual leaders. Two other terms—*watirirrirri* and *ngardarri-kirlangu*—are more generally invoked when identifying male ritual leaders. Because such terms of status are not entirely fixed along lines of gender, I have chosen to conflate them under the rubric of *yamparru* for purposes of clarity. When appropriate, the term is then modified by the descriptor *male* or *female.*

1. THE DREAMING AND ITS KIN

1. The term *dream-times* was coined by Francis Gillen in his "Report on the Work on the Horn Scientific Expedition to Central Australia" (1896:185); Spencer and Gillen used the term systematically in their work *The Arunta* (1927:592). The gloss was embraced wholeheartedly by Meggitt. "Ancestral times, ancestral period" was the phrase favored by Munn (1973:115). The origins of the synonymous but nontemporal *Dreaming* are more obscure. I share Stanner's preference for the last of these terms, for it is the

one most commonly employed by the Warlpiri themselves (1956:51). For further debates on the origins, meanings, and uses of the word *Dreamtime,* see Wolfe 1991; Morphy 1996; Mulvaney, Morphy, and Petch 1997; Christen 1993.

2. The often-quoted lines from Eliot's *Four Quartets* ("Burnt Norton") poeticize the Warlpiri conceit: "Time present and time past / Are both perhaps present in time future, / And time future contained in time past" (1943). The Warlpiri, however, would remove the "perhaps" to avoid tentativeness.
3. This multigenerational aspect of enfolding the dead into the Dreaming runs counter to some of observations made by Munn (1973:24–25) and Meggitt (1962:317, 329), who both noted that death provided an instantaneous merging with the Ancestral Realm. The nuances of this distinction are advanced further in chapter 2.
4. In her 1991 work, Glowczewski offers a particularly stimulating structural analysis of the sexual components of Warlpiri myth.
5. To complicate matters still further, there are often different Dreamings bearing the same name. The Fire Dreaming associated with Ngarna is but one of many Fire Dreamings; the other like-named *Jukurrpa* involve different itineraries and are thus composed of different segments.
6. Between 1983 and 1992 lengthy interviews with forty-two men and women over the age of fifty helped me trace specific nocturnal dreams to dreamers. On an average, a prolific dreamer was able to identify between forty and fifty-three *Jukurrpa* nocturnal dreams. Less prolific dreamers could recount fifteen, and the persons who described themselves as not often dreaming the *Jukurrpa* listed no more than six. The latter would explain that, unlike others, they were not *Tiyatiyapiya* or *Mungamungapiya;* that is, they did not dream of the *Tiyatiya* or *Mungamunga,* mythical agents who "gave" (*yungu*) nocturnal dreams.
7. For further discussion of the nature of this conflict, see Stanner 1966; Tonkinson 1974; Wild 1975; Bell 1983; Myers 1986a, 1986b; Glowczewski 1988, 1991; Gill 1998; Christen 1993.
8. Ian Keen has noted a similar expression used by the Yolngu people (1978: 160).
9. For a similar discussion of this concept among the Pintupi, see Myers 1986a:49.
10. See Hale, Laughren, Nash, and Simpson 1982–1988.
11. Aboriginalist literature since the 1980s has made great inroads in studying the impact of sedentarization on Aboriginal experiences. For a recent and insightful analysis focusing primarily on how urban Aborigines manifest their socioterritorial identities in the different phases of Australia after sedentarization, see Merlan 1998.
12. It is important to reiterate here that the four descent lines on the conven-

tional Arandic kinship chart are on terminological lines of descent and do not refer to four actual descent groups. The Warlpiri count many more than four.

13. Acceptance of this alternative marriage union among the Warlpiri appears to vary from one settlement to another. Meggitt (1962:86) indicates that such marriages were prohibited at Lajamanu while he conducted his fieldwork. Bell (1980:249) noted that at Warrabri, "Warlpiri women identified a third choice marriage with a mother's mother's brother (MMB) as acceptable although not preferable."
14. In my reference to the egocentric I employ the term found succinctly in Scheffler's work: "the ego-centric systems of social identities and statuses are described as kinship systems" (1973:756).
15. This emphasis on patrilineal descent rights in matters of ritual seems restricted to the Warlpiri. Myers's work on the neighboring Pintupi shows a group arranging its ritual life along lines of generational moieties (1986a). Other Aboriginal groups, such as the Walmajarri people, who inhabit Fitzroy Crossing in the nearby Kimberly region of Western Australia, situate their ceremonial activity within their subsection system. See Kölig 1981:91.
16. The utility of such terms as *patrilineality* and *patrimoiety* is a debate by no means restricted to Central Desert cultures. In the introductory remarks to their edited volume *Gender and Kinship* (1987), Collier and Yanagisako note that a number of the contributors, particularly Strathern, Shapiro, and Bloch, "illustrate the richness of understanding offered by analyses that attend to connections between concepts of personhood, gender, and descent." The editors go on to note, "By ignoring conventional interpretations of what might be considered 'patrilineal descent systems,' these authors demonstrate clearly how different systems of descent are constructed along with different systems of gender and personhood." They conclude: "In challenging the traditional boundaries of 'descent systems' to arrive at creative new understandings, this last trio of essays illustrates well just how productive it is to question kinship and gender as distinct fields of study" (12–13).
17. I use the verb *cleave* here because of the ambiguity of the term. The word can refer to objects that "adhere firmly and closely, loyally and unwaveringly," or it can suggest "a division in two parts by a cutting blow" (*Webster's Third Unabridged Dictionary*). The two senses capture the reciprocal force at work in the nurturance of the Dreaming, with the "owner" executing the work and the managers making sure it is *junga,* or "proper." This division, well documented in the literature, informs everything from inheritance of land and associated performative rights in ritual to the production of acrylic canvases loosely based on the Warlpiri iconography (see chapter 5). Indeed, this tethered bifurcation finds expression in most

domains of Warlpiri life, where social and economic obligations tend to be similarly constituted.

18. Note that references to one's *kurdungurlu* always refer to a member of the opposite patrimoiety, but may not necessarily imply an *actual* owner-manager relationship. This is just one of the many terminological pluralities that make description of Warlpiri kinship patterns confusing.
19. Nash's study of the twin terms is extensive. He notes, "The term *kirda* is clearly related to the kinship term *kirdana, kirdanyanu* 'father'" (1982: 143–45), and he observes a "historical connection between the term *kurdungurlu* 'other patrimoiety' and terms including *kurdu* 'child' and *kurduna* 'sister's child'" (1982:151).
20. In the ritual context *kurdungurlu* are the close uterine and affinal kin of *kirda*. See also Pink 1936:291, 300–3; Meggitt 1966:205; Peterson 1972: 23; Nash 1982:147; Hale 1980:5; Scheffler 1978:508.
21. This reductive synthesis of complex marriage and inheritance patterns would never be stated in these terms by the Warlpiri. They would explain that the reason they are *kurdungurlu* for their spouse is because they inherited these rights from their father and father's father, and that their spouse is *kirda* for the same country as their father's mother and father's father's mother.
22. The Nangala's male cross-cousins, mother's brothers, sons, husband, and brothers-in-law will also serve as *kurdungurlu* if the ceremony performed involves both male and female participation.
23. As noted, before, the Warlpiri notion of conception differs fundamentally from the non-Aboriginal use of the term. Conception sites register the geographic and ritually charged location where a fetus is animated by the life forces of the *jukurrpa*. See Merlan 1986.
24. See Spencer and Gillen 1899 for numerous examples found among most Central Desert Aboriginal groups.
25. There were, of course, other Europeans who encountered the Warlpiri prior to the Spencer and Gillen expeditions. Peterson et al. (1978:10) provide a list: "Penetration by Europeans of the Warlpiri, Kartangarurru-Kurintji domain began in 1856 with A. C. Gregory's exploration of Hooker Creek. In 1862 Stuart visited Arthur Hills just to the west of the Willowra and in 1873 Gosse visited the upper reaches of the Lander River and the site of Yuendumu, naming the hill that overlooks the settlement Rock Hill. Waburton was the first to cross through Warlpiri country in his journey from east to west." See also Gregory 1969; Stuart 1865; Gosse 1874; Waburton 1975; Meggitt 1962:19ff.
26. Peterson et al. (1978:9) argue: "From time to time there were major gatherings for ceremonies—150 men were seen 60 miles south of Tanami in 1910 holding a ceremony . . . but there is no information on the duration of such gatherings. However, it is difficult to conceive that they would have lasted

more than a week or two before a return to the small land using groups of three to five families numbering 15–25 people."

27. She described the remarks as being "mean-spirited" (*kulu-parnta*).
28. The relocation was a source of great suffering for the Warlpiri, evident even today when one asks about the matter. Concerning the establishment of a second settlement at Hooker Creek (which later became Lajamanu), residents of both settlements cite unilateral determinations by the white authorities and a process of dislocation prompted by lack of food rations. (Neither governmental records nor Warlpiri recollections offer any direct explanation of how the authorities selected who was to be relocated.) Meggitt, on the other hand, offers the following explanation: "Old feuds soon came to life and a long series of quarrels split the settlement into armed factions. Obviously another settlement was needed if bloodshed was to be avoided" (1962:29). While the residents of both settlements do not dispute that tensions existed, they do not accept that there was the risk of "bloodshed" that Meggitt invokes. They further state that they did not wish to be separated from each other, a severance far more dangerous than any of the risks attendant to mass settlement. Also missing from Meggitt's version are the social and religious implications of the breakup of kin groups, and the effect such social engineering had on Warlpiri ritual.
29. This account comes from conversations with the male performers and several women as well as with one of the geologists who was working for the mining company at the time, Frank Baarda.
30. Morphy notes also in his work with the Yolngu that progressively they came to make a connection between performance of Dreaming stories (bark paintings for the Yolngu) and "political" advocacy in a Western sense (1991:17).
31. The first Warlpiri land claim was initiated in 1974 and officially reviewed by a specially appointed Aboriginal Land Commissioner in 1978 (see Peterson et al., 1978). The Land Rights Act restricted the claims of indigenous groups to vacant Crown land. Successive efforts by the Warlpiri have proven successful. According to Tindale (1974:236), the original size of the Warlpiri territory was approximately 137,800 square kilometers (about 5,320 square miles). Over half of that is now Warlpiri land. The Mt. Doreen parcel, which represents less than 10,000 square kilometers (3,860 square miles), is now one of the most important held by non-Warlpiri people and currently under claim.
32. Exact population figures for Yuendumu's Warlpiri are impossible to gather, because of the flux of the settlement's inhabitants and the definitions of "Warlpiri" in the context of intergroup marriage. A 1985 survey listed 792 Warlpiri residing at Yuendumu proper, with another 457 in various outstations. No figure for non-Warlpiri residents was given, though the

number would be under 5 percent (Young and Doohan 1989:64). Fieldwork I conducted in 1992 indicated that some 850 Warlpiri lived at Yuendumu proper, with another 90 residing at Nyirrpi (an outstation that gained settlement status in 1991) and an additional 120 in satellite locations.

33. This will be explored in greater detail in subsequent chapters.
34. These outlying camps are not just spatial constructs; they are informed by issues of space, kinship, and gender. Warlpiri move throughout the settlement, in effect repudiating the external function imposed by governmental architectural constructs. There are very few houses at Yuendumu. In the camps, the quarters of families and single individuals are frail structures pieced together from sheets of corrugated iron and wooden poles. These tentlike structures are called "humpies" in Australian English. Humpies are used primarily to store possessions and as shelters during the rainy season. In the dry season, bedding and hearths are located outside the humpies.
35. Meggitt discusses in great detail the origins of the different groups of Warlpiri who were settled at Yuendumu, identifying the four main groups: the "Walmalla" to the west, the "Waneiga" to the north, the "Lander Yalpari" to the east, and the "Ngalia" to the south (1962:4); see also Munn 1973. When I did my fieldwork, distinctions between northern, western, eastern, and southern Warlpiri were not commonly made.
36. For example, Water Dreaming, Emu Dreaming, Kangaroo Dreaming, Fire Dreaming, and Snake Dreaming.
37. Bell argues that "locating Kaytej women at the centre of my analysis in this way involves no sleight of hand, for the Kaytej *jilimi,* the home of the ritually powerful and respected leaders, was the focus of activities in the main Kaytej camp for men and women alike" (1983:110).
38. Bell notes that the Kaytej *jilimi* constitutes "the area where women's authority is given its clearest expression" (1983:81).
39. The correlates of ritual power will be discussed later.
40. Though the physical space in which a widow resides is always called a *jilimi,* it should not be assumed that all references to *jilimi* imply residency in a large-scale camp of single women.
41. Though there is no doubt that in precolonial times succession patterns were open to manipulation, colonial contexts increased such transformation. See Peterson 1995.
42. Recently Smith, Frankhauser, and Jercher have been able to apply geochemical sourcing methods to ochre traces found at Puritjarra rock shelter in western central Australia. "Our work indicates that the red ochre in Late Pleistocene contexts at this rock shelter is from Karrku, a subterranean ochre mine still worked today by Warlpiri people" (1998:275).
43. Kumanjayi Jupurrurla's father had a special connection to the mine. His father, a Jakamarra, dreamt an important sequence that was integrated as a Dreaming segment of the *Karrku Jukurrpa.*

44. Peterson and Lambert, who visited the mine between 1972 and 1982, noted that the mine "lies on the border of a Jampijinpa-Jangala and a Jupurrurla-Jakamarra estate. While it is certain that permission has to be sought for access to the mine, there is some uncertainty whether this is the exclusive prerogative of the senior males of one or other of the estates, or shared between them" (1985:7). When succession was discussed in 1984, 1985, and 1987, the J/Nampijinpa-J/Nangala were often described as the *kirda* patricouple for the mine and the J/Napurrurla-J/Nakamarra subsections were regarded as *kirda* or *kuyuwurruru*—reflecting the interest of the speaker. It is clear that shifts of control from one group to another take place over time.
45. This situation will probably change again, since Kumanjayi Jupurrurla passed away in October 1999.

2. FROM TERMS TO TIMELINES

1. The phrase most commonly invoked to express this sense of tracing or replicating the movements of the Ancestral Beings is *jungarni mani,* which translates literally as "to follow in a straight line."
2. Foucault makes only passing reference to "a certain Chinese encyclopedia" and Borges; the English-language edition published by Vintage fails to trace the citation back to the Argentinean writer. Other liabilities of that edition, such as the rendering of "suckling pig" as "sucking pig," argue for a direct nod to Borges himself as rendered into English by Ruth L. C. Simms. "These ambiguities, redundancies, and deficiencies recall those attributed by Dr. Franz Kuhn to a certain Chinese encyclopedia entitled *Celestial Emporium of Benevolent Knowledge.* On those remote pages it is written that animals are divided into (a) those that belong to the emperor, (b) embalmed ones, (c) those that are trained, (d) suckling pigs, (e) mermaids, (f) fabulous ones, (g) stray dogs, (h) those that are included in this classification, (i) those that tremble as if they were mad, (j) innumerable ones, (k) those drawn with a very fine camel's-hair brush, (l) others, (m) those that have just broken a flower vase, (n) those that resemble flies from a distance." (See Monegal and Reid 1981:142). In point of fact, Borges's fiction, regularly invoked in Foucault and subsequently by numerous anthropologists (Sahlins most famously in *How Natives Think,* 1995) is saturated with language suitable to the paradoxes of the social sciences in general and the philosophy of language in particular.
3. In her book titled *Fictions of Feminist Ethnography* (1994), Kamela Visweswaran is particularly eloquent in her analysis of the relationship between ethnography and literature.
4. Such presumptive synonymity commonly found in early anthropological discourse between "sacred" and "secret" represents another point warranting attention. This is not a novel observation. C. H. Berndt was one of the

first to note the liabilities of conflating the terms. In her 1974 essay she argues, "To confine the label of 'sacred' is to distort the issues, and to exclude some of the most important ritual sequences that are performed in public in the general camp. It is much more realistic and more appropriate, to see this in terms of a continuum (or a series of continua), ranging from the mundane, or least sacred, though the ordinary-sacred to the most sacred: and this last, in Aboriginal Australia, most generally coincides with the sphere that is both sacred and secret—secret in varying degrees and in varying circumstances, but the especial province of fully initiated men" (1974:67).

5. Note that unfortunately Bell offers little substantiation regarding how "love magic" per se transforms female practitioners alone into "sex objects," especially since *yilpinji* are performed by both men and women. The liabilities of the translation exist for all who enact the *yilpinji,* and that includes me. Also problematic is the implicit uniform acceptance by Warrabri men of the rationale of the Philip Creek missionaries. Bell's observations do not detail what exactly is "defused."
6. This is a subject that warrants further documentation by linguists and specialists in proxemics. Adam Kendon has worked more than anyone else on Warlpiri sign language, and probably out of respect for his female informants he has omitted signs that are used to evoke restricted knowledge. For a general overview of Warlpiri sign systems, see Kendon 1988.
7. See Meggitt 1966 for an extensive description of the *Kajirri* cycle. However, Meggitt emphasized men's performance and only partially discussed women's involvement. Glowczewski mentions women's roles in the *Kajirri* in her 1981 article (1981:87–95).
8. This "lack of interest" by women in the ritual activities of men, well documented by both Munn (1973:23) and Meggitt (1962:210), is not unique to Yuendumu. Lederman (1986) makes a similar observation about Mendi women of Papua New Guinea.
9. My observations on the absence of a "secret" women's repertoire—that is, a body of ceremonial knowledge unknown to men—has at least one vocal critic among the ethnographers conducting fieldwork in the Central Australian Desert. Bell dismissed this observation (which I began to formulate in my dissertation) in a footnote to the second edition of her work *Daughters of the Dreaming:* "I would strongly challenge Dussart's assertion (ibid:41) that Warlpiri women have no secret knowledge or sites" (1995: 306). I would not presume to pass judgment on the rigor of Bell's fieldwork at Warrabri, having never worked there, and would welcome a similar restraint from those unfamiliar with the nuances of Yuendumu ritual life.
10. See, for example, C. Berndt 1950; White 1974; Hamilton 1981; Bell 1983, 1995; Tonkinson 1988, 1990; Anderson 1995.

11. Munn defines *kuruwarri* as "designs that constitute the wider category of men's designs. For the most part, women are not allowed to see these designs, but in some cases they can observe them from a distance, and less important body paintings may occasionally be seen at close quarters" (1973:49). And later in her glossary she writes that *kuruwarri* can be understood as a "[f]ertility essence, ancestral marks left in the country; men's ancestral designs" (1973:223).
12. C. Berndt notes a similar phenomenon in her influential paper "Digging Sticks and Spears, or the Two-Sex Model." She writes: "In a desert-fringe settlement, a woman walking along one of the tracks leading to the main camp tripped over a small stone, looked down at it, and exclaimed '*Darugu!*' [*tarruku*] (sacred, with an aura of secrecy). She glanced around, then stooped to pick it up, and examined it. It was not the shape or the chalk-pink colour of the stone that had attracted her attention, but the particular pattern of concentric circles that she identified at first glance as *darugu,* and specifically as *men's darugu*—in other words, knew that she shouldn't see" (1974:75).
13. I inject the comment about her manifesting more than an awareness of her own ignorance to invoke Morphy's subtle observations on the ontological discourse. Of the Yolngu he writes, "Although secrecy is important in the creation of men's power, it is equally important that women and uninitiated men know something of what men are controlling. This is what creates the power of secrecy" (1991:92).
14. The term used was *jirriny-pinyi,* "to bone," meaning to apply a curse (*yarda*) on an individual by pointing a bone that causes illness and eventual death. None of my informants ever provided any account of such an extreme sentence, and transgression generally resulted in milder punishment for men careless enough to expose their secret designs in the presence of women. This subject of transgressive transmissions will be explored in greater detail in chapter 5.
15. References to "exclusive" or "secret" women's material appears throughout Bell's 1983 book, but no substantiation of men's implicit ignorance regarding that material is provided.
16. This example is further detailed in chapter 5.
17. During my residency at Yuendumu almost no births took place at the settlement, either in "natural" contexts or at the small health clinic. Deliveries were almost uniformly undertaken at the Alice Springs hospital. See also Nathan et al. 1987.
18. Whereas the various initiation cycles of young men each took years to complete prior to sedentarization, they are now finished in a matter of weeks. See Meggitt 1962:285.
19. Sports Weekend is an annual event attended by many different Aboriginal

groups from the Northern Territory and Western Australia. On average five thousand people attend Sports Weekend, and a wide range of school and settlement teams compete during the four-day event. The following items are the official categories listed for competition: spear throwing (men only); women's corroboree (*yawulyu warrajanyanyi*); battle of the bands (country and western, rock and roll); basketball (men and women); softball (men and women); football (soccer); and athletics (men and women).

20. Fathers whose children were born in the bush are also knowledgeable about the process of child delivery.
21. The ethnographic literature describing these events dates back to Spencer and Gillen 1899:467. See also Berndt and Berndt 1944:225.
22. R. Berndt also noted the importance of the betrothal component of "male circumcision ceremonies" (1951).
23. Taboo relationships are established through preferred marriage declaration between initiands and their future mothers-in-law, and between a mother and her son's circumciser.
24. See Nash and Simpson 1981. Sometimes such speech taboos are prompted by external cross-cultural connection. When the film actor John Wayne died, all men named John at Yuendumu were identified as "no name" for a number of years.
25. The one cross-gender exception to this action I observed was when the fathers of a deceased child swept the grounds after the women had.
26. Women usually used sign language to refer to these finish-time ceremonies. The sign used refers to an action in the process of being completed.
27. Munn also noted that "Walbiri think of all ancestral ceremonial as contributing to feelings of happiness and well-being, and some men compared these functions of *yawalyu* [*yawulyu*] to those of the much more important *banba* [*parnpa*] fertility ceremonies controlled by men" (1973:45).
28. While both men and women explained that generally *yawulyu* ceremonies were not for "increasing" fauna or flora, the performance of certain Dreaming segments was said to help growth. Munn also noted that some paintings performed for *yawulyu* ceremonies are sometimes perceived as "increasing" the growth of bush food (Munn 1973:41–42).
29. For a description of these events in the early years of settlement, see Munn 1973.
30. For more details on myths and performances, see, for example, Spencer and Gillen 1904; Meggitt 1966; Peterson 1970; Sandall 1977; Glowczewski 1981; Lander 1993; Ross 1993.
31. The "brown bird" referred to here is more technically identified as the yellow-throated miner (*Manoria flavigula*).
32. For a detailed ethnography of a *Puluwanti* (*Buluwandi*) event focusing principally on men, see Peterson 1970:200–14.

33. Warlpiri reticence about these events is very strong. For more on *Jurlurru,* see Myers n.d.; Kölig 1979; Laughren 1981; Glowczewski 1983.

3. ON BECOMING A "BIG" BUSINESSWOMAN

1. To date, the most extensive discussion of the concept(s) of leadership among Australian Aborigines appears in a slim but influential issue of *Anthropological Forum* (1988, vol. 4). However, it should be mentioned that the authors offer insights on matters of leadership that are principally restricted to the domain of men.
2. For an exploration of the territorial and ritual disjunctures of control, see Bern and Labarlestier 1985:56.
3. Without access to male-only ceremonies, and the process by which winning is determined rarely appearing in the literature of Central Desert male events, no observations can be provided on how winning is decided within "dear" *watimipa* activity.
4. Meggitt was one of the first to isolate this notion of "straight" or "right" enactments of ritual knowledge (1962:251).
5. The language of shape-shifting is of little use in the context of Central Desert ritual. See also Munn 1986.
6. The links between economics and ritual, and the terminology they share, are noted by Glowczewski in her excellent essay "Affaire de Femmes, ou Femmes d'Affaires" (1981), and cited briefly in her book *Du Rêve à la Loi Chez les Aborigènes* (1991:83).
7. The following works eloquently address the place of rituals in Melanesia: Weiner 1976, 1992; Strathern 1987, 1988; Munn 1986; Godelier 1986.
8. The liabilities of the term have also been noted by Myers (1986a:221).
9. Nash (1982:155) observes: "Hale (1980a:3) described the ambiguity of 'the term "boss," borrowed in Warlpiri as *pawuju* . . .' as follows: 'in one of its uses, it functions as a gloss for *kirda.* In this usage, it is opposed to another term "worker," borrowed into Warlpiri as *warrkini,* which term, in the present context, functions as a gloss for *kurdungurlu.* . . . The other meaning which Warlpiri *pawuju* has acquired is closer to the English sense of "boss." . . . There is a verbalized form of the word in this usage—i.e., *pawuju-jarri-mi* . . . —which can be rendered in English as "to be boss of, to have authority over.'" . . . It is important, I think to note that this usage is appropriate for both *kirda* and for the *kurdungurlu.* That is to say, it is ethnographically correct to say both." The use of *boss* as a referent in non-Warlpiri Aboriginal contexts is also explored in Hamilton 1972:43; Myers 1980:203, 1986a:262–66.
10. Anderson adds, rightly, that his fourth characteristic is in fact a basic component of Aboriginal culture, one explored in great detail in Myers 1986a.
11. *Juju-ngarliya* is defined in the Warlpiri dictionary thus: "[K]nows all the

ceremonies. *Juju-ngarliya, ngulaji yangka kujaka yapangku mardarni juju, puwarrilypa—watingki marda, karntangku marda. Ngulaji yapa, wati manu karnta, nyinami pinangkalpa kuruwarriki manu langarrpa nyinami. Yangka kujaka juju warrarda-pinyi kurduyunpu manu yangka kujakajana yapakari jujungku pinjangku pina-pina-mani—jujungarliyarluju. Juju-ngarliya* is a person who keeps the ceremonies and designs and their meanings—either a man or a woman. It is a man or a woman who is knowledgeable about the Dreaming and understands it. Like a person who always performs the ceremonies for initiating young men and who teachers others by performing the ceremonies. That sort of person is said to be *juju-ngarliya.*" Hale et al. 1982–1988.

12. For explication of the issues of personal pride and selfishness among other Aboriginal groups, see also Chase 1984:117; Tonkinson 1988; Myers 1986a.
13. For similar investigations of leadership trajectory among various groups of Cape York Aborigines, see Anderson 1984, 1988; Sutton 1978, 1982; von Sturmer 1978.
14. As mentioned earlier, *warungka* means "unthoughtful" and is used for irresponsible or mentally disturbed adults and to identify children under about three years of age. It is also employed to refer to older and senile individuals, those temporarily physically handicapped (for example, suffering a broken arm), and adults who are unprepared to "see" certain segments of the Dreaming because they have lost permanently or temporarily parts of their consciousness. Such consciousness is located in the stomach area. Individuals often hold their stomachs in anticipation of "seeing" the Ancestral Beings during ritual. This gesture strengthens the individual's *pirlirrpa.*
15. Sorcery practices are mentioned in Meggitt 1962:36, 122, but the precipitant behavior for such curses is never provided. See also Myers 1986a.
16. Annette Weiner has made elegant use of various studies of kinship to reassess the underestimated bonds of sibling-ship. She argues: "Sibling intimacy reproduces social identities, rights to cosmological and material resources within the siblings' natal family, lineage or clan" (1992:116).
17. For more substantive investigations of acrylic production as a mirror of ritual relations, see Anderson and Dussart 1988; Dussart 1989b, 1997.
18. *Wayipi* (*Boerhavia diffusa*) is a floral creeper with an edible tuber.
19. *Watiya-warnu* is known botanically as *Acacia tenuissima.*
20. The individual wishes to remain anonymous.
21. Hair string (*wirriji*) can also be made of twisted crochet threads of mercerized cotton.
22. The list of potential ritual objects employed by women is much longer than the one cited here. Different Dreamings require slightly different materials. The enactment of the Initiated Woman Dreaming (*Karnta Jukurrpa*), for example, requires the hidden possession of special stones. Performance of

a certain segment of the Bush Carrot Dreaming (*Ngarlayiji Jukurrpa*) necessitates the brandishing of a boomerang, though in its absence, this principally male object may be replaced without liability by a dancing board (*yukurrukurru*).

23. See Glowczewski 1991. Other materials that are employed in ritual, such as feathers (from the Major Mitchell cockatoo, emu, and wild turkey), move between men and women, but in ways that defy any obvious exchange dynamic.
24. See Weiner 1992 on the importance of cloth in the Pacific.
25. For more a detailed discussion of Warlpiri aesthetics, see Sutton 1988.
26. The painting of *kirda* by their *kurdungurlu,* not very common at Yuendumu, is the norm in at least one other nearby settlement. Glowczewski notes that at Lajamanu it is *kurdungurlu* who typically paint *kirda* (personal communication, 1984).

4. HOW DREAMS ARE MADE

1. Cross-gender transmission in dreams and other contexts is the focus of the following chapter.
2. Sorcery practices are thought to be the cause of such displaced *pirlirrpa.*
3. Myers also discussed the importance of recounting dreams as soon as one wakes (1986a:51).
4. See also the work of Poirier on Western Desert residents of Balgo Hills (1990).
5. To provide but one example of dismissed dreams, in 1987 a businesswoman dreamt that an Ancestral Snake, while eating Bush Yams, transformed the Yams into several Emu Beings. Her dream was very quickly rejected by both *kirda* and *kurdungurlu* for the Snake Dreaming. They argued that such connections between the Ancestral Yam, the Emu, and the Snake did not make much sense, and they laughed at the idea that a Yam could become an Emu.
6. Poirier (1990:143) argues that young people from Balgo Hills between the ages of fifteen and thirty are unwilling to talk about their dreams if they evoke mythical elements.
7. For early observations on encounters between the living and the dead during dreams, see especially Howitt 1904.
8. They do, however, find replication in the newfound medium of Warlpiri "dot" painting. Many of the designs applied to the acrylic canvases sold internationally have their roots in such dreams.
9. Throughout this account the name of Topsy's spouse is avoided to respect the speech taboos of the dead.
10. The traditional form of this self-imposed punishment for women generally involves the painful application of digging sticks or a stone, but Topsy on

this occasion resorted to the employment of a crowbar, with which she repeatedly hammered at the top of her cranium—the ritually sanctioned locus of self-mutilation (see Meggitt 1962; Dussart 1989a).

11. Tonkinson (1978:112ff.) notes a distinction made by the Mardu between "finding" and being "given" (the quotation marks are his) new knowledge by "spirit being intermediaries" who come during dreams. Such a distinction is rarely, if ever, present among the Warlpiri. The Warlpiri are almost always "given" their knowledge and never "find" it, though the act of discovery may constitute a narrative component of the Dreaming that is given.
12. At the request of Dolly, the song texts are not replicated here. They are deemed too potent to allow for inclusion in a public document.
13. The permanence (and perceived irrefutability) of the nontraditional medium of audiotape has long been used to extend authority to the ritual in the negotiation surrounding ritual activity. As early as 1970 tape recorders were employed to register and replay songs that might enter the ritual arena. No substantial investigation of the effect of technology on ritual has been made, though work with the medium of videotape was investigated by Eric Michaels. See Michaels 1986, 1989.
14. See also Glowczewski's 1991 work on *Mungamunga.*
15. This is not always possible. Some designs may not be reproduced with or without songs for an uninitiated audience.
16. Morphy also reported a similar phenomenon in the Yolngu system. He cogently explores this conceit in an essay titled "What Circles Look Like" (1980b:3). See also Taylor 1987, 1996.
17. The exact relationship of Dolly's design to the designs presented in *Jardiwanpa* ceremonies is complicated by a temporal liability of fieldwork. The designs I took down in *Jardiwanpa* ceremonies were gathered *after* this event and I have no designs registered before it. Therefore it is possible, though unlikely, that later *Jardiwanpa* designs were themselves modified in response to the iconography that emerged from this innovated ritual.
18. The specific forms of well-being sustained by *yawulyu* can change depending on the specific Dreamings invoked and their relationship to the performers. See Dussart 1989a.
19. Faris makes a similar argument in his work on the Navajo (1990).
20. Emus have a predilection for desert berries of various kinds, most notably the *murnturru* (*Petalostigma quariculore,* var. *nigrum*).
21. I have opted for this nonliteral synopsis to avoid offending the owners of this song. Dolly expressed little reluctance that the "story" be presented; however, as mentioned earlier, she insisted that the song texts never find transmission among the uninitiated.
22. The oscillation between singularly and plurally invoked Ancestral Beings is common and unsystematic in storytelling and singing.

23. Research into specific intersettlement transmission of ritual data is still poor. For exceptions, see especially Kölig 1981; Glowczewski 1981, 1991; Poirier 1996.
24. Weiner has eloquently developed this argument in her last book (1992).

5. "ENGENDERING" KNOWLEDGE

1. Source: compact edition of the *OED;* see entry for *gender*. The definitions in the *OED* for *gender* and *engender* are multiple. The negative meanings that bring in the issue of disease are ones I have chosen to pass over.
2. Hamilton aptly understands women's activities in relationship to men. She writes: "[R]elations between husbands and wives, brothers and sisters, fathers and daughters, and sweethearts, provide a context of critical importance to individual women's chances of financial security, secure residential arrangements, access to resources of all kinds including vehicles and food, and above all physical security in the present context. These relationships need to be negotiated by women in relation to the men in their lives" (1986:15).
3. Though Peggy Nampijinpa granted permission to be photographed while "painted up," subsequent conversations indicated a measure of discomfort at having the photographs reproduced for publication. Her reasons are worth noting. Each of the images was deemed improper because of the inclusion of other women who are now deceased. When I asked if I could crop the images to exclude the *kumanjayi* women in question, Peggy said she felt *kuntangka,* or embarrassed. For that reason, I have relied on Peggy's feeling comfortable about having a line drawing published instead. Peggy also asked me not to have her face drawn, because she felt that the design could be drawn on a fictive Aboriginal person.
4. *Pandora doraxtoxylon.*
5. My account of this exchange is less than literal, since the man spoke Pitjantjatjara, which was then translated into Warlpiri for me by one of the women present.
6. I only saw four but it is possible that there were more. I did not confirm the number with the women who had seen them originally. They referred to what they had seen as *pirli,* which means "stone" without mention of number. As I mentioned earlier, it is usual for people to use a singular form to refer to objects or Ancestral Beings associated with the *Jukurrpa.*
7. Among the works that have addressed with eloquence the interculturality of Aboriginal art are Williams 1976; Megaw 1982; Morphy 1980a, 1983, 1991; Taylor 1987, 1996; Michaels 1988; Sutton 1988, 1992; Dussart 1988a, 1989a, 1993, 1997; von Sturmer 1989; and Myers 1989, 1994a, 1994b. For a history of early acrylic production at Yuendumu and Papunya, see Anderson and Dussart 1988.

8. Following Aboriginal use of language, Morphy employs the "inside"/ "outside" vocabulary in his scrutiny of the Yolngu. Morphy notes: "The spread of knowledge of the inside will, however, change its value to those who control it and may affect their position in society. Yolngu men must always maintain a delicate balance between holding and releasing knowledge. By releasing it too lightly, its value may be diminished and the power of the individual over others may be reduced. But the ultimate loss of power of knowledge is its non release through death of the possessor. It is true that in many circumstances, such power vacuums are soon taken up by new knowledge; but the potential power loss, as the loss of knowledge will be seen by the Yolngu, is an effective factor in people's lives, since to them it seems very real and undesirable" (1991:98–99). See also Glowczewski's insightful discussion of these terms (1991:98).
9. There are very few women's ground paintings "performed" today at Yuendumu. Those that are generally performed are not done by the Warlpiri but by women who are *kirda* for countries associated with southern Aboriginal groups, such as the Anmatyerre.
10. The measurement of male canvases ranged roughly between 120 cm by 80 cm (47 by 32 inches) and 150 cm by 100 cm (59 by 39 inches).
11. Munn argues: "Designs are thus channeled from men to women, *via* the marital relationship, but there are no designs that women teach to men for the latter to use in their rituals, an asymmetrical feature that is undoubtedly due to the relatively low ritual status and power of women" (1973:38).
12. See Trigger (1988:539) for an insightful commentary on cross-cultural performance as an expression of resistance to acculturation.

6. FROM *PURLAPA* TO *YAWULYU WARRAJANYANI*

1. Myers's seminal work on this notion of "relatedness" among the Pintupi can be applied to other Central Desert Aboriginal cultures (1986a). See also Dussart 1989a:177–80.
2. The juncture at which the indigenous and nonindigenous meet has been ably studied within the fields of Aboriginal anthropology and media studies. See, for example, Clifford 1985; Myers 1986a, 1986b, 1988, 1994b; Faris 1992; Ginsburg 1991; Povinelli 1994; Turner 1991, 1992; Thomas 1994; Hemming 1994.
3. The most sustained exploration of *yawulyu* among Central Desert Aborigines appears in *Daughters of the Dreaming,* Bell's book on Kaytej and Warlpiri women. Bell's conclusions warrant a note, for they are at odds with my data collected at Yuendumu. Of the *yawulyu* ceremonies, Bell writes: "Men approached neither the ground where *yawulyu* was celebrated nor the camps where the ritual items were stored, men's opinion on staging *yawulyu* were neither sought nor required" (Bell 1983:11). This characteri-

zation offers little latitude for the public *yawulyu warrajanyani,* which I found not only accommodated Aboriginal men, but nurtured the engagement of nonindigenous audiences as well. Bell's initial exclusionary observation is later softened somewhat by reference to public presentations of *yawulyu* performed for the Education Department (Bell 1983:27). How these performances connect to (or evade) the restricted *yawulyu* previously invoked is not made clear.

4. For example, public men's events did occur rarely in the late 1980s. However, the rare *purlapa* enacted tended to serve highly specialized, narrow ends, at odds with the broader goals guiding the *yawulyu warrajanyani.*
5. Berndt, in her 1950 and 1965 works on Aboriginal people who live in Balgo (Central Australian Desert), also notes the absence of women's public ceremonies during the early days of sedentarization.
6. These and many other observations synthesize comments made by twelve men and thirty-two women to whom I spoke about the place of public ritual. These include life histories registered between 1983 and 1992.
7. Nicolas Peterson confirmed that while he was conducting fieldwork at Yuendumu in the 1970s very few *purlapa* were performed (personal communication, 1999).
8. In 1983 women performed seven *yawulyu warrajanyani* and men one *purlapa.* In 1984 six *yawulyu warrajanyani* and one *purlapa* took place. In 1985, 1986, and 1987, an average of seven *yawulyu warrajanyani* were performed. Between 1989 and 1991, twelve *yawulyu warrajanyani* were performed, and two men performed a short *purlapa* at the local school.
9. See, for example, some of the reviews written on the Adelaide exhibition "Yuendumu" at the South Australian Museum, by L. Collins in the *Adelaide Advertiser,* March 21, 1988; P. Ward in *The Weekend Australian,* March 1–20, 1988; and Pamela Zeplin in the *Adelaide Advertiser,* March 20, 1988.
10. Ian Keen, in his most recent book, also notes that land rights and self-determination policies have brought new contexts for the exercise of intrakin group power based in religion. He argues that "[p]rocesses of settlement affected the ability of some groups to control access to their country and its resources, some becoming powerless, others gaining in power" (1994:300).
11. As one American anthropologist noted whimsically when I detailed the structural characteristics of Warlpiri ritual activity in the public sphere, "There's no representation without agnation."
12. See Sutton 1978; von Sturmer 1978; Trigger 1978; Anderson 1988; Tonkinson 1988; and Keen 1994. All these mention a similar phenomenon among the groups studied.
13. Myers raises similar issues on the relations and contexts of the production

and performance of "totemic," personal, and collective identities (1986a, 1994a).

CONCLUSION

1. The verb is defined as followed in the Warlpiri dictionary: "performs the ceremonial role appropriate to the matriline (see *kurdungurlu*) which involves material preparations: to work, perform, paint Dreamtime designs, prepare decorations, direct ceremony, get everything ready for performance."

BIBLIOGRAPHY

Anderson, C.

1984 The Political and Economic Basis of Kuku-Yalanji Social History. Ph.D. dissertation, University of Queensland.

1988 All Bosses Are Not Created Equal. *Anthropological Forum* 5(4):507–24.

Anderson, C. (ed.)

1995 *Politics of the Secret.* Oceania Monograph 45. University of Sydney, Sydney.

Anderson, C., and F. Dussart

1988 Dreamings in Acrylic: Contemporary Western Desert Art. In *Dreamings: Art from Aboriginal Australia,* edited by P. Sutton, pp. 89–142. Braziller, New York.

Bell, D.

1980 Daughters of the Dreaming. Ph.D. dissertation, Australian National University.

1983 *Daughters of the Dreaming.* McPhee Gribble/George Allen Unwin, Sydney.

1995 *Daughters of the Dreaming.* 2nd ed. University of Minnesota Press, Minneapolis.

Bern, J.

1979 Ideology and Domination: Toward a Reconstruction of Australian Aboriginal Social Formation. *Oceania* 50(2):118–32.

Bern, J., and J. Labarlestier

1985 Rival Constructions of Traditional Aboriginal Ownership in the Limmen Bight Land Claim. *Oceania* 56(1):56–76.

Berndt, C. H.
1950 Women's Changing Ceremonies in Northern Australia. *L'Homme* 1:9–87.
1965 Women and the "Secret Life." In *Aboriginal Man in Australia,* edited by R. M. Berndt and C. H. Berndt, pp. 236–82. Angus and Robertson, Sydney.
1974 Digging Sticks and Spears, or the Two-Sex Model. In *Woman's Role in Aboriginal Society,* edited by F. Gale, pp. 64–84. Australian Institute of Aboriginal Studies, Canberra.
1981 Interpretations and "Facts" in Aboriginal Australia. In *Woman the Gatherer,* edited by F. Dahlberg, pp. 153–204. Yale University Press, New Haven.
Berndt, C. H., and R. M. Berndt
1944 A Preliminary Report of Field Work in the Ooldea Region, Western South Australia. *Oceania* 14(3):208–37.
Berndt, R. M.
1951 *Kunapipi.* Cheshire, Melbourne.
Bradley, C.
1987 A Change in Status for Aboriginal Women? Aboriginal Women in the Australian Workforce. *Aboriginal History* 11(2):143–55.
Chase, A.
1984 Belonging to Country: Territory, Identity and Environment in Cape York Peninsula, Northern Australia. In *Aboriginal Landowners,* edited by L. R. Hiatt, pp. 104–22. Oceania Monograph 27. University of Sydney, Sydney.
Christen, K.
1993 "We Mob Gotta Hold up This Country": Warumungu Women's Ritual Responsibility. B.A. thesis, Arizona State University.
Clifford, J.
1985 Histories of the Tribal and the Modern. *Art in America* 1:164–77.
Collier, J., and S. Yanagisako (eds.)
1987 *Gender and Kinship.* Stanford University Press, Berkeley.
Dussart, F.
1988a Women's Acrylic Paintings from Yuendumu. In *Inspired Dream,* edited by M. West, pp. 35–39. Queensland Art Gallery, Brisbane.
1988b Notes on Warlpiri Women's Personal Names. *Journal de la Société des Océanistes* 86(1):53–60.
1989a Warlpiri Women's Yawulyu Ceremonies: A Forum for Socialization and Innovation. Ph.D. dissertation, Australian National University.
1989b Rêves à l'Acrylique. *Autrement,* March, hors série 37:104–11.
1992a Création et Innovation: Le Rêve de Tania. *Journal de la Société des Océanistes* 94(1):25–34.

1992b The Politics of Female Identity: Warlpiri Widows at Yuendumu. *Ethnology* 31(4):337–50.
1993 *La Peinture des Aborigènes d'Australie.* Parenthèses and Réunion des Musées Nationaux, Paris.
1997 A Body Painting in Translation. In *Rethinking Visual Anthropology,* edited by Howard Morphy and Marcus Banks. Yale University Press, New Haven.
1999 What an Aboriginal Acrylic Can Mean: On the Meta-Ritualistic Resonances of a Central Desert Painting. In *Art from the Land,* edited by Howard Morphy and Margo Smith Boles, pp. 193–218. University of Virginia and Kluge-Ruhe Aboriginal Art Collection, Charlottesville.
In Press The Politics of Representation. In *Oxford Companion to Aboriginal Art and Culture.* Oxford University Press, Melbourne and London.

Eliot, T. S.
1943 *Four Quartets.* Harcourt, Brace and Co., New York.

Faris, J.
1990 *The Nightway: A History and a History of Documentation of a Navajo Ceremonial.* University of New Mexico Press, Albuquerque.
1992 Anthropological Transparency: Film, Representation and Politics. In *Film as Ethnography,* edited by P. Crawford and D. Turton, pp. 171–82. Manchester University Press, Manchester.

Fleming, Rev. Tom
n.d. *A History of the Aboriginal Missions.* 57 pp. fscp roneo [Alice Springs].

Giddens, A.
1979 *Central Problems in Social Theory.* University of California Press, Berkeley.

Gill, S.
1998 *Storytracking: Texts, Stories, and Histories in Central Australia.* Oxford University Press, Oxford.

Gillen, F.
1896 Notes on Some Manners and Customs of the Aborigines of the McDonnell Ranges Belonging to the Arunta Tribe. In *Report on the Work on the Horn Scientific Expedition to Central Australia,* edited by B. Spencer. Dulan and Co., London.

Ginsburg, F.
1991 Indigenous Media: Faustian Contract or Global Village? *Cultural Anthropology* 6:92–112.

Glowczewski, B.
1981 Affaire de Femmes, ou Femmes d'Affaires. *Journal de la Société des Océanistes* 70–71:77–97.
1983 Death, Women and Value Production: The Circulation of Hairstring

among the Warlpiri of the Central Australian Desert. *Ethnology* 22:225–39.

1988 La Loi du Rêve. Thèse d'état ès lettres et sciences humaines. Université de Paris I-Panthéon-Sorbonne, Paris.

1991 *Du Rêve à la Loi chez les Aborigènes*. Presses Universitaires de France, Paris.

Godelier, M.

1986 *The Making of Great Men: Male Domination and Power among the New Guinea Baruya*. Cambridge University Press, Cambridge.

Gosse, W. C.

1874 *W. C. Gosse's Explorations, 1873*. Parliamentary Paper, South Australia 48. Government Printer, Adelaide.

Gregory, A. C.

1969 [1884] *Journals of Australian Explorations*. South Australian State Library facsimile. Government Printer, Brisbane.

Hale, K.

1967 Language, Kinship and Ritual among the Walbiri of Central Australia. Unpublished paper.

1980 Warlpiri: Traditional Aboriginal Owners. *Anthropology Resource Center Newsletter* 4(4):5.

Hale, K., M. Laughren, D. Nash, and J. Simpson

1982–1988 Warlpiri Dictionary. Massachusetts Institute of Technology, Cambridge.

Hamilton, A.

1972 Blacks and Whites: The Relationships of Change. *Arena* 30:30–48.

1979 Timeless Transformation: Women, Men and History in the Australian Western Desert. Ph.D. dissertation, University of Sydney.

1981 A Complex Strategical Situation: Gender and Power in Aboriginal Australia. In *Australian Women,* edited by N. Grieve and P. Grimshaw, pp. 69–85. Oxford University Press, Melbourne.

1986 Daughters of the Imaginary. *Canberra Anthropology* 9(2):1–25.

Hemming, S.

1994 In the Tracks of Ngurunderi: The South Australian Museum's Ngurunderi Exhibition and Cultural Tourism. *Australian Aboriginal Studies* 2:38–46.

Howitt, A. W.

1904 *The Natives of South-East Australia.* Macmillan, London.

Kaberry, P.

1939 *Aboriginal Women, Sacred and Profane*. Routledge and Kegan Paul, London.

Keen, I.

1978 One Ceremony, One Song: An Economy of Religious Knowledge

among the Yolngu of Northeast Arnhem Land. Ph.D. dissertation, Australian National University.
1994 *Knowledge and Secrecy in an Aboriginal Religion.* Clarendon Press, Oxford.

Kendon, A.
1988 *Sign Languages of Aboriginal Australia.* Cambridge University Press, Cambridge.

Kölig, E.
1979 *Djuluru:* Ein Synkretistischer Kult Nordwest—Australiens. *Baessler-Archiv* (neue folge) 27:419–48.
1981 *The Silent Revolution: The Effects of Modernization on Australian Aboriginal Religion.* Institute for the Study of Human Issues, Philadelphia.

Lander, N.
1993 *Jardiwanpa.* Film produced by City Picture, Australia.

Laughren, M.
1981 Religious Movement Observed at Yuendumu between 1975–1981. In unpublished proceedings of the AIAS Symposium on Contemporary Aboriginal Religious Movements, part 3, pp. 1–5. Canberra.
1982 Warlpiri Kinship Structure. *Oceania Linguistic Monographs* 24:72–85.

Leacock, E.
1978 Women's Status in Egalitarian Society: Implications for Social Evolution. *Current Anthropology* 19(2):247–75.
1983 The Origins of Gender Inequality: Conceptual and Historical Problems. *Dialectical Anthropology* 7(4):263–84.

Lederman, R.
1986 *What Gifts Engender: Social Relations and Politics in Mendi, Highland Papua New Guinea.* Cambridge University Press, Cambridge.

Lee, R. B.
1979 *The !Kung San: Men, Women, and Work in a Foraging Society.* Cambridge University Press, Cambridge.

Lévi-Strauss, C.
1986 *Structural Anthropology.* Penguin Books, Ringwood.

Megaw, V.
1982 Western Desert Acrylic Painting—Artifact or Art? *Art History* 5:205–18.

Meggitt, M. J.
1962 *Desert People.* Angus and Robertson, Sydney.
1966 Gadjari among the Walbiri Aborigines of Central Australia. *Oceania Monographs* 14:1–129.

Merlan, F.
1986 Australian Aboriginal Conception Beliefs Revisited. *Man* 21(3):474–93.
1998 *Caging the Rainbow: Places, Politics, and Aborigines in a North Australian Town.* University of Hawai'i Press, Honolulu.
Michaels, E.
1986 *The Aboriginal Invention of Television, Central Australia 1982–86.*
1987 Western Desert Sandpainting and Post-Modernism. In Warlukurlangu Artists, *Yuendumu Doors: Kuruwarri,* pp. 133–43. Australian Institute of Aboriginal Studies Press, Canberra.
1988 Bad Aboriginal Art. *Art and Text* 28:59–72.
1989 *For a Cultural Future: Francis Jupurrurla Makes TV at Yuendumu.* Art and Criticism Monograph Series 3. Art and Text Publications, Sydney.
Monegal, E. R., and A. Reid (eds.)
1981 *From Borges: A Reader.* E. P. Dutton, New York.
Morphy, F., and H. Morphy
1984 Owners, Managers, and Ideology: A Comparative Analysis. *Oceania Monographs* 27:46–66.
Morphy, H.
1980a The Impact of the Commercial Development of Art on Traditional Culture. In *Preserving Indigenous Cultures: A New Role for Museums,* edited by R. Edwards and J. Stewart, pp. 81–94. Australian Government Publishing Service, Canberra.
1980b What Circles Look Like. *Canberra Anthropology* 3(1):17–36.
1991 *Ancestral Connections: Art and an Aboriginal System of Knowledge.* University of Chicago Press, Chicago.
1996 Empiricism to Metaphysics: In Defense of the Concept of the Dreamtime. In *Prehistory to Politics,* edited by T. Bohyhady and T. Griffiths, pp. 163–89. University of Melbourne Press, Melbourne.
Mulvaney, J., H. Morphy, and A. Petch
1997 *My Dear Spencer: The Letters of F. J. Gillen to Baldwin Spencer.* Hyland House, South Melbourne.
Munn, N.
1964 Totemic Designs and Group Continuity in Walbiri Cosmology. In *Aborigines Now,* edited by M. Reay, pp. 83–101. Angus and Robertson, Sydney.
1986 [1971] The Transformation of Subjects into Objects in Walbiri and Pitjantjatjara Myth. In *Religion in Aboriginal Australia,* edited by M. Charlesworth, H. Morphy, D. Bell, and K. Maddock, pp. 57–82. University of Queensland Press, St. Lucia.

1973 *Walbiri Iconography: Graphic Representation and Cultural Symbolism in a Central Australian Society.* Cornell University Press, Ithaca.

1986 *The Fame of Gawa.* Duke University Press, Durham.

Myers, F.

1980 The Cultural Basis of Politics in Pintupi Life. *Mankind* 12:197–214.

1986a *Pintupi Country, Pintupi Self.* Smithsonian Institution Press and Australian Institute of Aboriginal Studies, Washington, D.C., and Canberra.

1986b The Politics of Representation: Anthropological Discourse and Australian Aborigines. *American Ethnologist* 13:138–53.

1988 Critical Trends in the Study of Hunter-Gatherers. *Annual Review of Anthropology* 17:261–82.

1989 Truth, Beauty, and Pintupi Painting. *Visual Anthropology* 2:163–95.

1994a Beyond the Intentional Fallacy: Art Criticism and the Ethnography of Aboriginal Acrylic Painting. *Cultural Anthropology* 6(1):26–62.

1994b Culture Making: Performing Aboriginality at the Asia Society. *American Ethnologist* 21(4):679–99.

1995 Re/writing the Primitive: Art Criticism and the Circulation of Aboriginal Painting. In *Meaning in the Visual Arts,* edited by E. Levin. Princeton University Press, Princeton.

n.d. What Is the Business of the "Balgo Business"? A Contemporary Aboriginal Religious Movement. Manuscript, Australian Institute of Aboriginal Studies, Canberra.

Nash, D.

1982 An Etymological Note on Warlpiri *Kurdungurlu. Oceania Linguistic Monographs* 24:141–59.

Nash, D., and J. Simpson

1981 No-Name in Central Australia. *Chicago Linguistic Society* 1(2):165–77.

Nathan, P., et al.

1987 Borning: *Pwere Laltyeke Awnerne Ampe Mpwaretyeke. Australian Aboriginal Studies* 1:2–33.

Ngaanyatjarra, Pitjantjatjara, Yankunytjatjara

1990 *Women's Council 1990 Report.* [Northern Territory:] Women's Council.

Peterson, N.

1969 Secular and Ritual Links: Two Basic and Opposed Principles of Australian Social Organization as Illustrated by Walbiri Ethnography. *Mankind* 7:27–35.

1970 Buluwandi: A Central Australian Ceremony for the Resolution of Conflict. In *Australian Aboriginal Anthropology,* edited by Ronald M. Berndt, pp. 200–15. University of Western Australia Press, Perth.

1972 Totemism Yesterday: Sentiment and Local Organization among the Australian Aborigines. *Man* 7:12–32.

1974 The Importance of Women in Determining the Composition of Residential Groups in Aboriginal Australia. In *Woman's Role in Aboriginal Society,* edited by F. Gale, pp. 16–27. Australian Institute of Aboriginal Studies, Canberra.

1995 Peoples, Islands and Succession. In *Anthropology in the Native Title Era,* edited by J. Fingleton and J. Finlayson, pp. 11–17. Australian Institute of Aboriginal and Torres Strait Islanders Studies, Canberra.

Peterson, N., et al.

1978 *Claim to Areas of Traditional Land by the Warlpiri, Kartangarurru-Kurintji.* Central Land Council, Alice Springs.

Peterson, N., and R. Lampert

1985 A Central Australian Ochre Mine. *Records of the Australian Museum* 37(1):1–9.

Pink, O.

1936 The Landowners in the Northern Division of the Aranda Tribe, Central Australia. *Oceania* 6(3):275–305.

Poirier, S.

1990 Les Jardins du Nomade. Ph.D. dissertation, Université de Laval.

1996 *Les Jardins du Nomade.* Lit Verlag and CNRS, Münster and Paris.

Povinelli, E.

1994 *Labor's Lot.* University of Chicago Press, Chicago.

Ross, Jampijinpa, D.

1993 Jardiwarnpa Jukurrpa. In *Aratjara.* Exhibition catalogue. Exhibition conceived by B. Lüthi and the Aboriginal Arts Unit of the Australia Council in Sydney. Kunstammlung Nordrhein-Westfalen, Düsseldorf.

Rowse, T.

1990 Enlisting the Warlpiri. *Continuum* 3(2):1–19.

Sandall, R.

1977 *Walbiri Fire Ceremony: Ngatjakula.* Film produced by Australian Institute of Aboriginal Studies, Australia.

Scheffler, W.

1973 Kinship, Descent and Alliance. In *Handbook of Social and Cultural Anthropology,* edited by J. J. Honingmann, pp. 747–93. Rand McNally, New York.

1978 *Australian Kin Classification.* Cambridge University Press, Cambridge.

Smith, M., B. Frankhauser, and M. Jercher

1998 The Changing Provenance of Red Ochre at Puritjarra Rock Shelter, Central Australia: Late Pleistocene to Present. *Proceedings of the Prehistoric Society* 64:275–92.

Spencer, B., and F. Gillen
1899 *The Native Tribes of Central Australia.* Macmillan, London.
1904 *The Northern Tribes of Central Australia.* Macmillan, London.
1927 *The Arunta.* 2 vols. Macmillan, London.
Stanner, W. E. H.
1956 Dreaming. In *Australian Signpost,* edited by T. A. G. Hungerford, pp. 51–65. Cheshire, Melbourne.
1966 *On Aboriginal Religion.* Oceania Monograph 11. University of Sydney, Sydney.
Strathern, M.
1987 *Understanding Inequality.* Cambridge University Press, Cambridge.
1988 *The Gender of the Gift.* University of California Press, Berkeley.
Strehlow, T. G. H.
1947 *Aranda Traditions.* University of Melbourne Press, Melbourne.
1971 *Songs of Central Australia.* Angus and Robertson, Sydney.
Stuart, J. M.
1865 *The Journals of John McDougall Stuart.* Edited by William Hardman. 2nd ed. Saunders, Otley, London
Sutton, P.
1978 Wik: Aboriginal Society, Territory and Language at Cape Kerweer, Cape York Peninsula, Australia. Ph.D. dissertation, University of Queensland.
1982 Personal Power, Kin Classification and Speech Etiquette in Aboriginal Australia. *Oceania Linguistic Monographs* 24:182–200.
1992 Aboriginal Art, The Nation State, Suburbia. *Artlink* 12(3):6–9.
Sutton, P. (ed.)
1988 *Dreamings: Art from Aboriginal Australia.* Braziller, New York.
Swain, T.
1988 The Ghost of Space: Reflections of Warlpiri Christian Iconography and Ritual. In *Aboriginal Australians and Christian Missions,* edited by T. Swain and D. Rose, pp. 452–69. Australian Association for the Study of Religions, Adelaide.
Taylor, L.
1987 The Same but Different: Social Reproduction and Innovation in the Art of the Kunwinjku of Western Arnhem Land. Ph.D. dissertation, Australian National University.
1996 *Seeing the Inside.* Clarendon Press, Oxford.
Thomas, N.
1991 *Entangled Objects: Exchange, Material Culture and Colonialism in the Pacific.* Harvard University Press, Cambridge.
1994 *Colonialism's Culture: Anthropology, Travel and Government.* Polity Press and Princeton University Press, Cambridge and Princeton.

Tindale, N. B.

1974 *Aboriginal Tribes of Australia.* Australian National University Press, Canberra.

Tonkinson, R.

1970 Aboriginal Dream-Spirit Beliefs in a Contact Situation: Jigalong, Western Australia. In *Australian Aboriginal Anthropology,* edited by R. M. Berndt, pp. 277–91. University of Western Australia Press, Perth.

1974 *The Jigalong Mob: Aboriginal Victors of the Desert Crusade.* Benjamin/Cummings, Menlo Park.

1978 *The Mardujara Aborigines: Living the Dream in Australia's Desert.* Holt Rinehart and Winston, New York.

1988 Egalitarianism and Inequality in a Western Desert Culture. *Anthropological Forum* 5(4):546–58.

1990 The Changing Status of Aboriginal Women: Free Agents at Jigalong, Western Australia. In *Going It Alone? Prospects for Aboriginal Autonomy,* edited by R. Tonkinson and M. Howard, pp. 125–47. Aboriginal Studies Press, Canberra.

Trigger, D.

1988 Equality and Hierarchy in Aboriginal Political Life at Doomadgee, North-West Queensland. *Anthropological Forum* 5(4):525–44.

Turner, T.

1991 Representing, Resisting, Rethinking: Historical Transformations of Kayapo Culture and Anthropological Consciousness. In *Colonial Situations,* edited by G. W. Stocking Jr., pp. 285–313. University of Wisconsin Press, Madison.

1992 Defiant Images: The Kayapo Appropriation of Video. *Anthropology Today* 8(6):5–16.

Visweswaran, K.

1994 *Fictions of Feminist Ethnography.* University of Minnesota Press, Minneapolis.

von Sturmer, J.

1978 The Wik Region: Economy, Territoriality and Totemism in Western Cape York Peninsula, North Queensland. Ph.D. dissertation, University of Queensland.

1989 Aborigines, Representation, Necrophilia. *Art and Text* 32:127–39.

Waburton, P. E.

1875 *Journey across the Western Interior of Australia.* Edited by H. W. Bates. Sampson Low, Marston, Low and Searle, London.

Warlukurlangu Artists Aboriginal Association

1987 *Yuendumu Doors: Kuruwarri.* Australian Institute of Aboriginal Studies Press, Canberra.

Weiner, A.
1976 *Women of Value, Men of Renown.* University of Texas Press, Austin.
1992 *Inalienable Possessions.* University of California Press, Berkeley.
White, I.
1974 Aboriginal Women's Status: A Paradox Resolved. In *Woman's Role in Aboriginal Society,* edited by F. Gale, pp. 36–46. Australian Institute of Aboriginal Studies, Canberra.
Wild, S.
1975 Walbiri Music and Dance in Their Social and Cultural Nexus. Ph.D. dissertation, Indiana University.
Williams, N.
1976 Australian Aboriginal Art at Yirrkala. In *Ethnic and Tourist Arts: Cultural Expressions from the Fourth World,* edited by N. Graburn, pp. 266–84. University of California Press, Berkeley.
Wolfe, P.
1991 On Being Woken Up: The Dreamtime in Anthropology and in Australian Settler Culture. *Comparative Studies in Society and History* 32(2):197–224.
Woodburn, J.
1982 Egalitarian Societies. *Man* 17(3):431–51.
Young, E.
1981 *Tribal Communities in Rural Areas.* Development Studies Centre, Australian National University, Canberra.
1987 Resettlement and Caring for the Country: The Anmatyerre Experience. *Aboriginal History* 11(2):156–70.
Young, E., and K. Doohan
1989 *Mobility for Survival: A Process Analysis of Aboriginal Population Movement in Central Australia.* Australian National University North Research Unit Monograph, Darwin.
Yuendumu Bilingual School
1983 *Junga Yimi,* newsletter of the Yuendumu Bilingual School, Yuendumu.

INDEX

Boldface page numbers indicate illustrations